William Howard Taft's
Constitutional Progressivism

AMERICAN POLITICAL THOUGHT

Jeremy D. Bailey and Susan McWilliams Barndt
Series Editors

Wilson Carey McWilliams and Lance Banning
Founding Editors

.

.

.

William Howard Taft's Constitutional Progressivism

Kevin J. Burns

 University Press of Kansas

Published by the University Press of Kansas (Lawrence, Kansas 66045), which was organized by the Kansas Board of Regents and is operated and funded by Emporia State University, Fort Hays State University, Kansas State University, Pittsburg State University, the University of Kansas, and Wichita State University.

Library of Congress Cataloging-in-Publication Data

Names: Burns, Kevin (College teacher), author.
Title: William Howard Taft's constitutional progressivism / Kevin J. Burns.
Description: Lawrence : University Press of Kansas, 2021 | Series: American political thought | Includes bibliographical references and index.
Identifiers: LCCN 2020042478
    ISBN 9780700632114 (cloth)
    ISBN 9780700632121 (epub)
Subjects: LCSH: Taft, William H. (William Howard), 1857–1930. | Judges—United States—Biography. | Presidents—United States—Biography.
Classification: LCC KF8745.T27 B87 2021 | DDC 973.91/2092—dc23
LC record available at https://lccn.loc.gov/2020042478.

British Library Cataloguing-in-Publication Data is available.

Printed in the United States of America

10 9 8 7 6 5 4 3 2 1

The paper used in this publication is recycled and contains 30 percent postconsumer waste. It is acid free and meets the minimum requirements of the American National Standard for Permanence of Paper for Printed Library Materials Z39.48–1992.

To David K. Nichols

Study the Constitution of the United States and see what the greatest instrument of fundamental law was and is, and how simple; how it has been elastic and has yielded to the demands of our increasing country, and yet is today the wonder of the world. . . . Our fathers builded even better than they knew, and we have not gotten in advance of them in the matter of laying down simple principles of constitutional law. We do not know more than our fathers, for in that respect they have proven what they knew by the usefulness of the Constitution of the United States.

—William Howard Taft, address at Prescott, Arizona, October 13, 1909

Contents

Preface

A century ago, in the summer of 1921, William Howard Taft was sworn in as chief justice of the United States. This, it has often been said, was the high point of his career because the ex-president and former circuit court judge thrived on the bench. In contrast, his tenure as president has often been deemed mediocre at best and disastrous at worst. Historian Mark Carnes demonstrated the textbook view of Taft's administration when he wrote Taft will "never be regarded as a great president or even a good one, but perhaps someday his obesity may cease to be his legacy."[1] Carnes jested, perhaps, but only slightly. Public knowledge of Taft now seems to extend little further than his weight and his alleged problems with bathtubs.

Let me take this opportunity to clear up one part of that particularly sticky issue. Despite the charming children's book titled *President Taft Is Stuck in the Bath* and despite the oversize bathtub installed in the White House to accommodate him, the only evidence for the myth of Taft's bathtub fiasco comes from White House chief usher Ike Hoover. In his memoirs, Hoover claimed that Taft would "stick" in the bathtub "and had to be helped out each time."[2] His story is amusing, but ultimately unconvincing; his impartiality is doubtful—he was a Theodore Roosevelt devotee who came to despise Taft—and no other evidence has ever come to light to support his claims. But there is at least a grain of truth to the story, for Taft was not bereft of bathtub-related disasters. A *New York Times* article from 1915 reported that ex-president Taft, while staying at a hotel in Cape May, New Jersey, filled his bathtub to the brim and then climbed in, displacing enough water to flood his second-story bathroom. The water eventually leaked through the floor and disturbed the guests in the hotel dining room. The *Times* recounted, "As Mr. Taft boarded his train this morning he glanced at the ocean and said: 'I'll get a piece of that fenced in some day and then when I venture in there won't be any overflow.'"[3]

But this book is not actually about bathtubs or Taft's weight problems. Instead, it describes the relationship between Taft's attachment to progressivism and his adherence to the Constitution. My work sits at the intersection of American political thought and constitutional law and explores the ways Taft's commitment to both the Constitution and progressivism drove his political career and the decisions he made as president and chief justice. Most importantly, where the vast majority of scholarship has seen Taft as a reactionary conservative and has tied his conservatism to his constitutionalism, I argue that Taft's devotion to the Constitution of 1787 actually contributed to his progressivism. Taft saw the positive role the Constitution played in American political life, recognizing that it created a strong national government and empowered it to enact broad progressive reforms. I show that his constitutionalism and progressivism were intertwined and mutually supporting; his devotion to the Constitution did not hinder his progressivism, but actually contributed to it.

Having spent half a dozen years studying him, I have developed an affection for Taft the man. Perhaps this has blinded me to errors or inconsistencies in Taft's thought. Ultimately, it is not my goal to praise or condemn Taft in this book—I do both at various points—but to explain Taft in his own terms and to demonstrate his contribution to American constitutionalism.

I am indebted to Mary Nichols, Jerold Waltman, Dave Bridge, David Smith, David Clinton, and Joseph Brutto for reading and commenting on earlier drafts of this project. Matthew Brogdon, Adam Carrington, Jordan Cash, and Mark Scully each provided advice on parts of the final drafts. Their guidance strengthened the argument and is deeply appreciated. My editorial assistants Milanna Fritz and Riley Damitz offered extremely detailed revisions and helped to smooth my prose. Both saved me from numerous embarrassing errors. I am also grateful to David Congdon of the University Press of Kansas for his guidance. The staff of St. John the Evangelist Library at Christendom College, and especially Stephen Pilon, was extremely helpful and secured much needed research materials.

Finally, I owe a great debt of gratitude to my teacher, David K. Nichols, to whom this book has been dedicated. This project originated in his seminars on jurisprudence and the presidency. With his typical mix of wisdom, sympathy, and sarcasm, he managed to provide both wise advice and incisive criticism on my work. He also somehow managed to tolerate some rather lengthy soliloquies on Taft with his usual gentlemanly patience. Since he is largely responsible for sparking my interest in the presidency and separation of powers, most of what is good in this project is a tribute to his teaching. It is my hope that this book lives up to the high standards he always set for the study of American constitutionalism.

Funding from the Institute for Humane Studies, the Charles Koch Foundation, and Christendom College's Faculty Mentorship Initiative permitted me to work with the Taft Papers and offset various research and publishing expenses. An earlier version of chapter 5 and a part of chapter 1 appeared in *Presidential Studies Quarterly*, and a version of chapter 8 was previously published in *Journal of Supreme Court History*; these chapters have been reprinted here with permission.

Introduction

The 1912 Republican presidential nomination contest pitted incumbent William Howard Taft against Theodore Roosevelt, his predecessor and political mentor. Both men attempted to claim the mantle of progressivism. Taft defended his administration's record as "progressive in the highest degree" and argued that it was "the duty of government" to undertake "wider . . . functions" and promote "real progress toward . . . greater human happiness." In response, Roosevelt insisted that Taft suffered from "narrow vision," "small sympathy," and the belief that "the people could not be trusted" to rule themselves.[1] Despite Roosevelt's accusations, Taft's claims were accurate: he was a progressive. In an era in which reformers "sought an enhanced role for government at all levels in regulating business, supervising morality, and purifying the political system," the Taft administration's policies fell comfortably within the progressive mainstream.[2]

Taft recognized that industrialization had radically altered social and economic conditions in the country and believed these developments, and the challenges that came with them, should be addressed by government action at the national level. However, unlike many of the most radical members of the Progressive movement, he did not believe the nation's written Constitution thwarted reform efforts. Instead, he insisted that the fundamental law "readily . . . lends itself to wider governmental functions in the promotion of the comfort of the people"; to this end, he declared his "one aim in the Presidency" was "to make a broad and permanent advance in the powers of the Federal government" through his "program of progressive laws." At the same time, he insisted on "wise progress," the "progress of the people in pursuit of happiness under constitutional government."[3] Taft believed that the Constitution could play a constructive role in promoting progressive initiatives, but he also thought that its restrictions demanded prudent, legal reform measures.

In this book, I argue that we can understand Taft more completely by recognizing the integral connection between his constitutionalism and his progressivism. Taft saw the Constitution as the means by which progressive policies could be safely advanced and permanently ensconced in the political life of the nation. Taft's account of the Republican Party's principles, enunciated during the 1912 election campaign, helps to elucidate the two sides of his political project. On the one hand, Taft insisted that he and his party had a duty "sacredly" to maintain "our Constitution and its guarantees." At the same time, he argued that the Republican Party should be "as progressive as possible in respect to what may be called humane legislation . . . for the promotion of human comfort" and that it had "a right to stand as progressives in *legislation*." Taft melded a conservative approach to the Constitution with a liberal attachment to progressive policy reforms.[4]

Taft's devotion to the Constitution of 1787 was sufficiently great to earn him the praise of Antonin Scalia, who lauded Taft's opinion in *Myers v. United States* as "a prime example of . . . the 'originalist' approach to constitutional interpretation." Taft adhered to the original public meaning of the Constitution, interpreting the text in light of the historical circumstances surrounding the transition between the Articles of Confederation and the Constitution, the debates at the Constitutional Convention in 1787, the views of particular Founders that seemed to represent the general public understanding of the Constitution, and the decisions and actions of the government during the early republic. He believed that alterations to the Constitution should occur through the formal amendment process of Article V and therefore regarded claims that the Constitution grew or evolved over time as lawless efforts to "break down that fundamental instrument and make it go for nothing."[5]

However, Taft's conservative constitutionalism did not prevent him from embracing dynamic reform. Instead, he saw the Constitution as a vehicle by which reform could be enacted. The Constitution, he argued, was an empowering "instrument" that vested the federal government with extensive authority in "general" and "comprehensive" terms. Rather than "load[ing] down" the government "with restrictions and limitations," the Constitution provided it with broad powers that were sufficiently "elastic" to meet "the demands of our increasing country."[6] According to Taft, the Constitution does not embody either a conservative or a progressive ideology, for it does not demand that national power be used to enact any specific set of policies; instead, it empowers the government to enact a variety of policies—conservative or liberal, progressive or reactionary. Further, in contrast to many radical progressives who were tempted to ignore constitutional restraints in order to more quickly enact reform policies, Taft recognized that the Constitution could play a constructive role, since reforms enacted through legal means and under the Constitution would be more permanent and lasting. The Constitution, he believed, could be open to change without itself changing.

My analysis of Taft's constitutional progressivism represents a significant revision of earlier scholarship that, Peri Arnold observes, has caricatured Taft as "a jovial conservative, more Gilded Age than Progressive Era in his sensibilities."[7] Most major works on Taft conclude that he failed as a political actor because his devotion to law and the Constitution made him incapable of adapting to changing political circumstances or enacting needed reforms. The scholarship has presented two interconnected strains of criticism: that Taft's great stumbling blocks were his "judicial temperament" and his constitutional formalism. We are told that Taft failed as president because of his judicial temperament; he adored the quiet stability of the judicial life, with its clear rules and procedures, and was uncomfortable in the hurly-burly of politics. This temperamental critique is closely linked to the second criticism: Taft was simply too attached to the written Constitution to be an able statesman in an era of reform. As a result, he has been pilloried as an opponent of progressivism. As president, it is said, his temperament made him incapable of providing the active and dynamic leadership the nation needed. And as both president and chief justice, his alleged attachment to legal formalism and a rigid understanding of the Constitution led him to block reform legislation.

Such a view is ubiquitous in the older biographical scholarship on Taft. Henry Pringle, in his *Life and Times of William Howard Taft* (1939), set the tone for future scholarship: "Taft worshiped the law; no understanding of him is possible without appreciation of that fact." Pringle claimed Taft's "judicial nature" made him a bumbling and inept president and that his "strict construction" of the constitutional powers of government limited his ability to respond to emerging challenges.[8] Following Pringle, Alpheus Thomas Mason's *William Howard Taft: Chief Justice* (1964) claims Taft's respect for "judicial stability" often led him to "fasten both the national government and the states in a constitutional straight jacket."[9] The most evenhanded of these early studies, Paolo Coletta's 1973 presidential biography, faults Taft's "juridical . . . conception of the presidency," which guaranteed that "with few exceptions, Taft proved unwilling to support federal intervention" to address social problems. Coletta concludes that Taft seemed to adopt progressive values "while under the spell of the dynamic Roosevelt," but "return[ed] to his basic conservative self" once freed from TR's influence.[10]

This older consensus has been revised by more recent scholarship, which has begun to narrow the temperamental critique and recognize that Taft had certain progressive sympathies. Most notable are Lewis Gould's studies, which examine Taft's presidency, the 1912 election, and the years between his time as president and chief justice. Gould writes that Taft was hindered by his "judicial temperament" and the vain hope that the president could rise "above partisan considerations," but Gould also convincingly challenges the claim that Taft's judicial experienced rendered him politically inept, if not virtually apolitical: Taft was "a creditable president" and "a competent chief executive." Gould also provides a more nuanced understanding of Taft's progressivism by arguing that Taft entered office marked by a "mild progressivism," but that his "instinctive" conservatism and belief in limited presidential powers eventually "muted the reform impulse."[11] Jeffrey Rosen offers a similar analysis and downplays the temperamental critique; he points to Taft's successes as president and chief justice and concludes that although Taft's constitutionalism was not inherently negative and limiting—Taft believed that the Constitution "both empowered and constrained" government—nevertheless his constitutional "scruples" and "strikingly restrained conception of the presidency" prevented him from exerting the influence needed to achieve his political goals.[12]

Taft's interest in progressivism has been most seriously analyzed by Jonathan Lurie, whose two books grapple with the complications of Taft's political views. In *William Howard Taft: The Travails of a Progressive Conservative* (2012), Lurie shows the president's genuine interest in advancing progressive policies, but also claims that Taft had a conservative attachment to "Gilded Age" legal values, reflecting "a fearful and frightened reaction by the legal order to very rapid change." Lurie concludes that Taft favored reform, but felt "oblig[ed] to make progress by incremental steps" in order to preserve the "social order, individual liberty, and Republican government."[13] In his recent study of Taft's chief justiceship, Lurie argues that Taft's progressivism faded as he aged. He attacks Taft's attachment to classical legal thought, which entailed an ideological devotion to property rights, a belief in near-absolute liberty of contract, and distrust of government regulations.

Although Lurie acknowledges that the Taft Court was not a "completely conservative tribunal," he argues that it rendered "steadfast ... obeisance to classical legalism 'with its unyielding rules that ignored social and economic' realities." Lurie therefore agrees with the older scholarship, and concludes that Taft's constitutionalism ultimately prevented reform: "For Taft the essential function of the Constitution was to protect against undesirable adaptation, not to facilitate it."[14]

In contrast to these biographical accounts, two political scientists have articulated a version of the temperamental critique. They de-emphasize Taft's conservative attachment to the Constitution and argue instead that his political training was responsible for his political failures. Donald Anderson's 1973 study argues that Taft's background as an administrator and judge failed to provide him the "political skills" he needed as president. Yet Anderson believes Taft was not truly devoted to the Constitution: although he often seemed conservative because he employed the "technical language of the law," ultimately Taft sought simply the "*appearances* of continuity" in order to guarantee popular respect for the nation's Constitution and traditional institutions.[15] Peri Arnold's *Remaking the Presidency* presents a similar assessment. Expanding on Anderson's argument, Arnold insists that many of Taft's weaknesses as president should be attributed to his political education as a bureaucrat and a judge, not to his alleged "conservative ideology" or "legalist views." Indeed, Arnold claims Taft lacked any "clear ideological stance" and is best understood as a flexible but conventional conservative.[16] For Anderson and Arnold, political education, not an ideological commitment to the Constitution, was the critical determinant in Taft's career.

My analysis of Taft diverges from these conclusions by demonstrating not only that Taft was genuinely committed to both the Constitution and progressivism, but also that his adherence to the Constitution actually contributed to progressive policy reforms by ensuring their legality and permanence. I contribute to an emerging body of scholarship that has analyzed Taft in his own terms. Both Sidney Milkis and Jonathan O'Neill have offered thoughtful studies of Taft as a constitutionalist in a progressive era. O'Neill writes that Taft respected constitutional limits, yet also shows that his "politically sophisticated" understanding of presidential power demonstrates "that a constitutional executive need not be a weak executive."[17] Milkis, for his part, follows Lurie in seeing Taft as a "conservative progressive" and details Taft's defense of "responsible constitutional government." Although Milkis believes that Taft had a habit of "privileging . . . forms over results," which did sometimes hinder reform, he also points out that Taft's attachment to law "paid dividends" in the realm of conservation policy.[18] Milkis and O'Neill both jettison the traditional unidimensional portrait of Taft as judicial, standpat constitutional conservative. By explaining that a constitutionalist could favor strong government action and promote reform, they show the need for a serious revision of older scholarship on Taft.

This book evaluates Taft's constitutionalism and progressivism throughout his national career, emphasizing both his presidency and his chief justiceship. Previous scholarship has focused on the negative and limiting side of the Constitution and stressed its restrictions on government power. In contrast, I demonstrate that Taft believed the Constitution could play a positive and constructive role, since it empowered the government to initiate and perpetuate dynamic progressive reforms. Taft's insights on the intersection of constitutionalism and reform speak to contemporary constitutional debates by cross-sectioning our modern political divisions and combining political progressivism-liberalism with constitutional conservatism. In this way, his career challenges our present assumption that conservatives will adopt an originalist approach to constitutional interpretation while liberals will embrace constructivism or a notion of a "living constitution." By melding progressive policy preferences with originalism, Taft shows, instead, that policy preferences need not determine a mode of constitutional interpretation. His constitutional vision remains relevant and helps to delineate the distinction between pragmatic policy arguments and doctrinal debates over the extent of the national government's constitutional powers. Moreover, by showing that the Constitution may remain stable even as change occurs at the policy level, Taft's perspective offers a principled means by which the United States can mature and adapt in the modern world without undermining the Constitution's integrity as a fundamental law.

Taft's Career to 1909: The Complications of Constitutional Progressivism

Taft's prepresidential career provides evidence of his political successes and, more importantly, demonstrates that he aligned himself with the reform movement in politics. His early career, and the reputation he gained as an up-and-coming Republican, may help us to better understand the apparent dichotomy between the young reformer and the allegedly reactionary president and chief justice. Taft never faltered in his commitment to progressivism, but this fact has been obscured by his complicated relationship with the Progressive movement's radical wing.

As a young man, Taft quickly rose to prominence in Ohio politics. He modestly attributed his successes to advantageous circumstances: "I got my political pull, first, through father's prominence; then through the fact that I was hail-fellow-well-met with all of the political people of the city convention-going type. I also worked in my ward." Although it is true that his father was a prominent Republican—he had served as a judge in the Ohio courts, secretary of war, attorney general, and minister to Austria Hungary and Imperial Russia—young Taft's claims more likely reflect feigned indifference than literal truth. Relying on personal connections and his own efficiency, he gained his first political office at the age of twenty-three, serving as assistant prosecutor for Hamilton County, Ohio (1881–1882) before accepting a federal post as collector of internal revenue in Chester Arthur's administration (1882–1883). Realizing to his disgust that he was expected to play an unsavory role in granting federal patronage, Taft resigned from office and informed Arthur he desired to practice law. Taft managed to maintain both his honor and his position with the party; Arthur raised no objections and apparently held no grudges. After two years in private practice, Taft was appointed assistant county solicitor for Hamilton County (1885–1887).[19]

During this early period, Taft was respected as a reformer in Ohio politics and was well known for opposing the spoils system and the machine politics and "boss" rule upon which that system relied. Even as he opposed the Republican political bosses, however, he managed not to alienate party elites. This delicate balance paid off. In 1887, Governor Joseph Foraker, a fellow Cincinnatian closely aligned with the Ohio Republican machine and with a history of personal animosity toward Taft, appointed him to fill a vacancy on the Ohio Superior Court. Despite his personal feelings, Foraker apparently understood that he would benefit politically by associating himself with the Taft family and that young William Howard Taft, with a promising political career ahead of him, should be pacified. Foraker wrote to newly appointed Judge Taft that, after serving out the unexpired judicial term and then winning election to a full term in 1888, Taft would be "so established in the confidence of the people that all other things will come naturally."[20]

But both Taft and Foraker knew that political advancement did not simply come naturally. Contrary to typical portrayals of Taft as lethargic or unambitious, he aggressively sought a place on the US Supreme Court in 1889. Despite his relative youth, he encouraged Foraker and other Republican allies to recommend his appointment to Benjamin Harrison. Although Harrison did not nominate Taft for a seat on the high court, he did appoint him solicitor general. Taft, still in his early thirties, became the third-ranking officer in the Justice Department.[21] When Harrison had the opportunity to nominate nine new judges to the federal circuit courts, Taft was appointed to the Sixth Circuit in 1892. Judge Taft handed down opinions on the major political issues of the day. Despite sometimes being painted as an antilabor judge, he authored decisions that limited the doctrines of assumption of risk and contributory negligence for railroad workers. Moreover, in *Thomas v. Cincinnati* he explicated and defended the rights of laborers to unionize and strike. Later, in the *Addyston Pipe* case, Taft became one of the first federal judges to implement the Sherman Act, delivering the "first great blow . . . for federal control of interstate commerce and the vitalization of the anti-trust law." As a judge, Taft showed that his love for the law was not in conflict with progressive goals.[22]

In January 1900, after Taft had served eight years on the federal bench, President William McKinley offered him a post on the Second Philippine Commission. There can be no doubt that Taft was surprised by the offer; he had opposed the US takeover of the islands and he hesitated to give up life tenure on the Sixth Circuit for a temporary posting to the Philippines. Taft enjoyed his judicial career immensely—his wife would later call his resignation from the bench "the hardest thing he ever did"—but he chose to give up his seat on the bench, even though McKinley optimistically suggested that he could take a leave of absence instead of resigning, quickly create a civil government for the Philippines, and return to the bench within a year. Notably, Judge Taft did not accept McKinley's offer until after the president had agreed to make him the president of the commission, despite his lack of executive experience—McKinley ultimately allowed Taft to approve the nominations of the other members of the commission—and with the expectation that he would eventually become civil governor. Taft took the post knowing he would be an executive, and he quickly proved to be an effective one. Throughout his administration of the Philippines, he basked in the "national political spotlight" and received widespread praise for his "impressive executive talents."[23]

Once in the Philippines, first as president of the Second Philippine Commission (1900–1901) and then as civil governor (1901–1903), Taft showed an understanding of political strategy and quickly consolidated power in the fledgling civil government. Faced with opposition by the commanders of US armed forces on the islands, Taft used his power of the purse and his influence with Secretary of War Elihu Root to gradually take over much of the military's authority and bring the islands under civil control. More importantly, Taft adopted a reforming progressive policy in the Philippines. He insisted that American rule should benefit the Filipino people, not American commercial interests. Taft worked to end tenant farming and encourage land ownership, sought to open good schools for the entire populace (only about 10 percent of Filipinos had received any formal education), and promoted racial integration socially and in the government. He ensured fair civil procedures in the local courts, worked to educate the people to prepare them for eventual self-government, steadily increased the number of Filipinos in the civil service, and gradually expanded the amount of political power held by the native population. It is some indication of Taft's obvious goodwill and efficiency that he was immensely popular with the Filipino people. When Roosevelt demanded Taft return to the United States to serve on the Supreme Court in 1902, thousands of Filipinos marched to the governor's palace and demonstrated so forcefully that TR was convinced to leave Taft in Manila.[24]

In 1904, Taft returned to Washington, not to don the ermine and sit on the bench, but to manage the War Department. Although he had previously refused judicial appointment because he believed it was his duty to stabilize the Philippine situation, as secretary of war Taft would retain control over US Philippine policy. Additionally, Taft's willingness to return to the United States was clearly influenced by strong hints from both Roosevelt and outgoing Secretary of War Root that he would be the likely Republican nominee for president in 1908. Taft's time as secretary of war offered him ample opportunities to prepare for the presidency. He gained extensive political experience during the 1904 and 1906 elections by campaigning for the Republican Party. More importantly, he became Roosevelt's "all-purpose troubleshooter," serving as a peace envoy to Tokyo at the end of the Russo–Japanese War in 1905, as provisional governor of Cuba in 1906, as the acting secretary of state when John Hay fell ill, and as the "pro tem president" during Roosevelt's absences. Before embarking on one voyage, Roosevelt remarked that "things will be all right, I have left Taft sitting on the lid."[25]

Roosevelt was happy to see this lid-sitting continue, and actively promoted Taft's presidential bid in 1908, announcing to the nation that Taft was his chosen heir and would continue the "Roosevelt Policies." When he entered the White House in 1909, Taft's professional and political reputation was excellent. He was a successful lawyer and talented judge, but he had also served with distinction in executive posts in the United States and abroad. Moreover, he was seen as an able executive with humane and progressive tendencies and had consistently aligned himself with the reform movement. In light of his prepresidential career, a question arises: How exactly did Taft's reputation as a successful politician with a distinctively progressive bent dissipate and give place to our current understanding of his career? How did we come to see Taft as a failed politician, a conservative constitutionalist who opposed—or at least slowed the pace of—progressive reform? The answer becomes clear when we recognize that Taft was committed to the key policy initiatives advanced by progressives, but he also rejected absolutely the radical plans for constitutional transformation proposed by the most extreme members of the Progressive movement.

Constitutional Means to Progressive Ends

As president, Taft broke with the radical wing of the Progressive movement, but this disagreement arose primarily from disagreements over constitutionalism rather than differences over public policy. Taft believed the national government existed to guarantee "life, liberty, property and the pursuit of happiness" against thoughtless or tyrannical action; moreover, he claimed the Constitution "rests on personal liberty and the right of property," including "the right of contract and the right of labor." Yet since he also insisted that these rights "are not obstructive to any reasonable qualification . . . in the interest of the community," we must consider his constitutional conservatism alongside his support for major progressive plans for social and economic amelioration. Because Taft believed that the massive industrial changes following the Civil War had created a plethora of socioeconomic ills, he worked to expand the national government's initiatives in the fields of trust-busting, land conservation, tariff reform, railroad regulations, and worker safety laws. He rejected the "laisser [sic] faire school," which taught that "the Government ought to do nothing but run a police force." The national government, Taft insisted, should promote "progress toward more perfect equality of opportunity and ridding society of injustice" by bringing "to a close this period of illegitimate corporate immunity" and forcing "an irresponsible plutocracy" to come "within the regulative influence of legislative and executive action." These calls for reform were not empty words; when conservatives within his own party were defeated in the 1910 elections, Taft wrote that they merited defeat since they had failed to "recognize the just demands of the people for a change and a reform."[26] Taft was attached both to the Constitution's guarantees of individual rights and to constructive progressive reform.

In contrast to the extreme members of the Progressive movement—the "vanguard of the Progressive movement," as Milkis has aptly labeled them—who insisted that the Constitution was a hindrance to real progress, Taft staunchly refused to support a transformation of the nation's fundamental law.[27] He disagreed with the radical views expressed by men of the stripe of Herbert Croly. As a leading progressive intellectual, Croly provided one of the bluntest and clearest attacks on the fundamental law when he wrote that the Constitution was "partly responsible for some of the existing abuses, evils, and problems" facing the country. Thus, Croly believed progressivism's "acid" had partially "disintegrat[ed] American political traditions," "challeng[ing] the old system, root and branch," and proposing a "new conception of the purpose and methods of democracy." In order to address modern challenges, he argued, the United States must emancipate itself from its past and unmoor itself from its inflexibly conservative fundamental law. To this end, Croly called for a "gateway amendment," which would permit a majority of Americans in a majority of the states to amend the Constitution, thereby doing away with the more difficult amendment mechanism of Article V and easing the process by which all future amendments would be enacted. Croly admitted that he was calling for revolutionary change; he sought the creation of a "new order" and desired not a "*re*birth" of the republic, but a wholly "*new* birth."[28] The *New Republic*, which Croly cofounded, was aptly named.

Croly may have been the most forthright critic of America's constitutional tradition, but he was not alone in his desire for constitutional transformation. During the 1912 election, Roosevelt argued that republican institutions must be updated to make way for "pure democracy." He mistrusted complex constitutional safeguards—representation, separation of powers, and checks and balances—because he believed they too often thwarted "the absolute right of the people to rule themselves." Setting aside an older constitutional tradition, TR proposed the states adopt a more democratic system to ensue that "the people . . . have the power to enact into law any measure they deem necessary." The Progressive Party platform of 1912 embodied a form of Roosevelt's ideas and called for change at both the national and state level. In addition to adopting a Roosevelt-authored pledge to secure "a more easy and expeditious method of amending the Federal Constitution," the party urged the states to adopt the initiative, referendum, and recall.[29] By the end of the 1912 campaign, Roosevelt had radicalized his position, blurring the line between reform at the state and national level as he called for applying the recall even to the president. Notably, Roosevelt believed these institutional reforms were "not . . . ends in themselves," but means for ensuring the people could enact a reform agenda. For Roosevelt, constitutional transformation was a necessary means to achieving the end of social progress.[30]

Taft's refusal to support constitutional transformation—the creation of Croly's "new order" and Roosevelt's "pure democracy"—marked his central point of disagreement with the extreme left of the Progressive movement. In 1912, the most important debate between Taft and Roosevelt was not over policy but over the fate of constitutional government. Taft stood for an older republican constitutional tradition, with its system of separation of powers and checks and balances, and he rejected radical demands for constitutional transformation because he feared, as Milkis writes, that "TR's progressivism threatened to sweep all intermediary institutions off the stage, to usher in a cult of personality."[31]

Taft explained his break with the radical progressives in a set of ten speeches delivered in 1912–1913 and later published together as *Popular Government*. He voiced his disagreement with what he called the "new school of progressives," who questioned "the wisdom and equity" of the Constitution because they believed reform was possible only through "a change in the fundamental structure of our Government." He insisted that he agreed with the "new school" as to "the *end* of government"—promoting "the happiness of the individual and his progress"—but diverged over "the *means* by which that government . . . [will] reach its end." Contrary to the radicals, Taft believed the constitutional system could "serve the purposes of honest government and of legislative and executive reforms" and argued that "all legitimate governmental purposes" sought by progressives could "be promoted and brought about" through the constitutional system.[32]

Taft stood for the Constitution of 1787, but his belief in the Constitution encompassed his understanding that the fundamental law was actually the source of the national government's powers; as a result, the Constitution and the institutions it created were not a hindrance to reform, but were instead "essential to further progress." Moreover, Taft recognized that if progressive policies were enacted through the institutions created by the Constitution and in accord with the Constitution's strictures, they would be more permanent and effective. He acknowledged that his insistence on regular legal processes did sometimes slow reform, but pointed out that "radical and revolutionary changes, arbitrarily put into operation, are not likely to be permanent or to accomplish the good which is prophesied of them." By putting progressive policies on firm legal footing, he would make them "permanent in the form of law." Taft therefore argued that the Constitution needed to survive and continue to function in the twentieth century because it would be the foundation for future reforms, embodying "the national idea" and empowering the government with powers sufficient to meet "all needed functions for national purposes."[33]

Even as Taft repudiated the radicalism of the extreme left, he also criticized the right's inflexible reading of the Constitution. Taft was a nationalist of the stamp of John Marshall and Alexander Hamilton. He called for a "liberal construction" of national powers, praising Marshall's recognition in *McCulloch v. Maryland* of the existence of "implied" powers of the national government and its right to use "any method of carrying out the express powers which was reasonably proper and adapted to the purpose." He therefore rejected a "strict construction" of the Constitution, which viewed the fundamental law as inherently limiting and time-bound and failed to recognize that the Constitution was actually capable of addressing "new conditions . . . which those who were responsible for the written law could not have had in view."[34]

Taft's defense of an enlarged role for the federal government rested on his belief that in the modern era "powers that under the Constitution were impliedly within congressional creation, but which had been allowed to lie dormant in view of the supposed lack of public necessity for their exercise" had become active as a result of "the necessities of modern government." Notably, he believed that the Constitution need not be rewritten or even reinterpreted to permit this expanding role: "Circumstances in the growth of the country have served greatly to increase the volume of Federal power. *This has not come from a new construction of the Constitution*, but it has come from the fact that the Federal power has been enlarged by the expansion of *the always conceded subjects of national activities*." He saw that the powers granted to the government could permit it to meet evolving circumstances, but that this expansion of the use of national power occurred without any alteration of the fundamental law. The Constitution's potential was stable and fixed, but the actualization of that potential could fluctuate tremendously in response to various circumstances.[35]

Additionally, Taft recognized that circumstances could change so much that the Constitution might need to be modified by amendments. As he said in 1912, he stood for "the Constitution as it is, with such amendments . . . as new conditions thoroughly understood may require." In contrast to Woodrow Wilson—who wrote in 1908 that the Constitution should be seen as "a vehicle of life" that grows and changes to meet "the exigencies and the new aspects of life"—Taft rejected any notion of a living constitution and insisted the Constitution was an unchanging legal document. Yet he respected the entire document, including the formal amendment process of Article V. As president, Taft supported enactment of the Sixteenth Amendment, which increased national tax power and therefore created a means by which expansive national programs could be funded, and also personally favored the Seventeenth Amendment, which mandated direct election of US senators. The Constitution might be difficult to amend, but he recognized that it could and sometimes should be amended to broaden national power and permit more extensive progressive reforms.[36]

Thus far I have emphasized Taft's belief in the flexibility of the Constitution and his desire for a liberal construction of governmental powers. Without losing sight of Taft's strong nationalism, it is important to remember that he did believe the Constitution imposed real limits on government action and at times restrained the momentary wishes of a democratic majority. Taft insisted that the Constitution's limitations were not undue restrictions on the popular will; instead, they protected safe and lasting popular government, since the fundamental law provides a basis of agreement between a ruling majority and ruled minorities. He therefore defended constitutional restrictions on popular and nationalist grounds, since he believed written constitutions "are the self-imposed restraints of a *whole* people upon a *majority* of them to secure sober action and a respect for the rights of the minority." The Constitution permits "a *majority* of the whole people" to rule, but its restrictions help guarantee "wise, just, and beneficent government for *all the people.*" Ultimately, he believed the limitations on majority power found in the Constitution were necessary to maintain popular government. Without essential agreement on the fundamental law, both the majority and the minority might have every incentive for violence: a majority may seize control of government and abuse the minority, but the minority may simply rebel after losing an election.[37]

Taft believed the early twentieth century was a time for testing America's constitutional system and hoped his own constitutional progressivism would "vindicate . . . [our] form of government and its capacity for progress and development toward higher civilization." Modern circumstances created an opportunity to prove that the Constitution's traditional restrictions and guarantees did not prevent the government from enacting substantive social reforms. He saw his own career as a chance to show the Constitution's potential, as an opportunity for "those of us who really believe in our institutions as essential to further progress . . . to remove real and just ground for criticism of our present system." Most importantly, Taft recognized that reform was necessary if the Constitution was to be maintained. Unless the constitutional system proved capable of permitting reform, he feared that many Americans would simply abandon the Constitution, seeing it as nothing but an oligarchic instrument of oppression. Taft hoped to take "away from the enemies of constitutional government . . . the only real arguments that they have." He therefore aimed to show that progressive reforms could be enacted under the Constitution, rather than in opposition to it.[38] Thus, Taft believed the Constitution and progressive reform could be mutually supporting. He was not a progressive in spite of his constitutionalism—to a certain extent, he was actually a progressive *because of* his constitutionalism, for he believed he had a duty to show that the two could work hand in hand. In this way, his constitutional progressivism offers us a keen insight into the nature of change and reform under a constitutional government by showing that progress may find an ally rather than an enemy in the Constitution.

The Plan of This Book

This book will examine Taft's constitutional progressivism throughout his public career, with the first half focusing on his presidency and the latter half on his work during his retirement at Yale and as chief justice. I will examine his success in expanding and consolidating the progressive policies he inherited from his predecessor, his views of the president's potential for governmental and partisan leadership, his postpresidency understanding of the chief executive's place in the constitutional order, and his influence as chief justice, in terms of both jurisprudence and structural reforms of the federal courts.

In the first two chapters, I consider whether Taft fulfilled his 1908 election pledge to continue the "Roosevelt Policies." These chapters emphasize his work to legalize and expand TR's efforts in both the executive/administrative and legislative arenas. As we will see, Taft consolidated and expanded Roosevelt's efforts in trust-busting, land conservation, and railroad regulations, and revitalized TR's attempts to promote a downward revision of the tariff. Although Roosevelt sometimes advanced his policies through extralegal or illegal means, Taft supplemented and legalized his predecessor's initiatives. In this way, he provided a constitutional and legal articulation of the work begun by Roosevelt and consolidated his predecessor's initiatives through longer administrative practice and additional legislation.

Chapters 3 and 4 turn to Taft's understanding of presidential leadership in modern American life. I reevaluate the traditional belief that he was a lethargic chief executive who lacked the ambition to engage in legislative leadership, but I also acknowledge the truth of claims that Taft lacked ability as a leader of the people. Chapter 3 considers Taft's interest in expanding and developing the president's role through institutional reforms, particularly his efforts to create a presidential budget and his plan to initiate a type of "cabinet government" by introducing heads of departments into Congress. Despite embracing creative ways of increasing presidential influence through governmental institutions, Taft had significant weaknesses as a partisan political leader, as chapter 4 demonstrates. Following Roosevelt's extremely active and personal presidency, the chief executive was expected to take on a more dynamic role in national politics, yet Taft too often viewed his role exclusively through the lens of government or party institutions and failed to see the importance of providing the nation with popular leadership. As a result, he was a capable party leader who successfully used his control of the Republican Party apparatus to beat off Roosevelt's primary challenge in 1912, but he failed as a popular leader and went on to lose a majority of rank-and-file Republican voters and place third in the general election. His instincts for institutional leadership were ultimately insufficient, since he never grasped the importance of active and personal presidential leadership in the early twentieth century.

The latter half of the book considers Taft's postpresidential career. After Taft's presidency, did he maintain his progressive standpoint? Or did he, as some scholars have suggested, become increasingly conservative and reactionary as he grew older? Chapters 5 and 6 bridge Taft's retirement at Yale and his ascent to the Supreme Court. These chapters explore his understanding of the constitutional presidency through a consideration of his book on executive power *Our Chief Magistrate and His Powers*, and his major executive power decision on the Supreme Court, *Myers v. United States. Our Chief Magistrate* analyzes the president's ability to respond to emergencies and rapidly changing circumstances and offers a viable alternative to Theodore Roosevelt's "stewardship" theory of the presidency. *Myers* presents a case for a robust executive in the context of presidential removal power, showing that a growing nation may create a strong national administration without undermining democracy and may hold even seemingly politically insulated administrators responsible to the public will. In both instances, Taft showed that the Constitution could empower the president to serve the nation's evolving needs without undermining legal limits on executive power.

The final two chapters analyze Taft's time as chief justice in order to explain his broader jurisprudence and work to reorganize the judiciary. As I explain in chapter 7, Taft's opinions on the commerce clause, regulation, and labor articulate the government's authority to regulate the national economy and protect labor without losing sight of the Constitution's basic limitations on national powers. As a result, his decisions display a principled constitutionalism that was open to progressive reforms. Finally, in chapter 8, I will analyze how Taft used his position as chief justice to spearhead one of the most significant judicial reorganizations in history: he formalized the judiciary's structure, centralized power in the Supreme Court, and promoted efficiency throughout the federal judiciary.

1 | "Maintenance and Enforcement"
Regularizing Conservation and Trust Policy

The 1908 election turned on the "Roosevelt Policies." Even Democratic nominee William Jennings Bryan, the populist agrarian making his third and final bid for the White House, could not escape from Roosevelt's shadow and was sometimes depicted as trying to out-Roosevelt Taft and the GOP. Unsurprisingly, the Republican Party platform unambiguously pledged "unfailing adherence to [Roosevelt's] policies," and Taft promised to prioritize "the maintenance and enforcement" of Roosevelt's political agenda. Specifically, Taft and his party pledged to continue and expand Roosevelt's work to conserve national resources and control trusts, and also promised tariff reform and new railroad legislation to regulate rates and protect laborers.[1]

Taft's promise to adhere to Roosevelt's policies was supplemented by his acknowledgment that his administration would serve a different function than TR's. Where Roosevelt had "quickened the conscience of the people, and brought on a moral awakening," the new president's task was to "complete and perfect the machinery by which these [Roosevelt's] standards may be maintained." He hoped to "clinch" Roosevelt's policies through "a progressive development" of his predecessor's work, a development characterized by regularizing administrative enforcement and securing additional reform legislation.[2]

This project of consolidating Roosevelt's policies will be the topic of chapters 1 and 2. In this chapter, I study Taft's administrative and executive actions in conservation and trust-busting, and in the next I examine the legislation he advanced, especially the Payne–Aldrich Tariff of 1909 and railroad regulations under the Mann–Elkins Act of 1910. Taft's work to constitutionalize and regularize Roosevelt's policies played a key role in buttressing and consolidating progressive reform. Roosevelt had launched a crusade and gained quick results, but had sometimes neglected legal and constitutional niceties. As president, Taft supported and extended Roosevelt's progressive policies, but he promoted them through legal methods. "It becomes my business," he wrote, "to put [Roosevelt's] reform into *legal* execution." Taft brought to the White House, the *New York Times* observed, "not so much a change of attitude on the great questions that have occupied public attention . . . as upon the methods by which the same policy will be followed." Roosevelt himself acknowledged this when he predicted that his successor's "system may be different, but the results will be the same." Taft's role was to follow behind and legalize TR's actions.[3]

Taft's divergence from Roosevelt's methods was not a betrayal of progressivism, nor did it denote mindless, legalistic formalism; instead, Taft's work actually buttressed and cemented Roosevelt's policies. Taft bemoaned TR's "disrespect for law when he felt the law stood between him and what he thought was right" because he recognized that had Roosevelt employed legal means to reach progressive ends, "he would be further along in some of his reforms."[4] By undergirding Roosevelt's initiatives with a robust constitutional and legal defense, Taft hoped to ensure that his predecessor's reforms could not be reversed by the stroke of a future executive's pen or a reactionary judiciary. His critique of Roosevelt's method was actually a contribution to the Roosevelt policies.

If Taft's contribution to American political life was less dramatic than Roosevelt's, nevertheless it was critically important for the maintenance and continuation of TR's policies. Stephen Skowronek's *Politics Presidents Make* argues that "reconstruction" presidents—those who substantially reform or remake the nation's political system—rightfully receive history's recognition for their towering contributions. In contrast, "articulation" presidents are "the orthodox-innovators" who "continue the good work of the past and demonstrate the vitality of the established order in changing times." Skowronek treats Roosevelt as an articulator of an older Republican tradition, but also acknowledges that TR defies easy evaluation since he initiated "major departures" from the established "institutional forms and routine operations of American party governance." Thus, although Skowronek insists there was no Roosevelt reconstruction, he concedes "there was a Roosevelt departure, and we appreciate that departure today as no less momentous than 'the birth of modern America.'" Roosevelt launched a reform crusade, but he left Taft the duty of articulating the details of that new reform movement. Skowronek points out that articulators such as Taft will never receive the acclaim of reconstructors, but he also cautions that "to dismiss presidents in such situations as [merely] presiding over a stable, 'normal' period

. . . is a mistake."[5] By articulating his predecessor's initial reform work, Taft's administration was able to protect Roosevelt's policies.

President Taft stepped into office at a time when the nation desired not a "reconstruction" or a new "departure," but further articulation of emerging reforms. In political terms, it seems that the nation was unwilling to replace Roosevelt with a similarly innovative and trailblazing successor. In 1908, voters both endorsed Roosevelt's policies by electing his handpicked successor and sought a period of relative calm by choosing Taft, who would administer, the *New York Times* predicted, "a Government of laws . . . enforced by an Executive of a just and deliberating mind."[6] In practical terms, Taft's "Government of laws" was necessary for the continuation of his predecessor's reforms. In a mere seven and a half years, even Roosevelt could not reshape political life in the United States; he needed a careful, legal-minded successor who would supplement his policies with further legislation and consolidate them through longer practice.

Conservation: Legalizing Land Withdrawals

During his tenure, Roosevelt had played a critical role in promoting conservation. But although his work earned the praise of progressives, he also garnered the condemnation of many members of Congress for using executive orders to withdraw millions of acres of public land from private settlement. As a general rule, Taft believed that Roosevelt's conservation efforts were good policy, but he recognized that TR's unilateral withdrawals were based on a legally tenuous doctrine of executive power. The Taft administration's concern for legality has often been written off as the foolish formalism of conservative lawyers. Donald Anderson, for example, writes that Taft adopted a "legalistic approach to conservation" that harmed him politically, while Paolo Coletta complains that Taft displayed a single-minded devotion "to the letter of the law" and ultimately "fragmented the comprehensive Roosevelt conservation program."[7] However, revisionist scholars have acknowledged that TR and his conservationist allies had shown a troubling lack of respect for law.[8] I argue that the Taft administration made a conscious and determined effort to maintain and expand Roosevelt's program by legalizing his environmental efforts and bringing them within the bounds of the constitutional order. By working with Congress, Taft not only secured explicit legislative authorization for executive withdrawals but also codified Roosevelt's extralegal actions.

Taft critiqued his predecessor's questionable methods while also remaining faithful to the conservationist cause. He differed from Roosevelt, TR's interior secretary James R. Garfield, and Chief Forester Gifford Pinchot primarily on the proper means and methods of achieving conservationist goals. Certainly, some policy disagreements did emerge, particularly between Pinchot, who Taft initially retained as chief forester, and Taft's interior secretary, Richard A. Ballinger. Ballinger was a self-made man who hailed from the Pacific Northwest; Pinchot was an easterner born into wealth. As a westerner, Ballinger had a greater concern than Pinchot for "balancing regional economic development with land and resource conservation." And as a self-made man and an opponent of monopoly, he feared that Pinchot was too willing to accept an alliance of "big government . . . with big business," which favored entrenched firms at the expense of their smaller competitors. As this tension shows, there were real policy debates within the Taft administration, but they represent differences of emphasis rather than fundamental disagreements over the goal of conserving and administering national resources.[9]

More important than these policy disputes was a deeper disagreement about administrative regularity and legal authority. Under Roosevelt, Pinchot had been permitted to function "as a virtual member of the cabinet for conservation" with a great deal of administrative autonomy. He had regularly circumvented the authority of his own direct superiors in order to work directly with the president. Additionally, he had advanced his priorities by brokering a number of informal temporary agreements between the Interior and Agriculture Departments. This informal and unrestrained style, which had blurred lines of responsibility and undermined centralized departmental control, was anathema to Taft and Ballinger. The new president believed his administration could chart a consistent policy only if it maintained clear lines of authority, from the president through department heads into individual departments and divisions. Ballinger, similarly, believed that a free-ranging administrator, who operated outside regular zones of administrative control, would undermine political responsibility and risk an unaccountable bureaucracy.[10]

Finally, and most importantly, Taft and Ballinger balked at Roosevelt's belief that the chief executive could violate the law in order to serve the nation. Although public lands had been opened to private settlement by statute, Roosevelt used executive orders to reserve millions of acres in order to protect valuable coal lands, potential waterpower sites, and timberlands.[11] TR insisted that presidential power to withdraw lands had been conceded him by Congress, and he consistently cited withdrawals made by past presidents as precedent for his own actions. However, Roosevelt's withdrawals differed quantitatively and qualitatively from those of his predecessors. Benjamin Harrison, Grover Cleveland, and William McKinley had together withdrawn about 50 million acres of land for forest reserves, whereas Roosevelt alone withdrew 230 million acres for forests and to protect natural resources. Moreover, past presidents had withdrawn tracts of land for discrete uses, sometimes by the government itself (typically for military bases, to expand Indian reservations, or to create bird reserves), whereas Roosevelt made mass withdrawals an integral part of his policy of placing resources "under the auspices of administrative experts" and facilitating "constructive management . . . [and] long-term productivity."[12]

Ultimately, Roosevelt's unilateral approach to conservation reflected his "stewardship" theory of presidential power. Roosevelt explained that the "laws were often insufficient" to allow him to protect natural resources, and because Congress had refused to expand his authority, he had found it necessary unilaterally "to supplement it [the law] by Executive action." In the end, Roosevelt's central justification for his actions depended not on statutory authority but on his belief "that the President could at any time in his discretion withdraw from entry any of the public lands . . . and reserve the same for . . . public purposes." His subordinates were even blunter. Secretary Garfield contended that since "full power under the Constitution was vested in the executive branch of the Government," the president's power to protect natural resources was limited only "by the discretion of the Executive, unless any specific act has been prohibited either by the Constitution or by legislation." Similarly, Pinchot admitted that Roosevelt "did not have, and could not get from Congress, specific authority for these withdrawals" but defended TR's acts as morally justifiable, albeit extralegal, uses of executive prerogative. Roosevelt and his allies "saw ethical principles and scientific information as fully adequate substitutes for laws," Peri Arnold aptly concludes.[13]

The practical repercussions of Roosevelt's assertion of virtually unlimited presidential power were demonstrated in the case of his midnight withdrawals. In 1907, the appropriations bill to fund the Department of Agriculture included a rider that proscribed executive land withdrawals in a half dozen western states. Instead of vetoing the bill, negotiating with Congress, or appealing to the public for support, Roosevelt quickly issued thirty-three "midnight proclamations" and withdrew 17 million acres of land to create twenty-one new national forests. Then, having already "preserved virtually all the land that the amendment had intended to put beyond the president's reach," he signed the bill into law.[14] As this incident shows, Roosevelt was more interested in attaining his goals than in attending to the niceties of cooperation with Congress. But his focus on immediate results actually damaged his reform agenda. His dramatic midnight withdrawals, made in "blatant . . . bad faith," spawned further congressional opposition to his policies, "drove a wedge" between the political branches, and ultimately "left unresolved the dispute about the appropriate federal role in managing natural resources."[15] He secured quick results in the field of conservation, but his refusal to work with Congress resulted in lasting harm to his policies.

By recognizing the tenuous legality of Roosevelt's approach, we can better see Taft's real contribution to the progressive environmental agenda. Conservation efforts, Taft believed, would be more permanent when "every step taken in that direction [is] within the law and buttressed by legal authority."[16] Taft helped to guarantee the permanence of TR's progressive project by ensuring conservation was carried out under the Constitution and with the support of statutory law.

When Taft entered the White House, the federal Geological Survey had begun to issue warnings that the US government was selling oil lands to private entities at token prices. Essentially, the United States was handing over valuable oil lands, unintentionally encouraging overproduction and waste, and parting with oil it might soon be forced to buy back to power its growing navy. Similarly, the government was selling waterpower sites and valuable timberlands to developers, some of whom sought to monopolize these resources.[17] To remedy these problems, Taft continued the policy of land withdrawals, but his own approach was more limited than Roosevelt's and more suited to collaboration with Congress. Taft made temporary withdrawals in order to give Congress time to legislate and determine which lands it wished to protect; in doing so, he both respected the constitutional separation of powers and avoided an inflexible and formalist approach to conservation.

A lengthy legal brief, authored by Oscar Lawler, assistant attorney general for the Interior Department, explained that neither the Constitution nor the laws granted the president power to withdraw lands permanently as a matter of policy. The Lawler brief argued that the president's powers were limited because statutory law had opened that land to private settlement. Lawler believed that the president could withdraw land for public use: for example, if Congress had appropriated funds for a military base and allowed the president to select the location. However, he claimed that withdrawing land as part of a general conservation policy would assume "the existence of a dispensing or suspending power in the Executive over laws," violating Congress's power to control federal lands, the president's duty under the take care clause to execute the laws, and the basic principles of separation of powers. Ballinger echoed many of these concerns when he insisted that "there exists no supervisory or discretionary authority . . . that will warrant the executive in doing what may seem to him to be best for the public interest independent of statutory direction."[18]

Taft was sensitive to these legal concerns and worked diligently to gain legislative authorization for land withdrawals, but he also saw room for limited presidential discretion in protecting resources from private exploitation in anticipation of congressional action. Thus, in September 1909 Taft issued a proclamation withdrawing from settlement all public oil lands in a 3 million acre tract in California and Wyoming. The Taft administration followed this up with more than a dozen additional withdrawals over the course of the next nine months.[19] Yet Taft tempered presidential authority by reassuring Congress that "these withdrawals are temporary . . . [and] made in order to permit Congress to legislate." His orders explicitly acknowledged legislative authority: "In aid of proposed legislation affecting the use and disposition of the petroleum deposits on the public domain, all public lands in the accompanying lists are hereby temporarily withdrawn from . . . settlement." Moreover, he affirmed that unless Congress decided to act, "it would be difficult for the executive to find the authority indefinitely to withhold these sites from settlement under the general laws."[20]

Essentially, Taft withdrew lands not to advance his own conservation policies but to ensure that Congress had time to address a problem before it was too late. But he promised to rescind his withdrawals if the legislature chose not to enact new statutes to control the disposition of natural resources. The president's understanding of executive power avoided both Roosevelt's refusal to recognize limits on executive power and a rigid formalism that would leave no room for executive discretion. In contrast, Taft admitted that the Constitution could place real limits on the chief executive's powers without destroying his discretionary authority to act "in aid" of Congress. Additionally, by wielding his independent powers in cooperation, not opposition, to Congress and its laws, Taft showed that the constitutional separation of powers may lead to constructive cooperation between the branches rather than unproductive gridlock.

Even as he exercised broad discretion, Taft made it clear that he respected Congress's legitimate authority to regulate national lands and asked Congress to provide him with clear legal authorization to withdraw land. As he pointed out, the president may "recommend" policies to the legislature, but Congress must lay down "general purpose[s]" and grant "general authority" in order to enable the president to regulate land withdrawals. Essentially, he recognized that the Constitution gave Congress power to control national lands, but he also believed that Congress could delegate some authority to the president and showed that the executive had a certain amount of discretion to aid Congress. In contrast, Garfield's claim that the president had power to act "unless any specific act has been prohibited either by the Constitution or by legislation" was an attempt to reverse this order and claim general presidential authority over public lands, which could be limited only by express statutory limitations.[21]

Recognizing the problematic nature of Roosevelt's claims, Taft understood that explicit legislative authorization would actually strengthen his ability to act. Indeed, his respect for legislative power ultimately redounded to the executive's benefit. In response to his request, Congress passed the Pickett Act, which gave the president the power "at any time in his discretion, temporarily [to] withdraw from settlement, location, sale, or entry any of the public lands of the United States . . . and reserve the same for waterpower sites, irrigation, classification of lands, or other public purposes . . . and such withdrawals or reservations shall remain in force until revoked by him or by an Act of Congress."[22] The Pickett Act gave the president explicit statutory authority to do the very things Roosevelt had done illegally. Taft's respect for law and willingness to cooperate with Congress ultimately resulted in expanded executive discretion. His constitutional approach to reform neither hindered progressive ends nor crippled executive power.

Nevertheless, Taft was excoriated by progressives because his approach had implicitly rebuked his former mentor's swashbuckling conservation methods. This theme of disagreement over constitutional means rather than policy ends was the critical factor in the Pinchot–Ballinger affair, the Taft administration's most damaging scandal. Pinchot, a favored member of Roosevelt's "Tennis Cabinet," swiftly became disenchanted with the Taft administration's conservation policy. To Taft and Ballinger, the disagreement with Pinchot was a result of Pinchot's disregard for legal limitations on his power. For example, in order to protect national lands from fires, Pinchot had been granted the power to authorize the passage of electricity lines through national forests; however, he used this power to bully electricity companies into adopting his own preferred schedule of rates. Similarly, Pinchot often requested withdrawal of lands he claimed would be used for ranger stations, but he later admitted that he actually had the land withdrawn because it could be used for waterpower sites. From Pinchot's perspective, his actions were justified by the good he achieved, while Taft's and Ballinger's scruples reflected the fussy anxiety of fastidious lawyers. Pinchot recalled that he broke from Taft because the new president had replaced Roosevelt's "sharp sword" with a "roll of paper, legal size."[23]

Taft entered office determined to maintain his credibility as a supporter of conservation and willing to keep the forester on in his administration. But Pinchot's disregard for law placed him on a collision course with the new president. By the fall of 1909, Taft had begun to see that he could not avoid a clash with Pinchot if he intended to control his administration's conservation agenda. Long-standing disagreements between Pinchot and Ballinger—some of which had originated years earlier when both served in Roosevelt's administration—quickly spiraled out of control. Pinchot began to publicly attack the interior secretary's integrity, claiming that Ballinger had permitted corrupt speculators illegally to gain control of coal lands in Alaska. Although he lacked significant evidence of the interior secretary's guilt, Pinchot permitted attacks against Ballinger by inferior officers and actively promoted denunciations of the Taft administration in *Collier's Weekly*. Eventually, Pinchot circumvented the president himself and sent a letter to Senator Jonathan Dolliver accusing the president of poor judgment. The Dolliver letter was more than a rhetorical thumb in Taft's eye; it violated the administrative "gag order," implemented by Roosevelt and expanded by Taft, which prevented bureaucrats from communicating with Congress except through heads of departments. Pinchot, Taft realized, was "looking for martyrdom."[24]

Taft has been blamed for his handling of the Pinchot–Ballinger affair and especially for waiting to dismiss Pinchot until after the Dolliver letter emerged and the forester had become openly insubordinate. To some extent, it is possible to sympathize with Taft's procrastination. Because Pinchot was one of Roosevelt's close friends and, as the nation's first chief forester, embodied the spirit of conservation, removing Pinchot would anger TR and create a perception that Taft was half-hearted in his support for conservation. Nevertheless, the criticisms of Taft's administrative style certainly have merit. Pinchot obviously deserved to be fired for working behind Taft's back and undermining his administration's credibility. Yet even when the president finally removed Pinchot, he committed severe administrative errors. As the conflict reached its climax, Taft and his attorney general, George Wickersham, predated a critical report that explained the administration's position on the affair. When Pinchot's supporters recognized that the report had been predated, the administration initially denied the charge, then backtracked and admitted the truth. The resulting press imbroglio embarrassed Taft and the administration enormously. As Lewis Gould notes, predating was neither unethical nor unusual, but the administration mishandled the issue, attempted to mislead the press, and was left "open to a charge of dishonesty."[25]

Regardless of Taft's administrative shortcomings, he fired Pinchot because of the forester's insubordination, not because of policy disagreements. Pinchot, the president wrote, had "destroyed [his] usefulness as a helpful subordinate of the Government" and had made "an improper appeal to Congress" through the Dolliver letter. Years later, Pinchot insisted on the justice of his cause but he also admitted that the Dolliver letter "from the narrowly official angle . . . was doubtless insubordinate," and he concluded that Taft "was perfectly justified in firing me." Despite the angry accusations from progressives who believed Pinchot's firing signaled Taft's betrayal of conservation, the president removed Pinchot in order to ensure that he could maintain control over the actions of his subordinates and coordinate a consistent approach to conservation. Taft blundered in his handling of the Pinchot–Ballinger affair, but his reputation as a conservationist suffered because of politics, not policy.[26]

Despite the political repercussions of Pinchot's removal, Taft's efforts were critical to legitimizing Roosevelt's conservation work. Roosevelt had notoriously withdrawn 230 million acres of land, often illegally and over Congress's objections. Taft worked with Congress to secure the Pickett Act, used that statute to confirm Roosevelt's ad hoc withdrawals, and withdrew more than 80 million acres in his own right. By providing a defense of Roosevelt's work, he undercut speculators who, acting "on the theory that . . . [Roosevelt's] withdrawing of lands . . . was not legal," had asked the courts to permit them to buy up lands withdrawn by executive order. As Taft recognized, these court battles "might have kept us in suspense for a long period" and could even have reversed prior withdrawals. Roosevelt's dramatic reforms garnered far more media attention, but Taft helped to integrate them into US law since, Paolo Coletta writes, Taft's conservation withdrawals "were the first to be legally authorized." Though Taft played a secondary role, his work was nevertheless necessary for maintaining Roosevelt's legacy.[27]

Revitalizing and Enforcing the Sherman Act

Roosevelt's presidency brought trust-busting to the fore of American political life when his administration's legal victories in *Swift & Co. v. United States* and *Northern Securities Co. v. United States* helped to resuscitate the 1890 Sherman Act, which had been seriously damaged by the Supreme Court's decision in *United States v. E. C. Knight.* Building on Roosevelt's initial successes, Taft systematized his predecessor's work by insisting on regularity and legality in the enforcement of the Sherman Act and by patiently pushing for expanded administrative authority to oversee corporate activities.

TR had utilized the Sherman Act more frequently than any previous president, initiating a total of fifty-four antitrust suits and proving the Sherman Act was still viable despite the *Knight* decision. However, Roosevelt had not set a clear course for combatting monopolies. He was impatient with the lengthy court battles required to break up large trusts under the act and often turned instead to informal methods of administrative oversight and unofficial gentlemen's agreements with certain big businesses. As a result, his legal victories were often weakened by his tendency to view the regulation of trusts as more important than the dissolution of monopolies. Overall, his approach to the trust issue resulted in a policy that was, Gould writes, "confused, vague, and often ineffective."[28]

When he entered the White House, Taft was forced to build upon this somewhat tenuous legacy of controlling monopolies and preventing business abuses. Where Roosevelt had employed informal arrangements, Taft and Wickersham were dedicated to enforcing the Sherman Act and bringing suit against corporations engaged in monopolistic activities. Their decision to enforce the law and break off TR's more informal approach has been frequently criticized. Coletta, for example, ridiculed the policy as "compulsive upholding of the letter of the law," and numerous scholars have pointed out that Wickersham's crusade against trusts alienated conservative members of the business community and cost Taft their support in the 1912 presidential election.[29] These criticisms miss the central reality confronting the new administration: the task of regularizing the nation's antitrust policies by replacing TR's government of men with Taft's government of laws. As I will show, Taft's decision to enforce the law was not itself problematic; however, the Sherman Act was flawed and contained vague provisions that confused and frustrated even honest businessmen.

Roosevelt's irregular approach to trusts sprang from his doubts about the Sherman Act's utility. Because the law simply banned "every contract, combination . . . or conspiracy, in restraint of trade," he believed it failed to distinguish between "bad" trusts, which harmed the public by seeking excessive and unreasonable profits, and "good" trusts, which were "useful to the country" despite their monopolistic character. Thus, he rejected on principle the Sherman Act's prohibition of "all combinations of whatever character, if technically in restraint of trade." Instead, he emphasized the role of government oversight, insisting that only by "a thorough and continuing supervision" of the trusts could the government prevent "improper forms of competition, and . . . wrongdoing generally." By 1911, Roosevelt believed the government ought to regulate, rather than dissolve, the trusts; he called for government price controls and essentially planned to treat these conglomerates as public utilities or common carriers, permitted to control the market in exchange for government oversight. If these trusts could be regulated and required to promote the national interest, Roosevelt would not oppose their continued existence.[30]

Roosevelt therefore favored increased executive discretion to allow the president to distinguish between "good" and "bad" trusts and demanded additional legislation to give the administration the power to supervise and control, rather than break up, large trusts. When he failed to gain this new oversight power from Congress, he determined to move forward on an ad hoc basis and began initiating informal investigations and negotiations with various trusts. For example, in the fall of 1905, then Bureau of Corporations head James Garfield worked closely and discreetly with the U.S. Steel Corporation, examining their records and, with Roosevelt's direct intervention, working out an informal agreement to gain the company's cooperation with the government. Similarly, in 1906, when J. P. Morgan's International Harvester Corporation came under scrutiny, the administration secured the company's cooperation with the investigation in return for a promise of confidentiality (but not immunity). In some ways, these methods were likely beneficial. Such agreements relied on "administrative techniques in regulating business [rather] than . . . on the Sherman Antitrust Act" and circumvented normal legal channels, but they could produce quick results and cooperation from the firms under investigation.[31]

Yet TR's policy suffered from significant administrative and legal weaknesses. Although Roosevelt's Bureau of Corporations entered into informal understandings with industry, his Department of Justice sought to take a harder line on enforcing the Sherman Act. These differing approaches produced interdepartmental conflicts within his administration. In some cases, Roosevelt stepped in to call off the Justice Department—even requiring Attorney General Charles J. Bonaparte to end an investigation and withdraw the suit he was prepared to file. Moreover, the president's informal approach essentially wrote his own definition of good and bad trusts into the Sherman Act. This, in turn, "often meant that his personal reaction to an issue or corporation determined where the White House stood." Because the administration ignored the letter of the law and did not rely on any legal definition of an illegal monopoly, the distinction between a "good" and "bad" trust could sometimes be determined by Roosevelt's personal perceptions and a company's willingness to cooperate with the government. Despite his honest motives, TR's political pragmatism sometimes obscured his progressive principles.[32]

Taft agreed with Roosevelt's contention that the executive needed additional oversight and investigatory authority, and he also acknowledged that the law might be clarified by specifically defining prohibited business activities. However, he rejected Roosevelt's extralegal practice of distinguishing between good and bad trusts by executive fiat. Instead, Taft insisted that the Sherman Act be consistently enforced. From Taft's perspective, enforcement of the law, in combination with expanded oversight and regulatory powers, would provide a more permanent solution to the trust problem. Moreover, Taft's approach could prevent the abuses that might arise when haphazard negotiations and bargaining between the White House and Wall Street replaced consistent enforcement of the antitrust law. As Wickersham explained, the Taft administration's approach relied on law, not personal reactions: the administration "enforced the laws . . . without discrimination and without fear" and even prosecuted the president's "personal friends."[33]

To ensure consistent enforcement of the Sherman Act, Taft sought a steady and experienced hand at the tiller in his Department of Justice and so turned to Wickersham. Taft has often been criticized for appointing a number of former corporate lawyers to cabinet positions, with the typical biography suggesting that he stocked his cabinet with conservative, business-friendly attorneys. Donald Anderson, for example, believes Taft's administration trended away from progressivism because of "the conservative-legalistic bias" of his cabinet. Whatever merit these concerns may have, Taft explained that he selected attorneys such as Wickersham not because of their associations with the corporate world, but because of their legal acumen: he saw no reason "why the United States should not have the benefit of as good a lawyer as the corporations." Despite his former career as a corporate lawyer, Wickersham quickly proved himself as a crusader against illegal trusts and "launched an antitrust crusade to which Roosevelt's paled in comparison."[34]

Taft's administration both enforced the Sherman Act and consistently pushed Congress to expand the administration's investigative authority. In his inaugural address, Taft pledged to ensure "effective cooperation" between the Department of Justice, the Bureau of Corporations, and the Interstate Commerce Commission in order to "secure a more rapid and certain enforcement" of the law. Throughout his presidency he sought to expand national oversight over large corporations and create an option for national incorporation of businesses.[35]

The dissonance between Roosevelt's and Taft's methods of controlling trusts came to a head in October 1911, when Taft's Department of Justice brought suit against the U.S. Steel Corporation. This action demonstrated to the general public that the Taft administration was willing to prosecute the very same trusts that Roosevelt had tolerated. The issue reached back to the financial panic of 1907, when Roosevelt had inadvertently approved the creation of a steel trust. At the height of the crisis, Moore & Schley, an important brokerage house, was tumbling toward bankruptcy. To save the firm, J. P. Morgan arranged for his U.S. Steel Company to buy up Moore & Schley's shares in the Tennessee Coal and Iron Company (TC&I). This would save Moore & Schley from bankruptcy and also bring one of U.S. Steel's competitors under Morgan's control. Eager to restore economic stability, Roosevelt approved the sale after receiving assurances that U.S. Steel was buying the stock at an exorbitant price and would not benefit substantially from the arrangement. He later defended his actions by explaining that he believed that U.S. Steel would derive "little benefit" from the arrangement, would not gain monopoly control of the steel industry, and that the proposed sale "was emphatically for the general good."[36]

It is almost certain that Roosevelt had acted with the best of intentions. Yet his hasty approval of the sale and his later insistence that he saw "no public duty . . . to interpose any objections" illustrate the weaknesses of his antitrust policy. Because he chose to ignore the Sherman Act and to rely instead on executive discretion in a case-by-case basis, Roosevelt created a situation in which presidents would be forced to make snap judgments about the legality of corporate acquisitions. In 1907, he had acted swiftly to restore economic stability, believing that U.S. Steel was a "good" trust. But, contrary to the information TR received, U.S. Steel did not pay an exorbitant price for TC&I's stocks (it paid only $45 million to acquire stocks worth close to $1 billion), and the sale ensured U.S. Steel a near monopoly on steel production. Even if Roosevelt believed that he was serving the common good, his policy of expanding executive discretion at the expense of statutory law "was never any better than his capacity to grasp the facts of a specific issue." Regardless of his good intentions, Roosevelt had actually sanctioned the illegal consolidation of a steel monopoly.[37]

The Taft administration thus had legitimate grounds to bring suit against U.S. Steel in 1911. Yet the Justice Department created a tremendous political headache for the Taft administration, since the bill against U.S. Steel named Roosevelt and—without accusing him of actual wrongdoing—asserted that he had been misinformed when he approved the TC&I acquisition. The suit was brought in the wake of damaging hearings in the Republican-controlled Senate and of investigations in the Democratic-controlled House into U.S. Steel's control of American steel markets after its purchase of TC&I. As a result of these hearings and its own investigation, the Department of Justice concluded that the company had "eliminated a competitor and unlawfully acquired a power which is a menace to the welfare of the country and should be destroyed." Roosevelt had been misinformed in 1907 and the Taft administration's suit, "the most sweeping antitrust action ever brought by the Department of Justice," was in accord with the Sherman Act. Setting aside political considerations, the decision to bring suit was clearly correct.[38]

The U.S. Steel case is the most famous of the Taft administration's antitrust suits because of its political ramifications, but it was only one part of the attorney general's crusade against trusts. The Taft administration concluded prosecutions begun under Roosevelt and won major lawsuits against the Standard Oil and American Tobacco trusts. In only four years, Wickersham initiated ninety antitrust suits, nearly double the fifty-four brought by the Roosevelt administration in seven and a half years. He broke up trusts left untouched at the end of Roosevelt's term and attacked the "beef trust," the "shoe trust," the "electrical trust," the "bath tub trust," the "sugar trust," and the "powder trust," among others. As the *National Tribune* wrote in late 1911, Taft's Department of Justice was a "juggernaut rolling over the trusts."[39]

Taft's decision to enforce the law instead of relying on virtually unlimited executive discretion was a valuable contribution to antitrust policy. Nevertheless, the scholarly consensus that Taft alienated conservative business interests by enforcing the act does point to a weakness in his policy. Because the Sherman Act's prohibitions were quite vague, some businessmen were left confused. What sort of combinations were legal and which were prohibited? Taft never provided a clear answer to this question. He initially admitted the law's weaknesses and suggested that Congress should pass additional explanatory legislation, yet his support for such legislation seems to have been half-hearted. Taft himself evidently felt that supplementary legislation was not truly necessary since he believed "the slow course of judicial decision" had helped to clarify the act. Specifically, he believed that the Standard Oil and American Tobacco cases had laid out a clear and workable "standard for judging" whether a corporation's act was "intended to and does result in a suppression of competition, in an enhancement of prices, or in monopoly."[40]

The president was apparently genuinely convinced that the law's meaning had been clarified; Taft wrote to one businessman, "I confess that I don't see where the uncertainty arises in respect to future business. The decisions of the Supreme Court are easily interpreted and anyone can follow them."[41] The president failed to grasp that businessmen without legal training remained confused even after the Court handed down these decisions. When he later attempted to explain the allegedly clear "standard for judging," he found it necessary to produce a book-length study, *The Anti-Trust Act and the Supreme Court* (1914), which belies his claim that "anyone" could easily understand the law by its density and complexity. In refusing to earnestly seek further legislation, he showed that at times his legal training and judicial experience did hinder his policies. Ironically, even as Taft did his best to enforce the law as interpreted by the courts, his failure to make the act's meaning clear risked creating the impression that his administration had adopted a discretionary and arbitrary approach to antitrust prosecutions—precisely what he sought to avoid.

In addition to enforcing the Sherman Act, Taft consistently requested legal authorization to use oversight powers like those TR had informally employed. As we will see more fully in chapter 2, he successfully lobbied for legislation to expand the rate-setting powers of the Interstate Commerce Commission. Moreover, as a result of a small tax on corporate incomes, enacted in 1909 alongside the Payne–Aldrich Tariff, the government gained important oversight powers over businesses engaged in interstate commerce. Taft pointed out that the tax "incidentally" granted the government the authority to investigate corporate financial records to "make the law effective over the annual accounts and business transactions of all corporations." This empowered the national government to inspect "the real business transactions and the gains and profits of every corporation in the country," taking a "long step toward that supervisory control of corporations" necessary to prevent future monopolistic abuses. Taft's goal was clearly progressive: he sought to use national administration to control private interests and bring them in line with the general welfare of the nation.[42]

Despite disagreements over other aspects of antitrust policy, both Taft and his predecessor agreed on the importance of administrative regulatory power over corporations in interstate commerce. Thus, in order to replace TR's informal oversight efforts with a more regular system, Taft worked with Congress to broaden the formal administrative power of the federal government to oversee and regulate big business. As a result, Roosevelt's complaint that Taft had attempted to address the trust issue "by a succession of lawsuits" rather than by administrative oversight fails to recognize that a significant part of Taft's project was directed towards increasing the power of the government to oversee and control trusts.[43]

Roosevelt and Taft disagreed—sometimes vehemently—over the method by which trusts should be suppressed and controlled, but these disagreements should not blind us to the political interreliance of their antitrust policies. Taft owed a great deal to Roosevelt's initial work to bring trust-busting to the forefront of American politics. Without Roosevelt's initiation of the antitrust crusade, Taft's own work would have been more difficult and less effective. Roosevelt and his policies, in turn, were indebted to Taft's insistence on regularity and legality, which avoided the pitfalls of Roosevelt's extralegal approach and led to numerous important legal victories against major trusts. If Roosevelt had initiated the headline-grabbing work of corporate reform, it was Taft's and Wickersham's slow, plodding work that made Roosevelt's policies more effective and consistent.

Constitutionalism and the Taft Policies

Taft jettisoned Roosevelt's methods, but did so in order to consolidate and expand TR's policies. He did not reject or cripple TR's progressive agenda, but instead sought to strengthen it by alleviating the conflicts between progressivism and law that had become prevalent during his predecessor's term. As Taft said in his speech of acceptance in 1908, his administration would "secure the country against a departure" from Roosevelt's policies.[44] By tweaking Roosevelt's work, gaining additional ancillary legislation, and altering the methods by which Roosevelt's progressive policies were carried out, Taft helped to consolidate those policies. Taft's practice of consolidation and legalization was a rejection of Roosevelt's disdain for the Constitution's limitations on executive power. But by demanding that reform be continued in an orderly and legal manner, he helped to cement the Roosevelt Policies in the political life of the nation.

Taft was deeply attached to law and the Constitution, yet his constitutionalism cannot be fully understood without recognizing the role it played in protecting and expanding progressive policy goals. Taft's legalism and constitutionalism did not result in a cramped understanding of the national government's powers. Instead, he recognized and employed the robust powers for the national government, albeit within the restraints imposed by the Constitution. Taft saw that Roosevelt's progressive policies could be implemented by constitutional means and successfully showed the promise of lasting liberal-progressive policy reforms within legal restraints and under the aegis of the Constitution. In the end, Taft's constitutionalism played a positive role in his administration; rather than hindering his reform efforts, it empowered him to maintain a progressive agenda through the structure created by the fundamental law.

2 | Party Leadership and Legislation
Tariffs and Railroad Regulations

In chapter 1, I argued that Taft's demand for legality in the administration
and execution of policy reinvigorated and strengthened his predecessor's
progressive initiatives by ensuring their constitutionality. This chapter
will examine Taft's expansion of the "Roosevelt Policies" through
further legislation, emphasizing the Payne–Aldrich Tariff of 1909, the
Mann–Elkins Act of 1910, worker safety legislation, and the proposed
employers' liability bill of 1912. Taft has typically been depicted as a
rigid and judicial legalist whose cramped view of the Constitution led
him to underestimate both national legislative power and the president's
ability to lead his party in the legislature. This study of his legislative
accomplishments will show, in contrast, that Taft supported a broad
array of progressive legislation and worked diligently to push his agenda
through Congress.

Theodore Roosevelt had reveled in the national limelight, enjoying
his "bully pulpit" and the influence it gave him over his party and
Congress. Yet even Roosevelt could not accomplish everything he hoped
for in a mere seven and a half years. Having begun the task of reform,
he left critical work to his successor. As Taft wrote in early 1909, "It
is the business of my Administration to do something, and to embody
what we do in statutory form. . . . [Roosevelt] has preached a crusade
and has nerved the people up to demand reform. Now it falls on me to
clinch the matter by securing the necessary statutes, and that is a very
different thing from carrying on a popular propaganda."[1] Taft oversaw
the enactment of many of these "necessary statutes": in addition to
securing a significant tariff bill and numerous new railroad regulations,
he gained a barrage of new legislation that addressed issues as diverse as
food and drug safety and "white slavery."

Legislative and Party Leadership

Taft's efforts to broaden the scope of the Roosevelt Policies were intimately linked to his understanding of the party system, since his belief in responsible party government helped define his understanding of the president's role as a party and legislative leader. Taft argued that parties were a necessary part of the political system, because they helped to create and maintain national majorities united behind a political program. A nation divided into "small groups with no majority control" by any party, he insisted, results in a coalition government and "paralyzes a government into doing nothing, into weak compromises." His belief that parties played a useful role did separate him from more radical progressives, who, as Sidney Milkis points out, disliked the party system because they feared it was "grounded in local perspectives" and therefore hindered strong national administrative power. Yet the president's defense of the party system rested on his understanding that parties were needed to ensure the government could express the will of the majority. Parties unite the people into groups large enough to govern by encouraging moderation and requiring the voters to "yield their views on the less important and less essential principles" in order to focus their efforts on commonly held "main policies." Thus, parties animate the "machine of government" and provide the "cohesive power" needed to unite a majority around a set of key policies. Parties, for Taft, did not simply reflect the sectional desires of different locales, but helped to unite the various sections of the country around a constructive policy.[2]

Moreover, in contrast to radicals who thought that "mediating institutions" such as parties undermined political responsibility by creating too much distance between the people and their representatives, Taft believed that parties actually helped to promote responsible representative government. Because any party's legitimacy with the people depends on the public's ability to hold it accountable to a clear statement of policy, party platforms play a critical role in maintaining a popular system of government. The party therefore had "no higher or more sacred duty" than to carry out its preelection pledges; moreover, its responsibility in government and its adherence to its platform pledges established its "claim to the confidence of the public and to its continuance in political power." Thus, in 1909, Taft insisted the Republican Party was not only morally bound to carry out the pledges made in its 1908 platform, but that its success in doing so was the only means by which it could maintain popular support and hope for victory in the 1910 and 1912 elections.[3]

This understanding of party leadership heavily influenced the way Taft viewed the president's role as a legislative leader: as head of his political party, he believed it was his responsibility to play an active role in galvanizing congressional Republicans to carry out the pledges made in the party's platform. Some scholars have claimed that Taft saw little room for executive intervention into partisan legislative affairs. For example, Henry Pringle complained that Taft frequently adopted a policy of "presidential noninterference" in legislative matters; Jeffrey Rosen argues that Taft refused to discuss "substantive [policy] issues" with Congress because of his belief that the president could perform no action beyond "what the Constitution explicitly allowed."[4] In reality, Taft's understanding of the president's duties as the leader of his party was neither formalist nor rigidly restrained.

Taft recognized that the president received political power and influence not only from the Constitution's explicit text but also from the political structure it created and from the party system that had emerged in the United Stated. Because the Constitution grants the chief executive the veto power and permits him to recommend legislation, Taft asserted that the president wields "both legislative and executive power" and becomes constitutionally "a part of the legislature." Additionally, he is "the head of our government," and the influence he holds through his enumerated legislative powers make him "head of the party" within the legislature. He must lead the members of "his party in both Houses" in order to "accomplish any progress dependent on affirmative legislation." Thus, Taft insisted, our political system "not only justif[ies] but require[s]" presidential party leadership, if the president is to fulfill "his responsibility . . . for carrying out [the] ante-election promises" of his party.[5]

The Constitution created an executive with limited powers and separated the legislative and executive branches; at the same time, the structure of the Constitution allowed the president to wield tremendous informal influence. The Constitution's logic, Taft believed, points to the president as the chief of party, since his unity and influence over the legislature make him a powerful figurehead around which parties coalesce. Taft's understanding of presidential power over legislative affairs cannot fairly be termed formalist. It is true that he based his arguments for presidential party leadership on the Constitution and the political system it created, but in doing so he showed that the constitutional grant of legislative power to the chief executive was the basis for more extensive presidential influence over Congress, not a rigid limitation on the executive's interaction with the legislature.

The Payne–Aldrich Tariff

The Republican platform of 1908 had promised a special session of Congress to revise the tariff downward according to what it called the "true principle" of protection: "the imposition of such duties as will equal the difference between the cost of production at home and abroad, together with a reasonable profit to American industries." Taft enthusiastically endorsed this policy of revision and explicitly linked tariff revision to trust-busting; as he saw it, a "needlessly high tariff" merely "nourishes monopoly" and "holds forth a constant temptation to the formation of little trusts." To his mind, a government that imposed excessive duties could foster monopolies just as surely as business conglomerates could by illegally conspiring to artificially inflate prices.[6]

Taft's desire for revision played a critical role in the Republican Party's pledge to revise the tariff. The GOP had favored high tariffs since its inception, and even Roosevelt had failed to convince his party to embrace reform. Although Roosevelt occasionally threatened tariff revision to manipulate conservative Republicans, he quickly abandoned serious plans for tariff reform after Speaker of the House Joseph Cannon warned him that the party responsible for tariff revision usually lost the next election. Nevertheless, Roosevelt encouraged Taft to take up the tariff issue and hoped his successor might be able to succeed where he had failed. Recognizing the truth of Cannon's warnings, Roosevelt argued that tariff reform should occur in the first year of a new administration. According to his theory, a tariff bill in 1909 might lead to significant Republican losses in the 1910 midterm elections, but Taft could still have a chance to secure reelection in 1912 if the benefits of the revision had by then become clear.[7]

Despite Roosevelt's support, Taft's demand for tariff reform was a significant deviation from the Republican Party's long-held attachment to high tariffs. Aside from the risk of electoral disaster, the difficulty of tariff reform was compounded by divisions within the Republican Party. Republican opposition to reform ran high in many quarters for vastly different reasons. Taking the party as a whole, the more liberal Republicans from the Midwest generally favored a downward revision, but the conservative old guard in the East supported high duties. However, these divisions were complicated by local and regional interests. For example, western suppliers of raw hides demanded protection, but eastern shoe manufacturers insisted hides should be duty-free. Many progressive Republicans, known as insurgents, fought to lower rates on cotton, wool, and industrial goods, but they were stymied by a coalition of western wool growers and eastern clothiers. And midwestern progressives both claimed that they favored a general downward revision and voted for higher duties on the foodstuffs produced by their own constituents. Because of these internal divisions, Taft found himself immediately faced with the task of uniting his fractured party around a politically dangerous policy revision. Even after the party's platform promised reform, a successful downward revision was far from certain in early 1909.[8]

Knowing that he could enact his policies only with the help of congressional leadership, the president-elect seriously considered supporting insurgent Republicans in a bid to unseat the conservative Speaker of the House. However, even if Taft had thrown his full weight behind the effort to remove Cannon, the chances of defeating the Speaker would have been slim at best. Of 218 Republican congressmen, Cannon commanded the loyalty of at least 165 against about 30 insurgent members and a dozen fence-sitters. Under such circumstances, the *New York Times* predicted, "There is, in fact, no reasonable prospect of defeating Mr. Cannon for the Speakership." Moreover, even if Taft's support had somehow tipped the balance against Cannon, the ex-Speaker and his allies would have retained significant power in the House. As Roosevelt warned, a "sullen and hostile" Cannon, deprived of the speakership, would remain powerful enough to bring Taft's administration "to grief." Taft therefore recognized that ousting Cannon would have only resulted in "a factious and ugly [old guard] Republican minority, willing and anxious to defeat all progressive measures, and with the power to defeat them." Thus, instead of attacking Cannon head-on, Taft accepted the advice of Roosevelt and outgoing secretary of state Elihu Root and reached a working agreement with the cantankerous Speaker.[9]

Shortly after the inauguration, Taft and Cannon brokered a compromise. They agreed that the president would remain neutral in the election of the Speaker of the House, and, in return, Cannon and his conservative allies would adhere to the party's 1908 platform and loyally support the president's agenda. Essentially, the agreement meant that if Cannon and the old guard would back the president's legislative priorities, Taft would put aside his personal dislike of Cannon for the sake of party unity and in order to advance the party's agenda. As he wrote to Root, if Cannon and his allies would "play fair, I will play fair, but if they won't then I reserve my rights to do anything I find myself able to do." Taft's decision to work with Cannon was prudent and necessary for the success of his legislative program. Yet the president's alliance of convenience with the conservative Speaker angered insurgent Republicans. Many insurgents, ignoring political reality, had conjured up fantasies of their ability to defeat Cannon with Taft's support. When Taft compromised with Cannon, they were left feeling betrayed. Their anger would simmer throughout the rest of Taft's presidency.[10]

On March 16, 1909, Taft called Congress into special session and urged it to pass the tariff reforms promised in the Republican platform. His decision to send a short message to the legislature—his missive calling for tariff reform was only 324 words—has drawn criticism from both politicians and scholars who believe such a brief message showed the president's incompetence as a legislative leader. Yet as Lewis Gould points out, Taft's brief message was actually well received by the contemporary press and was the result of Taft's recognition that Roosevelt's many "long, insistent messages had wearied Congress." In fact, Taft's approach was a part of a prearranged strategy worked out with House leadership. At the request of Republican leaders, the president did not directly intervene in the deliberations of the House. This decision was a strategic response to a promise of congressional cooperation with the party platform, not a bow to formalism. If Congress would enact his agenda without his interference, the president would gladly remain placid in the White House. By and large, Taft's restraint paid dividends: Speaker Cannon abided by his pledge and played fair. The House Ways and Means Committee, chaired by Sereno Payne of New York, produced a revision bill on March 17 mandating substantial reductions. Overall, the committee bill lowered rates on about 400 products and raised rates on only 75. After reducing a few schedules further, the whole House approved the Payne Bill on April 9 with only one dissenting Republican vote.[11]

The Republican House had given Taft most of what he wanted in a tariff bill, but convincing the Senate to do likewise would pose a new challenge. Republicans enjoyed a 61–31 seat advantage in the upper house, but the majority caucus lacked unity. Eight to ten insurgent Republicans would likely demand lower duties and oppose the bill; should the insurgents peel away from the majority, a group of protectionist Republicans might also vote against it, destroying any chance of passage. An additional complication arose because of disagreements over taxation. Everyone recognized the need to provide new sources of revenue to offset reduced tariff revenues, but the Senate rejected the House's proposed 1 percent tax on incomes over $10,000 without agreeing on an alternative tax. As a result, Republican Senate leader Nelson Aldrich and his conservative allies added more than 800 amendments, including 600 rate increases, to the Payne Bill in order to maintain the votes of protectionist senators and to offset future deficits. This conservative position was not popular, but it did have the support of a significant number of senators. In contrast, Democrats and insurgent Republicans could not reach agreement on any coherent plan for securing alternative sources of revenue and splintered into factions supporting either personal or corporate income taxes.[12]

Taft had agreed to stay aloof from the tariff battle, but that agreement hinged on congressional cooperation. When the Senate balked at the House's tariff bill, Taft intervened to break the deadlock, undermining Aldrich's opposition to new taxes and convincing Senate conservatives to support not only a corporate excise tax but an income tax amendment (the eventual Sixteenth Amendment). Taft personally favored a graduated inheritance tax, but he recognized that Congress preferred to levy an income tax. However, in *Pollock v. Farmers' Loan & Trust Company* (1895), the Supreme Court had struck down an income tax as an unconstitutional direct tax. Taft voiced serious reservations about the Court's ruling and believed that the national government should be able to levy an income tax since that power "might be indispensable to the nation's life in great crises." However, despite his misgivings about the Court's precedent, he refused to support the plan of House progressives to enact an income tax in violation of *Pollock* because he feared that a war with the judiciary would damage the Court's prestige.[13]

In the tariff battle, Taft saw an opportunity to expand federal tax power and simultaneously lower duties in the Aldrich Bill. Knowing the idea of an income tax was anathema to Aldrich and the old guard, he offered the Senate leader an ultimatum: either Aldrich could whip the votes to enact an excise tax on corporate earnings and additionally propose an income tax amendment, or Taft would support the insurgents' plan for a direct income tax. This threat, Taft's military aide Archibald "Archie" Butt wrote, caught Aldrich "entirely unprepared." In order to avoid immediate passage of an income tax bill, the Senate leader agreed to Taft's demands. Taft had initiated a process that would eventually override *Pollock* via constitutional amendment and ensure the national government a robust nontariff revenue source. Despite the complaints of insurgents who were angered by his refusal to support their income tax bill, the income tax amendment received wide bipartisan support; the Senate voted unanimously for the proposal of the Sixteenth Amendment, and the House favored it by a vote of 317–14.[14]

Taft's masterful maneuver ended the legislative deadlock over taxes and allowed tariff reform to move forward, defeated two warring factions in Congress, and obliterated *Pollock* as a precedent. By providing a new revenue stream, he effectively undermined Aldrich's arguments for a higher tariff. Further, by threatening to support a direct income tax bill in 1909, Taft frightened the old guard into supporting a corporate excise tax. Last, by convincing Congress to propose the Sixteenth Amendment instead of simply enacting a direct income tax, he not only forced the insurgents to avoid a confrontation with the Supreme Court, but also voided the Court's *Pollock* decision and ensured that future income tax laws could not be successfully challenged as unconstitutional. His victory in securing the proposal of the income tax amendment was critical, for it permitted Taft to avoid a bruising contest with the judiciary, which would have either damaged the Court's credibility, if it reversed *Pollock*, or resulted in a second defeat of an income tax law, thereby cementing judicial precedent against such a policy.[15]

Taft therefore secured a constitutional amendment in addition to a tariff reform. In fact, it is not an exaggeration to say that the Sixteenth Amendment owes its existence to Taft; not only did he pressure conservative legislators to support it, his administration played a major role in drafting the amendment's language.[16] In addition to his victory on the tax provisions of the bill, Taft gained two substantial administrative features in the Senate bill. First, it contained the so-called maximum and minimum clause, which allowed the president to raise duties by up to 25 percent of an article's value to penalize nations whose rates discriminated against American goods. Second, it funded the creation of a tariff board that could provide expert recommendations for future tariffs. Since a tariff bill typically encouraged localism and political hypocrisy in Congress, Taft hoped the board would dramatically improve tariff policy over time. As he argued, the major powers of Europe determined rates based on unbiased studies of production costs at home and abroad, but in the United States, Congress's rate-setting was informed almost exclusively by "the warped and biased testimony of the men to be affected by their schedules." He believed a tariff board could replace this "notoriously unscientific and wrong" system and shift future tariff reforms from a political to a scientific basis. Overall, even aside from the proposal of the Sixteenth Amendment, Taft won substantial concessions from the Senate by gaining these important administrative powers.[17]

However, Taft was not satisfied with the Senate bill, which had raised a significant number of rates above those proposed by the Payne Bill. Even as he acknowledged the bill's shortcomings, Taft hoped at least some of the Senate's amendments could be modified in the conference committee. Meaningful revisions, however, stalled as Cannon packed the conference committee with conservatives and Aldrich was repeatedly forced to allow higher duties to pacify the various factions of his disunited caucus. In response, Taft pressured the conference to agree to reductions on coal, iron, steel, tin plate, leather, and shoes. Even after these concessions, the committee deadlocked by the end of July, whereupon Taft again interjected. He insisted on free hides, substantial reductions on rates for other leather goods and lumber, and the defeat of an exorbitant glove schedule. To ensure compliance, he threatened to veto the bill and call another special session of Congress unless the committee agreed to his demands. Both the conference committee and Congress as a whole accepted the president's requirements, and the Payne–Aldrich Tariff was enacted in early August. Archie Butt hailed the result as a "complete victory" for Taft and a "humiliating defeat" for Cannon. Taft, the first Republican president to seek a downward tariff revision, had managed to bend a largely conservative Republican caucus to his will through skillful party leadership.[18]

Some insurgents demanded that Taft veto the bill rather than sign an imperfect tariff revision. Senator Robert LaFollette of Wisconsin, for example, insisted that Taft could force Congress to accept rates lower than those proposed by either the House or the Senate. Taft rejected this dramatic—and likely pointless—recommendation. As he wrote to his brother, Horace Taft, "I could make a lot of cheap popularity . . . by vetoing the bill," but a veto "would leave the party in bad shape." Moreover, he feared that vetoing the bill would alienate congressional Republicans, exacerbate the widening divisions within his party, and destroy any chance of enacting "the entire program of progressive legislation, to which I had dedicated the whole strength of my administration." Finally, vetoing the Payne–Aldrich Bill would have undermined the substantial reductions secured in the final bill. Like the insurgents, Taft was not satisfied with the bill; in fact, he even publicly admitted that some duties—particularly the rates on woolens under Schedule K—were so high that they violated the spirit of the Republican platform. Despite this, he believed that the bill was the best that could be secured under the circumstances. Congress had agreed to reduce rates on 654 items and raised duties on only 220; moreover, he insisted that these increases fell almost entirely upon luxury goods rather than essentials, providing an additional revenue stream for the government through what amounted to an excise tax on imported luxuries. As a result, Taft signed the bill, believing he had gained a substantial victory in line with the Republican promise of a revision. He admitted that the tariff "does not go far enough in certain respects," but concluded that "a tariff bill no one can be entirely satisfied with."[19]

In the twenty-first century, it is difficult to judge the importance or political effect of a tariff bill from 1909. The press was inclined toward Taft's efforts, but the country was less than aroused by the passage of the bill. Taft traveled widely in the fall of 1909 to speak on the tariff. His swing through the country was not simply a victory lap; he was defending the bill to the public. However, it is notable that conservative Republicans, who had traditionally supported high tariffs, requested he appear in their states and explain the new law. For example, Representative James Tawney of Minnesota, chairman of the House Appropriations Committee, wrote the president, "I sincerely hope that you . . . [will] deliver your first speech in defense of the Payne tariff bill in my home city. There is nothing that I could suggest that would, in my judgment, contribute more to the alignment of the republicans of Minnesota in support of that law than a strong, forceful statement from you on that occasion." This episode suggests the extent of Taft's success in forcing a badly fractured party to compromise. Tawney was the only Republican congressman from Minnesota to support the tariff and desperately needed the president to provide him with political support by endorsing the act to his more progressive constituents.[20]

Taft made a good faith effort to defend his supporters by publicly praising the Payne–Aldrich Tariff. Yet his efforts have been overshadowed by a single speech delivered in Winona, Minnesota. In that speech, Taft claimed the bill was "the best tariff bill that the Republican party has ever passed, and therefore the best tariff bill that has been passed at all." And he concluded, "I think that we ought to give the present bill a chance. After it has been operating for two or three years, we can tell . . . the necessity for any amendment."[21] The press instantly latched onto these statements and thoroughly lambasted the president. Although he had just convinced the Republican Party to accept a significant downward revision, Taft's claims were unduly grandiose. By heaping such pretentious praise upon the bill, the president angered insurgents who believed the new tariff law did not go far enough. And his desire to give the law "a chance" sounded like a determination that the tariffs should not be revisited in the near future. Moreover, Taft's words would appear increasingly tone-deaf, as the cost of living actually rose in the wake of the Payne–Aldrich Tariff. This was a result of worldwide causes, not the Republican tariff, yet Taft and his party would nevertheless be roundly punished for the rise of prices in the 1910 elections.[22]

Despite Taft's stumble at Winona, it is worth noting that he was fully dedicated to completing tariff reform and eliminating excessive rates such as those levied by Schedule K. If his own party would not faithfully enact its platform pledges, he was willing to work even with congressional Democrats to fulfill his promises to the American people. Following the Republican defeat in the 1910 midterm elections, Taft called the newly elected Democratic House into special session to consider trade reciprocity with Canada. Because the costs of production in the United States and Canada were nearly identical and made protection unnecessary, Canadian reciprocity would have acted as a supplement to the Payne–Aldrich Tariff. Rather than pursuing a treaty, Taft and Canadian prime minister Wilfrid Laurier attempted to convince Congress and the Canadian Parliament to pass identical trade legislation. Taft campaigned actively for the bill—he met extensively with individual members of Congress, appealed to the public on a lengthy swing through western states, and gained the support of the press—and secured its passage. But his efforts were ultimately defeated when the Laurier government fell in the autumn of 1911, eliminating any chance that the Canadian Parliament could enact the needed legislation.[23]

The Payne–Aldrich Tariff did not lower rates as far as Taft believed it should, and the failure of the Canadian reciprocity plan was a real blow to Republican policies. Nevertheless, the tariff bill and the proposal of the Sixteenth Amendment were both substantial legislative victories for the president. Some scholars have argued that Taft's handling of the Payne–Aldrich Tariff polarized and divided the Republican Party and led to the eventual party split in 1912.[24] Whether or not the tariff battle was the critical first step toward Republican disunity during the 1912 election, it did not leave Taft a lame duck. Of course, internecine feuding during the special session did sharpen the divisions within the Republican Party, and Taft's Winona speech was a public relations disaster. Yet the tariff and its consequences did not significantly hamper Taft's success as a legislative leader. Instead, his agenda moved forward steadily, and he continued to achieve significant legislative successes throughout his term.

The Mann–Elkins Act and the Employers' Liability Bill

Samuel Gompers labeled Taft the "father of injunctions" for his allegedly antiunion opinions as a circuit court judge, but Taft's record as president belies this charge. Taft pledged to expand Roosevelt's efforts to curb business abuses and protect workers, and he emphasized the need for more thorough railroad rate and safety regulations. As president he fulfilled this promise, convincing Congress to regulate railroads and protect their employees by expanding the reach of the Interstate Commerce Commission (ICC), creating the Commerce Court, enacting new worker safety legislation, and pursuing an extensive health and life insurance plan for railroad workers engaged in interstate commerce.[25]

The Hepburn Act, passed under Roosevelt in 1906, gave the ICC authority to set "just and reasonable" carrying rates for common carriers engaged in interstate commerce and to prohibit "unjustly discriminatory, or unduly preferential or prejudicial" rates. Broadly speaking, the law sought to outlaw unfair price setting by which railroads granted special rates to favored companies to the detriment of their competitors. As secretary of war and a candidate for the presidency, Taft had defended the Hepburn Act and linked it to the government's trust-busting efforts. The act's prohibitions prevented monopolies, he explained, since it outlawed the "secret rebates and unlawful discrimination" that benefited "large combinations . . . to the disadvantage of the smaller competitors."[26]

However, the Hepburn Act was less effective than Taft had anticipated. The ICC's power was severely crippled when the railroad companies realized they could gain temporary relief from the rates set by the ICC simply by seeking an injunction from a federal court. As Taft pointed out in a special message to Congress, the railroads had brought a total of sixteen suits in 1908, challenging virtually every consequential order issued by the ICC. Moreover, the courts had granted preliminary injunctions in six of the suits brought by the railroads, seriously undermining the ICC's ability to regulate effectively. In a similar vein, Wickersham complained "under the present workings of the law, many of the important orders of the [Interstate Commerce] comission [*sic*] . . . are suspended by injunctions"; as a result, "the benefits anticipated from the passage of the Hepburn act have not yet been realized."[27]

To remedy these problems, Taft urged Congress to strengthen the Hepburn Act by enacting what came to be known as the Mann–Elkins Act. Although the scholarship has sometimes downplayed Taft's support for this progressive legislation, Mann–Elkins owed much to the Taft administration's backing.[28] The original plan for the law was drafted by a committee that consisted of Wickersham, Commerce and Labor secretary Charles Nagel, Solicitor General Lloyd Bowers, ICC commissioner Charles A. Prouty, and Representative Charles L. Knapp of New York. Its work was approved by Taft and presented to Congress in 1910. Moreover, Taft and his attorney general actually played a key role in garnering public and congressional support for its enactment. In an attempt to preempt the pending legislation, twenty-five western railroads announced a 20 percent rate increase over the summer of 1910. Their decision gave Taft the opportunity he needed to publicize his battle with the railroads. An investigation by the Department of Justice found that the proposed increases "were the result of special conferences and agreements . . . made under such circumstances as to amount to an . . . agreement in restraint of interstate commerce, in violation of the Sherman Act." Taft therefore ordered Wickersham to seek an injunction against the railroads; as Michael Bromley points out, this essentially forced the railroads either to "submit to the [rates] rules of the bill—as not yet passed" or face the threat of an antitrust suit. In response to this threat, the railroads folded and the resulting public support for the president ensured quick passage of the Mann–Elkins Act. Senator Chauncey Depew of New York observed, "The whole atmosphere of the Capitol was charged with the idea that the people were behind President Taft as they had been behind Roosevelt and that it was dangerous to defeat his program."[29]

In early 1910, Taft had requested the creation of a specialized commerce court capable of quickly hearing rates cases and deciding them with uniformity. The Mann–Elkins Act created this court as a part of the larger policy of expanding the ICC's power to regulate shipping rates. In so doing, the new law constructed a simple and speedy means for appealing the decisions of the ICC to a specialized court, promoting efficiency and also maintaining critical procedural rights and the right of appeal to the Supreme Court. The Commerce Court was to be made up of five circuit judges appointed for five-year terms on the court by the chief justice of the United States. It had jurisdiction to hear all cases related to the enforcement of the ICC's orders, except those involving criminal sanctions or the payment of fines. This eliminated the older procedure, which permitted appeals to any US district court, resulting, Wickersham observed, in "conflict of decision and delay beneficial only to the railroad." The Commerce Court acted as an expert tribunal to hear appeals against ICC regulations, helping to relieve the congestion in the federal courts and hastening decisions affecting rates. Also, because the court focused solely on rates cases, its judges would quickly gain the expertise necessary to render just and uniform decisions in cases that were "technical in their character [and] require a knowledge of the [railroad] business and the mastery of a great volume of conflicting evidence."[30]

The Mann–Elkins Act remedied a critical failure of the Hepburn Act and maintained important procedural safeguards. Under the Hepburn Act, suits challenging an ICC order could effectively suspend the contested regulation if a district court granted an injunction; in contrast, Mann–Elkins prevented superfluous litigation from hindering the actions of the ICC. Mann–Elkins made it harder for the railroads to secure a preliminary injunction, although the Commerce Court and appellate courts had the power to suspend the regulation pending a final decision "in cases where irreparable damage would otherwise ensue" to the company.[31]

Moreover, the procedural rights of the railroad companies were guaranteed. Although the ICC itself functioned as an administrative tribunal, the act preserved the right of common carriers to appeal the rulings of the Commerce Court to an Article III court, even permitting direct appeals to the Supreme Court. Thus, Taft insisted that the law would guarantee the "constitutional right" of "every carrier affected" to a full judicial hearing. Notably, Mann–Elkins distinguished between the procedural rights of corporations and individuals employed by the corporation. Because the Commerce Court had power to hear only regulatory issues and could not directly impose criminal sanctions, it lacked the power to try individuals. Any corporate employee or officer accused of violating the law could be tried in federal district court and could be subject to criminal penalties. In this way, individuals accused of committing crimes would be answerable to Article III courts, guaranteeing the benefits of the full array of procedural protections, but they would not be subject to either an administrative tribunal or the specialized Commerce Court.[32]

Taft's approach to railroad regulation, which recognized a place for an expert commission and also a specialized commerce court, highlights the different regulatory approaches progressives adopted in their attempts to rein in business conglomerates. Some, such as Roosevelt, believed that the judiciary would simply hamper the ICC and favored expanding administrative powers while limiting judicial oversight. Others, Taft and Prouty among them, recognized that the courts could hinder reform by limiting the power of administrators, but they also believed that specialized courts, such as the Commerce Court, could play "an important role . . . in administrative regulation." Specialized courts would understand and quickly enforce the technical decisions of administrative experts and would also develop "a new body of administrative law and procedure." In this way, Skowronek points out, the Commerce Court could actually play a critical role in "Progressive state-building reform." Taft's support for the Commerce Court thus shows both his progressivism and his constitutionalism; he hoped that the court would "upgrade the quality and responsibility of judicial decision making in an era of administrative specialization" and also "reaffirm constitutional guarantees at a time of expanding administrative discretion."[33]

The act did not, however, secure the physical valuation of railroads as a basis for setting rates—a longtime progressive desire. The Republican Party platform of 1908 had promised legislation that would prevent future overissue of stocks, and Taft had endorsed a plan for the physical valuation of railroads as early as 1907. Wickersham later explained that no other portion of the Mann–Elkins Act created so many difficulties, including both legal concerns about the constitutionality of the specific language proposed and fears of unjustly and unintentionally harming businesses. Despite the eventual failure of this part of the bill, Congress did appropriate money permitting Taft to appoint a commission to further study the issue. The commission's findings recommended national incorporation of railroads, which would have permitted far greater national regulation of the conglomerates. Taft continued to push for regulation of stock issue throughout his term.[34]

Overall, Taft's plans for railroad reforms—never enacted in their entirety—were incredibly broad. The president secured additional legislation to protect railroad workers with the Safety Appliance Act of 1910. Although this legislation was not groundbreaking, it was a valuable supplement to earlier legislation from 1893 and 1903. The act mandated the installation and upkeep of critical safety features on railcars and delegated power to the ICC to "designate the number, dimensions, location, and manner of application" of safety appliances, in accord with the needs of specific types of cars and the development of equipment.[35]

Yet Taft's most ambitious project was the proposed employers' liability bill of 1912. Taft advocated such policies throughout his presidency. In his inaugural address, he pointed to Roosevelt's successes in gaining workmen's compensation legislation for federal workers and announced his intention to "promote the enactment of further legislation of this character." This theme was reiterated in his annual messages, in which he repeatedly demanded legislation to improve the "thoroughly unsatisfactory system of employers' liability" and guarantee "certain and definite relief to all employees who are injured in the course of their employment in those industries which are subject to the regulating power of Congress." By 1912, a federal commission headed by Senator George Sutherland of Utah had drafted legislation that would essentially require interstate employers to insure each of their employees against accidents. This bill—similar to the progressive liability laws that were already in force in California, Kansas, New Hampshire, New Jersey, Ohio, and Washington—made four important improvements to extant liability and compensation laws.[36]

First, the bill altered the rules of liability. Whereas Roosevelt had succeeded in limiting the contributory negligence rule, Taft hoped to eliminate it entirely. Taft argued that limiting the liability of an employer had "been abandoned in most civilized countries" because modern technology "with its vast complexity and inherent dangers arising from complicated machinery and the use of the great forces of steam and electricity" had obviated the previous utility of contributory negligence rules. Thus, the Sutherland Bill would have guaranteed an injured worker compensation "without reference to his contributory negligence," except in cases of drunkenness or intentional self-injury.[37]

Second, Taft hoped to modernize and streamline the means by which injured employees were compensated. Under the proposed legislation, most claims for compensation would be settled by an impartial federal adjuster according to a predetermined schedule. The bill set ongoing compensation rates based on the employee's income, the degree of disability, and, in the case of death, the relationship of the deceased to any surviving dependents. Disabled workers would be paid up to half of their salaries for the remainder of their lives. The family of a deceased worker would be paid up to 50 percent of his wages for a period of no more than eight years; the extent and length of benefits was determined by the closeness of the relationship and number of dependents, with widows and orphans receiving the highest compensation. This system, Taft hoped, would streamline the amount paid to workers based on the severity of their injuries, creating uniformity and guaranteeing reasonable recoveries on a set scale.[38]

Third, standardizing the process would make the system less expensive for the worker. By standardizing the payment of damages, the law would not only promote uniformity but also quicken the proceedings, thereby rendering the entire process more economical. As Taft pointed out, the unreformed system was faulty, as "recoveries of verdicts of any size do not result in actual benefit to the injured person because of the heavy expense of the litigation and the fees charged by the counsel." By encouraging the litigants to forgo expensive jury trials in favor of quick settlements by an adjuster, the plan would substantially reduce the cost accrued by an injured worker in legal fees. Overall, Taft argued that such procedural flexibility would "secure justice to the weaker party under existing modern conditions."[39]

Fourth, Taft's system would reduce the number of liability and disability cases heard in court without denying either the employer or the employee due process. The adjusters would normally hear claims in a court-like setting: both parties could be represented by counsel and their claims could be supported by the evidence of physicians and witnesses. Moreover, if either party was dissatisfied with the decision rendered by the adjuster, it had the option to appeal the decision into federal courts; provision was even made to permit an appeal up to the Supreme Court.[40]

The liability bill, Taft observed, would have essentially forced railroad companies "to insure the lives of their employees" while they were employed in interstate commerce. Taft's support for what amounted to a nationwide health and life insurance plan for railroad workers shows his understanding of the potential for the national government to advance progressive causes within the constitutional structure. The legislation was incredibly far-ranging, especially for its time. Yet it accorded with the Supreme Court's decisions in the 1908 and 1912 *Employers' Liability Cases* and Taft contended that the interstate commerce clause provided the national government a general "police power" to regulate interstate commerce and control the companies engaged in it. Taft read the commerce clause in light of the necessary and proper clause—as had, indeed, the Supreme Court in the liability cases.[41]

The Republican-controlled Senate passed this groundbreaking employers' liability bill in 1912, but the bill had not been approved by the Democrat-controlled House when the legislative session ended. Nevertheless, the liability bill remains one of the best examples of Taft's constitutional progressivism. It has sometimes been claimed that Taft became less progressive as his term wore on. Paolo Coletta, for instance, claims that Taft "appeared to be a progressive" so long as he was under Roosevelt's influence, but quickly became more conservative once Roosevelt left the presidency.[42] Yet Taft's support for such progressive legislation late in his term shows that he did not become less progressive after assuming the presidency or suddenly align with the reactionary right as Roosevelt's primary challenge loomed in 1912. Ironically, TR would later become famous for his support of a national system of social insurance against old age, sickness, and unemployment during the 1912 election; yet it was not Roosevelt, but his allegedly ultraconservative successor, who came close to actually enacting a broad life insurance plan.[43]

Taft's Constitutional Articulation

This evaluation of Taft's legislative successes shows his attachment to progressive causes, provides evidence of his abilities as a party and legislative leader, and demonstrates the potential for progressive reforms to be enacted constitutionally. It has been said that Taft gained few concessions from conservative members of Congress and that his interventions into the legislative process were sometimes pointless since "he was like a child in the hands of cunning politicians."[44] These claims must be reconsidered in light of his impressive legislative record.

During the first half of Taft's term, the Republican majorities in Congress boasted impressive legislative achievements. The major items of Taft's agenda—conservation, trust-busting, tariff reform, and railroad regulations—formed a broad front in the progressive movement's efforts to regulate the business conglomerates that were coming to power during the Progressive Era. I have thus far emphasized these four leading policy initiatives, but Taft's efforts bore fruit in other areas. During his term, Congress strove to improve conditions for workers by creating a separate Department of Labor, a Bureau of Mines, and a Bureau of Children, and by mandating an eight-hour workday for laborers on federal projects. It sought to promote morality in politics and American life by enacting new regulations for corporate campaign contributions and requirements to publicize campaign contributions and expenditures, by passing a new federal corrupt practices act, and by implementing the Mann Act, which imposed harsh federal penalties on "white slavery." Congress also enacted limited criminal justice reforms, passing legislation that allowed federal prisoners to be paroled and creating a probation system in the District of Columbia. Finally, Congress created a postal savings bank system, passed a strengthened Pure Food and Drugs Act, and banned the production of phosphorous matches—all projects meant to aid and protect the common man.[45]

Taft's legislative record actually equaled or surpassed Roosevelt's. The *New York Times* praised the bevy of reform legislation as "a personal record for the President not equaled by a Chief Executive in a great many years" and tacitly endorsed Taft's effective but low-key style of legislative leadership by noting that his successes had been "accomplished by methods utterly unlike those used by the White House in the preceding seven years."[46] Despite common misconceptions, Taft was not a phlegmatic president who rejected reform and refused to lead, but an active chief executive who initiated and secured a significant legislative program.

These legislative efforts to strengthen the federal government's hand in addressing emerging problems show Taft's broad understanding of national power and demonstrate his ability to meld his constitutionalism to his support for progressive policies. His work to undergird progressive causes with law and the Constitution reached its high point with the passage of the Sixteenth Amendment. Taft questioned the Supreme Court's decision in *Pollock* and publicly suggested that a modern Court might be willing to reverse itself and uphold a similar tax law, but he nevertheless refused to side with insurgent Republicans who wanted to pass an income tax bill in defiance of *Pollock* and provoke a confrontation with the Court.[47] His willingness to play the long game resulted in the Sixteenth Amendment, which made the *Pollock* decision a constitutional nullity, permanently expanded Congress's tax power, and guaranteed that no future Court could rule a progressive income tax unconstitutional. The breadth of Taft's achievement cannot be underestimated. The Sixteenth Amendment is almost certainly the most important of the four "Progressive amendments," for it guaranteed the national government the ability to finance its expanding role in American life. Taft not only secured a means of funding progressive reforms but showed that the Constitution's amendment process was not so rigid as to foreclose significant constitutional reforms.

Taft's constitutional and policy initiatives remind us of the critical role played by presidents in Taft's situation—presidents tasked with articulating the achievements of their predecessor. Skowronek acknowledges that the critical role of articulation presidents is usually eclipsed by the reputations of presidents who usher in a reconstruction. We might add that articulators such as Taft are typically eclipsed by previous presidents who, like Roosevelt, ushered in a "departure." Nevertheless, Skowronek points out that the task of articulation is important and that presidents should be evaluated in light of their circumstances and the political context they faced during their terms. It is certain that Roosevelt will always be considered a more impressive and important president than Taft. At the same time, the criteria by which Taft should be judged must be different from those by which Roosevelt is judged—just as TR himself should hardly be judged by the same criteria one would apply to George Washington, Abraham Lincoln, or Franklin Delano Roosevelt.[48]

Considered in this light, the extent of Taft's successes are quite notable in light of the political terrain during his term. Taft's situation was hardly enviable. Having campaigned as TR's successor, he was placed in the difficult position of making his own mark while building on the work of his predecessor. Taft's task was made more difficult by divisions within his own party. Roosevelt had secured significant gains for progressivism, but he had also caused tremendous political disruption and schism within the Republican Party. Having juggled reform for more than seven years and legitimated the insurgents' internecine feuding against the old guard, Roosevelt left office just as his party's unity was collapsing. He bequeathed to Taft the undesirable job of holding together an increasingly fragile and rebellious Republican coalition while also attempting to protect and expand on his predecessor's legacy.[49]

Under the circumstances, the very fact that Taft could secure so much substantive work for progressivism represents a considerable accomplishment. Taft's role was the articulation of Roosevelt's "departure," but he was a success in his own right as he spearheaded a barrage of legislation aimed at curbing errant businesses. His task, as Donald Anderson aptly puts it, was "to transform the ideals of Roosevelt into permanent social institutions and policies," and Taft made a valuable contribution to progressivism that helped cement his predecessor's initiatives by legalizing and constitutionalizing them. Taft has often been remembered as a one-term failure, but his accomplishments in articulating and consolidating Roosevelt's policies point to the potential even single-term presidencies hold. He may not have been too far from the mark when he claimed that "a number of our best Presidents have had only one term, and there is nothing disgraceful in not having two."[50]

3 | To "Perfect the Machinery"
Modernizing the Executive Branch

Modern scholarship often admits that Taft was a reformer insofar as he was attuned to progressive desires for scientific management, yet he has sometimes been depicted as capable but half-hearted, an administrator attached to "efficiency progressivism" but uninterested in providing the executive leadership needed to promote broad social reforms or expand popular rule. Paolo Coletta, for instance, writes that Taft understood administration from a purely "mechanistic" viewpoint and saw the government's "formalistic structure as an end in itself." Because Taft had administrative skill but not executive ability, Coletta claims, he failed to provide "the leadership and spirit management requires" and only rarely saw his administrative renovations as means by which social reforms could be furthered.[1]

In this chapter, I examine Taft's administrative reforms and his efforts to modernize the executive branch. In his 1908 speech of acceptance, Taft insisted that the "chief function" of his administration would be "to complete and perfect the [government] machinery" necessary to sustain Roosevelt's progressive initiatives.[2] Taft's program for modernizing the national government's administrative machinery, however, went beyond mere mechanistic tinkering to secure structural efficiency; as I demonstrate, the president recognized that administrative reform would facilitate substantive progressive projects, because it would strengthen the voters' ability to hold their elected representatives accountable and also permit the government to expand its efforts to promote social welfare. Moreover, Taft's administrative initiatives involved a serious effort to broaden the president's role in leading the nation. His interest in technical matters of governmental reorganization and scientific management was a critical step in freeing the chief executive from relatively minor administrative duties in order to allow him to serve as a national political leader and a strong voice in favor of progress and reform.

This chapter will first consider Taft's Commission on Economy and Efficiency, which proposed sweeping reforms to the government's administrative structure. The commission proposed significant departmental reorganization schemes and the introduction of business methods into administrative work; moreover, it recommended a centralized budget process for the federal government. Taft understood the political implications of these administrative reforms, for he recognized that the presidential budget would both increase efficiency and make the government's financial information more available to the voters, thereby allowing them to better hold their government accountable. Moreover, he hoped a more efficient and economical government could take on new social projects and expand its reform activities.

Second, this chapter will analyze civil service reform and Taft's expansion of the merit system. As president, Taft attempted to replace the outdated and inefficient patronage system with a modern civil service system, but his efforts for comprehensive civil service reform were hindered by congressional opposition. Remarkably, Taft's proposals called for an extension of the merit system to the very highest grades of the federal administration and the creation of something comparable to the British senior civil service. By expanding the authority of apolitical expert administrators, he hoped to disencumber the president and his cabinet from routine administrative burdens and allow them to focus on the more important task of promoting a constructive political agenda for the nation. His civil service reform plans, especially when considered alongside his attempt to expand executive leadership through a form of "cabinet government," show us that he aimed to transform the administration and make it more capable of providing the efficient, transparent leadership the nation expected in the twentieth century.

This administrative reform program demonstrates the breadth of Taft's constitutional progressivism. Taft was opposed to radical progressive plans to transform the Constitution and implement direct democracy through the referendum, recall, and initiative, yet he was not averse to instituting changes that would make the institutions of government more efficient and more responsive to the popular will. His progressivism led him to see the importance of such modifications, but his constitutionalism led him to seek to bring these reforms about within the constitutional structure and in accord with a traditional understanding of separation of powers and republicanism.

Economy and Efficiency: The Presidential Budget

In light of the national government's expanding activities, Taft recognized the need to modernize the federal administration to promote greater economy and improve its efficiency. He therefore hoped to centralize authority in the federal administration, clearly delineate lines of authority and responsibility, and ensure a more regular and systematic organization of departments and bureaus. Taft was "more of an innovator" than either Theodore Roosevelt or Woodrow Wilson when it came to "his vision of how the federal government and the role of president should be changed," Gould argues.[3] His reform agenda was remarkably broad: he sought to streamline the administrative organization and allow the nation's political leaders to set overall administrative policy for a modernized government machine.

The most complete statement of Taft's own efficiency policy came in a special message to Congress. He appointed the Commission on Economy and Efficiency on March 8, 1911, and the president sent a detailed report of its findings to Congress in early 1912. Taft hoped to implement a dramatic reorganization of the national bureaucracy, based on a detailed analysis of the duties and activities of every government entity, from departments in Washington to the smallest local offices. To this end, the commission proposed a broad array of reforms to secure greater managerial expertise, promote general efficiency, and introduce modern business methods into government work. On the commission's recommendations, Taft advocated the expansion of the merit system to all local offices; general consolidation of bureaus performing overlapping or redundant tasks; the elimination of superfluous local offices; regularization of office work methods across the government by adopting uniform methods for mail, reducing travel and document copying costs, standardizing office equipment, and introducing new labor-saving devices; and the adoption of a uniform method of accounting procedures (the Treasury Department alone had nineteen different accounting methods) to make financial information more accessible to every branch of the government.[4]

The commission's work was groundbreaking and made Taft the first president to launch a full-scale study of the federal administration as a united and coherent organization. Taft ultimately intended the creation of a truly "unified organization for the most effective and economical dispatch of public business." The technical reforms he advocated were necessary to modernize a government that had expanded piecemeal "with little or no reference to any scheme of organization of the Government as a whole" and lacked a "comprehensive plan" for organizing existing departments and bureaus or planning the creation of new ones. Critically, the Commission on Economy and Efficiency also sought to centralize power in the presidency. Peri Arnold has shown that the commission itself relied primarily on "staff expertise in the White House," consciously excluded department heads from involvement, and worked on the general assumption that "good administration entailed the capacity of a president to guide it."[5]

Most of the proposed reforms could only be implemented with congressional support. Although Taft recommended significant civil service reforms in all four of his annual messages, Congress largely ignored his suggestions.[6] Despite this, the president and his cabinet managed to carry out significant department-level reorganization schemes in line with the commission's general call for efficiency and centralized authority. Secretary of State Philander C. Knox and his first assistant secretary, F. Huntington Wilson, reorganized the State Department into four geographical divisions, permitting the creation of separate bureaus staffed with experts on Latin America, Europe, the Far East, and the Near East. Additionally, they initiated training programs for diplomats, created a Division of Information to transmit intelligence from Washington to American posts abroad, and brought in trade advisers. Significant centralization and efficiency reforms also occurred in the army and navy. Secretary of War Henry Stimson and Secretary of the Navy George von Lengerke Meyer both updated their service's decentralized and outdated bureau system, which had granted vast power to entrenched senior offices and often undercut civilian control. The new, centralized and hierarchical systems they implemented consolidated civilian control over military policy and helped to ready the military to meet twentieth-century challenges.[7]

¶ Overall, then, the Taft administration implemented modest departmental reforms even without congressional support. However, the most important outgrowth of the Commission on Economy and Efficiency was Taft's decision to take up the commission's recommendation that the president propose a unified national budget. By 1909, the United States was spending hundreds of millions every year but lacked any central authority to assemble a unified budget or control national spending. Prior to the Budget and Accounting Act of

1921, financial control was decentralized, with each department head submitting budget estimates to Congress without the direct involvement of the president and without serious analysis of the government's overall expenditures. The *New York Times* lamented, "Unlike other nations, the United States has no budget, and appropriations are made by Congress without any relation to [the government's] income." Department heads requested funding, Donald Anderson writes, with "no responsibility to gear their estimates to expected revenues or to propose new revenues to meet added expenditures." Accordingly, the federal government lacked any central authority capable of coordinating budgets and of considering the relation between the nation's income and expenditures.[8]

Throughout his term, Taft and Treasury Secretary Franklin Mac-Veagh oversaw departmental estimates and demanded reductions. As early as 1909, reports circulated that the president had forced one department—likely the Department of Agriculture—to cut 15 percent from its proposed budget. But in 1912, based on the findings of his Commission on Economy and Efficiency, Taft took a more public position and articulated the importance of creating a unified executive budget for the entire national administration. Ultimately, Taft presaged the eventual creation of the Bureau of the Budget in 1921; he hoped to create a Central Division of Budgeting in order to be able to present "a definite understandable program of [government] business . . . to be financed" that would be laid out in a "well-defined, clearly expressed financial program."[9]

To this end, the president ordered his cabinet to submit their proposed budgets directly to him, used the recommendations of his commission to eliminate waste from the initial estimates, and sent Congress a unified national budget. Sensing an institutional challenge to its pecuniary power, Congress moved to limit the president's discretion over budgetary matters by adding a rider to a key appropriations bill: "Until otherwise provided by law, the regular annual estimates of appropriations for expenses of the Government of the United States shall be prepared and submitted to Congress, by those charged with the duty of such preparation and submission, only in the form and at the time now required by law, and in no other form and at no other time."[10] Put plainly, Congress commanded department heads alone, that is, "those charged," to prepare and submit their departmental budgets. Congress also evidently sought to forbid presidential involvement in formulating, reviewing, or altering the department budgets by declaring it would receive estimates "only in the form" required by law. Essentially, the legislative branch attempted to maximize its control over the power of the purse by destroying the chief executive's control over his own cabinet. Taft rebelled against this attempt to limit his power, pushing back against both Congress and cabinet heads who hoped to avoid presidential interference in their budget estimates. Taft signed the appropriations bill, but publicly voiced his determination to ignore the rider's provisions.[11]

In a public letter to Treasury Secretary Franklin MacVeagh, Taft laid out a detailed defense of the president's power to control his cabinet. His argument drew out the implications of the executive vesting clause generally, but he relied specifically on presidential power under the opinions in writing clause and the State of the Union requirement. Taft insisted that Congress had no power to prevent the president from consulting with his subordinates and preparing a unified national budget. He argued that since the president controls "heads of departments, and their subordinates," he may "use them to assist him in his constitutional duties, one of which is to recommend measures to Congress." Indeed, to Taft's mind, the president would be unable to conscientiously carry out his obligations if he were unable to consult with his cabinet. In executing his duty to recommend legislation, the complexity and size of the modern federal government virtually required the president "to acquire information from his subordinates . . . [in order] to illustrate the utility of his recommendations, and to emphasize and point out the application of proposed reforms to existing conditions." Thus, Taft argued that the executive power granted by the Constitution establishes the president's own authority and also guarantees him power to use subordinate officers as he exercises his constitutional functions.[12]

Taft also challenged the rider by asserting that it trampled on the president's legitimate authority to control the executive branch. The proposal, he insisted, barred the president from supervising or directing the activities of his own cabinet officers while at the same time subsuming department heads under the legislature. Taken to its logical conclusion, Congress's position would allow the legislature, but not the president, to consult with executive branch officials, making the "heads of departments . . . the ministerial agents of Congress." Commanding department heads to submit their budget directly to Congress permits "the legislative branch of the Government to usurp the functions of the

Executive and to abridge the executive power in a manner forbidden by the Constitution," thereby robbing the president of the authority to control his own administration.[13]

Finally, Taft insisted that Congress may not "forbid or prevent" the president from submitting a unified budget to the legislature, since a budget proposal is nothing more than a recommendation of policy. Because Taft classified the proposal of legislation as a discretionary rather than ministerial function, he argued that Congress had no power to determine the manner in which the president exercised his authority. However, despite his constitutional objections to the legislature's overreach, Taft did believe that as a general matter Congress could create a ministerial duty for department heads and require them to report information to the legislature, and he conceded that the president could not directly control his subordinates in the execution of such ministerial duties. He did not "question the constitutional right of Congress to prescribe the manner in which reports of expenditures and estimates shall be submitted to it *by department officers*," but he did insist that the chief executive had sufficient discretion to consult with his subordinates and submit an additional presidential budget. Taft eventually permitted the department heads to submit budgetary estimates directly to Congress, but he also submitted his own unified budget separately. Unsurprisingly, Congress ignored his financial proposals and retaliated against his initiative by slashing funding for the Commission on Economy and Efficiency.[14]

It is ironic that Taft, the president famous for his alleged formalism, recognized how the implications of two ostensibly minor constitutional grants of power could justify a presidential budget. And a presidential budget, one scholar has noted, makes the president the "general manager of the administration." During his brief retirement, Taft continued to advocate executive control over the budget process by suggesting a constitutional amendment that would give the president the duty to formulate a budget, which Congress could revise downward, but not upward. Despite the failure of his presidential budget and the fact that his proposed amendment never gained traction, Taft was vindicated a decade later with the passage of the Budget and Accounting Act of 1921. Taft's work to advance a presidential budget "eventually led to the creation of the Bureau of the Budget," now the Office of Management and Budget, which has become "one of the most powerful centralizing tools the president has today at his disposal."[15]

Taft's understanding of presidential power and executive leadership, Jonathan O'Neill shows, demonstrates his belief that the president was "empowered to undertake, and was politically responsible for, the systematic administration of the executive branch."[16] Taft's argument presupposes presidential responsibility for leading the nation by advancing a coherent policy agenda. Yet his budget dispute with Congress may have obscured the larger issue of maintaining political responsibility as the size of the national administration increased and its role expanded. Taft insisted that a consolidated presidential budget would better serve the public by reducing waste, providing the people with more accurate information about the government's activities, and allowing the government to take on more extensive reform projects.

Because he insisted that members of Congress representing diverse states and districts would be more attune to the particular interests of their constituencies than the good of the whole nation, Taft argued that the president is particularly well suited to formulating an equitable national budget. Since the president's constituency was the American people and his position allowed him to survey the whole field of government activity, Taft believed it was appropriate that the president should propose a unified budget and curb "legislative extravagance." A unified presidential budget, he insisted, would better serve the entire nation and help to reduce wasteful expenditures that benefited only factional interests. At least with respect to national budget decisions, Taft agreed with Woodrow Wilson's claim that the president "is the representative of no constituency, but of the whole people. When he speaks in his true character, he speaks for no special interest."[17]

Even more importantly, Taft recognized that the president, as "head of the Administration," is "held accountable by the public" for the efficient exercise of the government's duties. Thus, the presidential budget was geared toward public responsibility, since the "constitutional purpose of a budget is to make government responsive to public opinion and responsible for its acts." The Commission on Economy and Efficiency report similarly pointed out that a unified presidential budget would "impress" the proposed plan of government work "upon the attention of the people, through the public press" and thereby "arouse discussion and elicit comment" in order to keep the political branches "in touch with public opinion . . . [and to] best meet welfare demands." By laying a plan for government expenditures before the people, Taft hoped, a presidential budget would increase public awareness of the government's activities and imbue the government itself with a greater sense of responsibility to the voters.[18]

Finally, a centralized budget would better serve the public because it would make political leaders more responsive to the nation's growing needs. Although Taft's call for financial responsibility and his excoriation of legislative extravagance came in response to burgeoning deficits, his efficiency drive had little to do with fiscal conservatism or a belief in small government. He even argued that the nation had "passed beyond the time of what they call the laisser-faire [sic] school." He objected to waste, but he was no disciple of economic conservatism; instead, he promoted efficiency in government explicitly in order to expand government activities:

> We want economy and efficiency; we want saving, and saving for a purpose. We want to save money to enable the Government to go into some of the beneficial projects which we are debarred from taking up now because we cannot increase our expenditures. Projects affecting the public health, new public works, and other beneficial activities of government can be furthered if we are able to get a dollar of value for every dollar of the Government's money which we expend.

In his second annual message, he had voiced a similar theme, insisting that "in handling Government expenditure the aim is not profit—the aim is *the maximum of public service at the minimum of cost.*" Especially when considered alongside his support for greater national tax power under the Sixteenth Amendment, this call for economy was explicitly progressive; Taft and his administration sought to increase efficiency in order to broaden the government's role in promoting social progress and reform.[19]

Civil Service Reform and Cabinet Government

Under the deservedly maligned spoils system, administrative appointments were often given to party leaders' "political henchmen," resulting in corruption and gross inefficiency. Naturally, many people received offices for their political loyalty rather than their administrative expertise, and the patronage system encouraged the proliferation of offices with duplicate and overlapping functions in order to allow party elites to reward as many supporters as possible. This problem, together with the increasing size of government, slowly eroded political responsibility. By 1913, the president was personally responsible for appointing about 10,000 federal officers. However, because no president could be expected to know the qualifications of the pool of applicants for so many offices, the recommendation of a member of Congress typically determined who would be appointed to a local post. This practice divided power from responsibility: it permitted individual legislators to bestow offices but left the president technically responsible for the behavior of "his" appointees.[20]

The Commission on Economy and Efficiency proposed sweeping expansions of the merit system in the federal bureaucracy. Taft and the commission called for a vast extension of the merit system and recommended placing most local officers in the Treasury, Justice, Interior, Postal, and Commerce and Labor Departments on the classified list, thereby protecting those officers from partisan removals. Congress blocked the proposals, but had this plan succeeded, Taft's administration would have brought about the most significant civil service reform since the Pendleton Act of 1883.[21]

Although congressional inaction prevented Taft from implementing his most ambitious initiatives, he was able to take unilateral action to reform the lower grades of the administration. In contrast to his predecessor, who had made "widespread use of executive orders to exempt federal employees from the civil service law," Taft used his power under an 1871 statute to add thousands of civil servants to the merit system by executive order.[22] In 1910, he classified assistant postmasters, clerks in first- and second-class post offices, consular officers, and subordinate diplomatic officials up to the rank of embassy secretary. In 1912, he continued this project by placing an additional 20,000 workers in navy yards and 35,000 fourth-class postmasters under the merit system. Overall, Taft added a total of 70,000 positions to the merit system. By the end of his term in 1913, there were approximately 460,000 federal bureaucrats, of whom 282,000 were on the classified list; of these, 172,000 had been classified by executive orders. The 70,000 positions added by Taft therefore represent almost a quarter of the entire classified service and just over 40 percent of all classifications made by executive order.[23]

Additionally, the president tried to implement some version of a merit system even for those offices he could not classify by executive order. Many members of Congress favored a system of short terms for local offices, a practice that allowed them to reward more of their political allies by rotating supporters through lucrative positions. This system of terms served the political aspirations of some congressmen, but it was prone to corruption and sacrificed efficiency for political expediency. Taft refused to remove officials from office simply because they had reached the end of their traditional two- or four-year "term," and instead retained capable political appointees during good behavior. He even vetoed legislation that attempted to limit these officers to seven years of service. His system decreased the role of partisanship in appointments and created greater stability and expertise in government.[24]

Despite occasional dalliances with withholding patronage appointments from insurgent Republicans, by the end of his term Taft was holding himself to a high standard, retaining industrious and efficient civil servants even when their partisan leanings diverged from his own. Even in the heat of the 1912 presidential canvas, when Roosevelt's insurgent campaign attracted the support of many members of the federal administration, Taft sought to preserve the principle of apolitical administration. He made no attempt to conduct a general purge of the civil service or to root out his political opponents; instead, he tried to limit removals to those officials whose open partisanship hindered the government's activities because their public engagement in the campaign had undermined their ability to function as useful public servants.

He removed one postmaster for his political tirades against the attorney general and fired another who had accused him of stealing Roosevelt's delegates at the 1912 Chicago convention.[25] He was willing to remove an officer for his "vicious" and "partisan" attacks on the administration, but tried to avoid overtly political removals. For instance, Taft ordered an investigation of a Kentucky postmaster for engaging in open political activity. Since the postmaster opposed Roosevelt's candidacy, his activities may have actually benefited Taft politically; nevertheless, Taft believed his activities were "so active and vicious politically as to interfere with the discipline of the [Postal] Department." Although we may legitimately wonder how often Taft's personal feelings played a role in removals, the fact remains that he was apparently willing to fire even his own supporters when their partisanship undermined administrative efficiency.[26]

Moreover, Taft made an honest attempt to retain political opponents whose opposition to his administration did not prevent them from serving the government. He counseled John Lord O'Brian, then a rising federal prosecutor in New York, not to resign, and assured him that "I have no desire that you should tender your resignation because you . . . feel it necessary to vote for Mr. Roosevelt." Further, when a young Felix Frankfurter sought to resign his position in the Department of War, Stimson assured Frankfurter "that he [Stimson] was authorized by the President to say that simply because I [Frankfurter] was support-ing Colonel Roosevelt and not President Taft there was no reason why I should leave office." Frankfurter remained in office, "unashamedly, though not offensively . . . support[ing] Mr. Roosevelt." Although there is evidence that Taft's subordinates were far less principled about the use of government patronage during the 1912 election, the president himself attempted to limit removals to those civil servants who used their government posts for partisan activities, and he was willing to retain even his adversaries when their partisan opinions did not affect their work.[27]

Broadly speaking, Taft sought to recognize the realities of a bureau-cracy made up of political appointees while also avoiding blatant partisanship in appointments and removals. He hoped that eventually virtually every official in the civil service would be added to the classified list and insulated from partisanship. However, because Congress refused to implement civil service reform, Taft recognized that the federal administration would remain rank with partisanship. He therefore compromised with the imperfections of the national bureaucracy, but he apparently recognized that by doing so he surrendered his principled position: "Personally, I should be glad if there were no local patronage and every such office were covered by the civil service law. . . . But as long as the question practically presented is whether patronage shall be used against the Republican administration and its policies or not, I propose to take measures to prevent the first of these alternatives." As a result, he conceded that until the civil service was fully protected from partisan influences, "the only thing we can do is to see to it that the conduct of the offices is not impaired by too great activity in political matters and that the power of officers in the use of offices for political purposes is not abused." This was hardly a perfect solution, but Taft hoped it was nothing more than a temporary concession.[28]

Thus, despite the fact that he was often forced to use informal means and work without the support of Congress, Taft advanced the cause of civil service reform. Taft's initiative undercuts the accusation of strict formalism often leveled at him. A formalist president would likely have seen little role for the president as an administrative reformer; at best, he might petition Congress to enact reform policies. Yet Taft promoted civil service reform unilaterally in the face of congressional opposition. Ironically, Taft's expansion of the merit system was both statutorily permitted and in direct defiance of Congress. The president had legal authority to expand the classified list by executive order, but Taft's efforts to gain congressional support for his reforms had been rejected. He evinced his broad understanding of the executive's power to initiate reform by acting under law, but in the face of congressional intransigence.

Furthermore, even as Taft circumvented Congress's desire to preserve its influence over patronage, he also understood that the president acting alone was less capable of promoting meaningful reform than both political branches operating together. After initiating reforms in the State and Navy Departments, he asked Congress to embody "in a statute the principles of the present executive order" in order to "make permanent" the advantages gained by his reforms. The president had authority to advance his program on a small scale by executive order, but he recognized that his reforms would only be permanent if they were supported by legislation. Just as Taft could initiate change by executive order, so too could any one of his successors rescind his orders and return thousands of civil servants to the patronage system. As the *New York Times* observed, legislative sanction would make reform lasting and encourage even unprincipled or politically isolated presidents to maintain the improvements in the State Department: "Of course there is no doubt that MR. TAFT, as long as he holds the office of President, will enforce the merit system. . . . But it is well to fix the system within the protection of the law . . . in order that the successive Presidents and Secretaries of State shall have its sanction to strengthen and sustain them." Taft's unilateral initiatives were legal, but he understood that statutory reform was far more permanent.[29]

Although the president made significant formal and informal improvements at the lower levels of the civil service, the legislature's refusal to cooperate left him unable to initiate his more ambitious plan for a senior civil service. Taft had hoped to classify even "the higher administrative positions in the service at Washington," including all ranks up to departmental assistant secretaries and bureau chiefs. He recommended limiting the president's appointment power to cabinet officers, a single political undersecretary in each department, and important ambassadors and foreign ministers. These "most important offices" would not be classified because they required "discretion in the carrying out of the political and governmental policy" of the administration. As he argued, this system would ensure stability and expertise in the national administration because under it most administrators would remain in office even when control of the White House shifted between presidents or parties.[30]

Taft's proposals for creating a senior civil service sought to promote administrative efficiency generally, but also would have secured more significant political results. First, by vastly expanding the classified service and limiting presidential appointments to a relatively small number of officials, the president could carefully select his subordinates and the public could justly hold him accountable for their conduct. Second, because day-to-day ministerial and administrative duties would be delegated to career officials, the highest officers in the executive branch—the president, his cabinet, and the chief subordinates of department heads—would be freed to perform discretionary and political tasks. As a result, Taft's proposal would have had tremendous ramifications. It called for the destruction of the spoils system and the introduction of a system similar to the British senior civil service.[31]

The full implications of Taft's reform proposals may be best understood when considered alongside his plan to give cabinet secretaries seats in both houses of Congress. In his fourth annual message, he proposed that department heads be allowed to speak on the floor of Congress, answer questions during debates, and even introduce legislation, although they would not be permitted to vote.[32] Taken together with his civil service reform plans, this proposal displays Taft's desire to dramatically readjust the institutional powers held by the political branches. If Taft's bureaucratic reforms could be put in place, the president and his cabinet would be freed from many ordinary administrative duties and be more able to provide energetic public leadership. The "cabinet government" plan, in turn, would have empowered the president to use his cabinet to forcefully advocate the administration's legislative program before Congress and significantly increased the president's ability to lead his party, the legislature, and the nation as a whole.

It is true that Taft's proposal was in some ways radical, yet his plan was constitutional and could have been enacted by statute. Indeed, similar proposals had been recommended by select committees in the House in

1864 and the Senate in 1881 and had been endorsed by Justice Joseph Story's *Commentaries on the Constitution of the United States.*[33] The proposal would have significantly expanded the president's influence over the entire government, yet it followed the constitutional logic of America's system of separation of powers. Under Article II, the chief executive is required to recommend legislation to Congress. This, in addition to his veto power and the fact that the president is the de facto head of his political party, already permits the president to wield significant influence over the legislative branch, particularly when his own party is in the majority.

By permitting department heads to initiate legislation, the plan would strengthen the president's hand in promoting his agenda by giving him "what he ought to have, some direct initiative in legislation." Taft explained that it would provide the president with "a greater means of bringing about what he wishes in the character of the legislation to be considered by Congress." Even beyond the ability to introduce legislation, the mere presence of the cabinet secretaries would allow the administration to more effectively advocate for its policies, for it would grant it "greater powers of persuasion to secure the adoption of . . . [its proposed] legislation" and "contribute to the enactment of beneficial legislation." The cabinet would therefore have the ability to spearhead the administration's agenda and ensure that the president's policies would have pride of place and a solid chance of passage.[34]

Taft argued that this new influence was necessary because of popular expectations for greater executive leadership. The president's status as the most visible figure in the government ensures that "the whole government is so identified in the minds of the people with [the president's] personality that they are inclined make him responsible" for the actions of the entire government. Additionally, Taft insisted that because the president's "constituency is the electorate of the United States," he often "more truly represents the entire country" than do members of Congress, who represent only particular states or districts. Thus, the "strongest reason" for increasing presidential authority in Congress was to ensure "that the influence that the Executive shall have in shaping legislation shall be more in harmony with the responsibility that the people hold him to in respect to it."[35]

This cabinet government scheme shows that Taft understood modern demands for executive leadership in Congress. Contrary to typical narratives of his presidency, Taft did not eschew public leadership in government; instead he called for institutional reforms that would make that leadership more effective and forceful. Yet he attempted to increase the president's influence while also respecting Congress's independence under the constitutional separation of powers. As Taft pointed out, his scheme would not confer on the president any real "power" over the legislature, but would simply increase his "influence" in advancing legislation. Ultimately, the proposal would have resulted in only two formal changes. First, it would have permitted the administration to write and set forward its own legislation on the floor of Congress, rather than having to find a congressional sponsor for an administration bill. Second, it would have provided for an American version of British "question time" following the executive branch's proposal of a policy agenda. The basic constitutional system would not be altered. Save for the ability to initiate debate on an administration bill, the cabinet would have no formal legislative power. Instead, cabinet officers would simply be treated as favored guests of Congress and would lack any official status within the legislature.[36]

In fact, although the plan would have increased presidential influence, it also would have yielded benefits to Congress and the general public. Taft's proposal, as he recognized, would have given the legislature a greater ability to pry into the workings of the executive branch and forced the cabinet to undergo a "public and direct inquiry" into the business of the administration. As a result, the plan was not lopsided from an institutional standpoint, for it strengthened the president's influence over legislation and also increased Congress's oversight powers. This in turn would lead to increased publicity and responsibility, creating "an opportunity for the public to judge of the Executive" and giving the voters a greater ability to grasp the complex inner workings of the federal government.[37]

As a result, Taft's plan would have increased cooperation between the two political branches by readjusting the relationship between the president and Congress. Taft argued that his plan would help "facilitate" the "functions" of the political branches while also maintaining each branch's independence. He explained: "It was never intended" that the executive and legislative branches "should be separated in the sense of not being in constant effective touch and relationship to each other." The arrangement would have increased cooperation and coordination between the political branches, Taft explained, by correcting the practice of "rigid[ly] holding apart . . . the executive and the legislative branches." However, aside from the cabinet's ability to initiate legislation, Taft called for no actual changes to institutional powers under the Constitution.[38]

It is useful to compare Taft's proposal to Woodrow Wilson's famous plan for "cabinet government." Both men shared the same basic concerns: power and responsibility were divided, a lack of information harmed Congress's ability to deliberate and legislate prudently, the division between the executive and legislative branches was too great, and the public was often ignorant of the actions of the government.[39] Yet their solutions, despite the similarities of their concerns, would have produced markedly dissimilar results. Taft's proposal would have increased efficiency, but it would have done so without undermining the constitutional tension between the branches. Wilson's system, in contrast, would have united the executive and legislative branches and fundamentally altered our governmental system.

In contrast to Taft's relatively modest proposals, Wilson's plan for cabinet government would have transformed the tripartite American system into a parliamentary system. Wilson hoped to allow the cabinet to absorb the executive power of the government by requiring the president to choose his cabinet secretaries from among the members of Congress. In theory, this could have been accomplished through only a single constitutional amendment, which did away with the prohibition on executive officers serving in Congress. By making cabinet members the leaders in Congress and the focal point of government, Wilson believed the executive's agenda and Congress's agenda could be wholly united and the legislative process quickened.[40] Perhaps more importantly, the system would have concentrated power in the cabinet in Congress and sidelined the president. As Wilson acknowledged, he saw nothing wrong with a legislative-centric system that reduced the president to a mere administrative clerk, "the first official of a carefully-graded and impartially regulated civil service system." Walter Lippmann suggests that Wilson believed the president "would become a kind of republican monarch, the head of state, but no longer the Chief Executive."[41]

Ultimately, Wilson's goal was to transform the tripartite system of separation of powers. Because the Founders were adherents of Montesquieu, Wilson wrote in *Constitutional Government*, they had created a government controlled through a system of separated, balancing powers. Wilson overemphasized the negative side of separation of powers and worried that three separate institutions would check each other and hinder the government's ability to act swiftly and energetically.[42] Since Wilson believed America's divided institutions prevented adequate action, he insisted that the government should be transformed and reconceived as an organic "living thing" rather than a "machine"; it should be made "accountable to Darwin, not Newton." More tellingly, he insisted that "corrective interference," that is, constitutional transformation, was necessary, since the belief "that our system is self-adjusting" was no more than "a vain hope."[43] Taft's plan recognized the importance of promoting concerted action by the political branches, but it sought to make the government function more effectively while also maintaining the separate institutions and functions of the political branches. Wilson, for his part, sought to undermine that system by wholly uniting the two political branches.

In contrast to Wilson's scheme for constitutional transformation, Taft's proposal remained conservative in its constitutionalism even as it promised a significant readjustment of authority within the government. It would have vastly strengthened the president as a political leader, but it would have done so by rebalancing, rather than replacing, the system of separation of powers. Taft tried to preserve the constitutional system in part by showing that separation of powers can play a positive role insofar as it can incite creative tensions and encourage fruitful cooperation between the branches. He hoped to increase cooperation, but his proposal ensured that the political branches would retain separate structures and functions. Yet the fact remains that Taft's scheme was clearly progressive and was moderate only in comparison to Wilson's. In the end, his proposed system did maintain its allegiance to Montesquieuean separation of powers, but it would have buttressed the president's ability to lead, drastically increased the potential efficiency of the political branches, provided a conduit for informing the public, and allowed the executive branch to be held more fully accountable for its administration of the government.

Efficiency Progressivism and Social Reform

In this chapter, I have examined Taft's administrative and bureaucratic initiatives, showing the link between his interest in economy and efficiency and his advocacy for social reform and popular sovereignty. Taft's successful administrative reforms were technical and even

mechanistic in their character. However, when this work is seen as part
of a coherent plan of governmental reform, replete with a presidential
budget and a system of cabinet government, it becomes clear that Taft's
program involved far more than tinkering with the formal structure
of the government. Taft famously rejected the radical progressives'
project of constitutional transformation through the initiative, recall,
referendum, and a simpler amendment process. Yet as this chapter
shows, if Taft was unwilling to transform the Constitution, he was
nevertheless willing to substantially alter the way the institutions created
by the Constitution operated—albeit in a manner that respected the
integrity of the Constitution and its system of checks and balances.

Taft's demands for economy and efficiency were a springboard for a
larger project of reform, which would have made the national government stronger and more answerable to the voters. His efficiency drive
was aimed at cutting costs and reducing government waste. However,
as seen especially with the proposal of the federal budget, economy was
pursued not only for its own sake and to eliminate budget deficits, but
also because administrative waste reduced the government's power to
initiate further policies for social amelioration. Similarly, because he
recognized that the president was expected to take on an increased
leadership role, his civil service plans and cabinet government proposal
would have paved the way for more expansive presidential leadership
and allowed the chief executive to promote a comprehensive plan for
progressive legislation. Seemingly banal administrative alterations, Taft
showed, may actually aid and advance social reform.

Moreover, Taft's administrative reforms pointed to increased government responsibility to the people. His comprehensive study of the
administrative apparatus made information more readily available to
government officials, the press, and the public. He argued that the primary reason to create a presidential budget was to make the government more responsive to public opinion, allowing the American people
to understand more fully the government's financial decisions and to
be more capable of holding their representatives accountable for the
nation's fiscal policy. In the same vein, his calls for eliminating the spoils
system and his scheme for cabinet government sought to unite power
and responsibility. As Milkis has pointed out, a more radical strand of
progressive thought sought to eliminate the "space created by institutional devices such as the separation of powers and federalism" in order
to promote a more pure version of democracy.[44] Although Taft was un-

willing to jettison these traditional constitutional features, he was nevertheless sensitive to increasing demands for popular leadership and political responsibility to the people.

In chapters 1 through 3, I have reevaluated Taft's presidency, pointing to his administration's forgotten achievements in execution and administration, legislative leadership, and institutional administrative reforms. In chapter 4, I will turn to his abilities as a partisan leader, specifically considering his actions as a party and popular leader during the 1912 election.

4 | Partisanship and the Presidency
Party and Popular Leadership

Before he became president, Taft had served in a variety of executive and judicial offices at the state and national level. Notably, he initially secured every one of these offices by appointment; his sole experience as a candidate for office came in 1888 when, having already been appointed to complete an unexpired term on the Ohio Superior Court, he won an uncompetitive statewide election for a full term on that court. When Taft ran for president in 1908, it was the first time he sought office in a contested, partisan election. Perhaps for this reason, he often downplayed his own political abilities and ambitions and complained about the burdens of campaigning. "A national campaign for the presidency," he famously declared in 1904, "is to me a nightmare."[1]

Taking such complaints at face value, many scholars have characterized Taft as an inept politician and an apolitical judge who loathed partisan competition and lacked the practical skills needed to employ the "bully pulpit" and navigate a partisan election. Donald Anderson, for example, laments Taft's "atrophied political skills" and memorably writes that "unlike Roosevelt, Taft had no political instinct for the jugular"; Doris Kearns Goodwin finds Taft was reluctant "to passionately embrace his political ambition" and "did little in his own behalf to invigorate his popularity."[2] However, Lewis Gould and Michael Korzi have recently challenged this unidimensional understanding of Taft. They offer a more complete picture of his abilities and argue that he was a capable campaigner who did much of the work in assuring his nomination and election in 1908, managing his own campaign and proving his ability to "win in his own right."[3]

This more nuanced analysis of Taft's capacity for partisan leadership requires us to recognize apparent contradictions that require further explanation. Taft's successes during the 1908 general election belie the charge of atrophied political abilities and undercut his stated hatred of campaigning. In that contest, Taft broke from tradition and became "the first victorious presidential candidate to have engaged in a full-scale speaking tour" through the nation. Moreover, Taft won the electoral votes of Indiana, Minnesota, Montana, North Dakota, and Ohio, even as Democratic gubernatorial candidates were elected in each of those states; he also outpaced his party in Michigan, Illinois, and New York.[4] However, if Taft was a proficient campaigner, we might raise serious questions about his actions during the 1912 general election. How could he watch his party break apart, make few efforts during the general election, and win a mere eight electoral college votes, despite his proven ability to "win in his own right"?

In this chapter, I will evaluate Taft's strengths and weaknesses as a candidate and political leader. A complete understanding of his career requires us to distinguish between his approaches to party leadership and to popular leadership. I first consider Taft's skill as a leader of the Republican Party and show that, although he was not a brilliant party leader, he was adept at managing intraparty affairs. I examine his successful campaign in 1908 and his strategy for achieving renomination in 1912, when his understanding of party management allowed him to control the party's structure and defeat Roosevelt's insurgent challenge. Taft understood that the president played an important role as head of the party as an institution. Even though Taft went on to lose the general election, he did win the support of the party machine and retain the loyalty of most party elites.

Second, I will consider Taft's failure as a popular leader. After winning renomination in 1912, Taft refused to engage in the general election campaign. He offered various justifications for his inactivity, excusing himself by explaining that he did not want to launch a public attack against his former mentor, hated the idea of lowering the presidential office by engaging in partisan rhetoric, and had already done enough simply by denying Roosevelt the Republican nomination. This final excuse holds the key to explaining Taft's approach to the campaign and to understanding his political weaknesses. In contrast to many more radical progressives, who believed political parties were corrupt and outmoded, Taft firmly believed in the importance of political parties, as evinced by his explanation of the "cohesive power" of parties and dedication to fulfilling his party's platform pledges (chapter 2) and his cabinet government scheme (chapter 3). He felt that it was his duty to lead his party and protect it against Roosevelt. Yet, bafflingly, he apparently recognized no similar duty to lead his nation and defend it against Roosevelt and Wilson during the general election.

We will understand Taft more completely if we recognize the connection between Taft's partisan abilities and his understanding of his partisan duties. The standard critiques of Taft's abilities exaggerate his lack of both public speaking skills and political savvy, yet they are correct insofar as they demonstrate his weaknesses as a leader of the people and explain his overarching devotion to the Republican Party. Peri Arnold, for instance, keenly observes that Taft was reticent "to promote himself" through popular addresses, but he "was able to publicly promote his party."[5] As I show, Taft believed he had a duty to lead his party and therefore found ways—some of them innovative—to increase the president's influence and control over his party. In contrast, because he attached less importance to popular leadership through direct appeals to the voters, he also made fewer efforts to develop his abilities as a leader of the people. This partisan astigmatism was largely responsible for his lopsided and often puzzling approach to the 1912 election.

Party Leadership: 1908 and 1912

As we have seen, Taft was not blind to the need for innovative reforms to buttress the president's influence as a leader in government and as the head of his party in Congress. His presidential campaigns in 1908 and 1912 show that he was a reasonably skilled party organizer. By utilizing the power of incumbency, Taft managed to control the workings of the Republican Party throughout his term of office. Ultimately, even in 1912, it was not Roosevelt but Taft who controlled the Republican Party apparatus.

In 1908, when he defeated William Jennings Bryan's third and final bid for the White House, Taft successfully took over leadership of the Republican Party from Roosevelt. Despite exaggerated claims that Roosevelt foisted Taft's nomination on the party and orchestrated the whole campaign to ensure his election, Taft generally controlled his own presidential campaign. In the months preceding the Republican Convention, he successfully courted party elites, overcame a significant challenge for party control in Ohio, and handily stacked up a delegate lead by winning a string of state primaries and conventions.[6] Roosevelt's influence certainly helped his secretary of war succeed, but Taft took responsibility for his nomination as he seized the reins of party power.

Moreover, Taft set his party's course and, together with TR and a few close advisers, drafted a document that formed the backbone of the party's platform. Even when more conservative party elders convinced the Republican Convention to reject or weaken proposed progressive planks favoring publicity for campaign donations, physical valuation of railroads, injunction reform, and direct election of senators, Taft all but ignored them and stated his own support for each of these policies in his speech accepting the Republican nomination. Bryan's political positions were clearly further left than Taft's: he favored the recall, initiative, and referendum, and he famously endorsed government ownership of railroads. Yet the Republican nominee's relative moderation should not blind us to the fact that he took control of a more conservative party, bent its agenda toward his own preferences, and went beyond the platform when his own position was more progressive than his party's.[7]

Taft's ability as a party chief would again be shown in 1912, when he had to fight for control of the Republican Party in direct opposition to his former mentor. Roosevelt and his ultraprogressive allies sought to weaken judicial power, expand direct democracy, and lessen the power of political parties. In contrast, Taft was conservative in his belief that political parties, as mediating institutions that collected groups of voters around a set of major policy priorities, continued to play a valuable role in public life. Notably, however, Taft focused on the parties as *national* institutions, which represented the will of the national majority; indeed, Milkis has shown, Taft actually agreed with the progressive critique of parties, insofar as he favored decreasing the power of local parties and local party bosses.[8] However, because he believed in the importance of parties and saw an urgent duty to preserve the Republican Party as a vehicle for constitutional progressive reform, Taft used every tool at his disposal to deny Roosevelt the nomination and control over the party.

In 1912, Taft used his authority over party elites and the party apparatus to defeat Roosevelt. His renomination at the GOP's Chicago convention was largely a result of Taft's program for developing the power of the West Wing over the party machine. As president, Roosevelt had relied on his personal secretaries, George Cortelyou and William Loeb Jr., as chiefs of staff. Taft continued this practice and began to institutionalize the office of secretary by making the role more prestigious, dramatically increasing the secretary's political authority, and building up the White House staff into a more professional and organized body. Charles D. Hilles, who served as Taft's secretary in 1911–1912, played an active role in the election, helping win over critical party support and going on to serve as chair of the Republican National Committee (RNC) during the general election.

Hilles's political influence rested on a White House reorganization plan that released the president's personal secretary from most administrative duties and allowed him to focus on political tasks. When Taft entered office in 1909, the president had the support of only a small group of assistants and lacked a real policy staff. The White House executive staff was composed of the president's personal secretary, two assistant secretaries, seventeen clerks, and eighteen assorted messengers and doorkeepers. By 1911, Taft convinced Congress to reorganize and professionalize the executive office. White House office space doubled with the building of the Oval Office, and the president's staff was professionalized and refocused on executive work, as doorkeepers and messengers were replaced by clerks, stenographers, correspondents, and an accountant.[9]

Additionally, the newly professionalized staff permitted the creation of a chief of staff system and concentrated political power in the hands of president's secretary. Previously, the secretary had played an administrative role: he was tasked with overseeing the personnel and budget of the White House, directing the Secret Service detail attached to the president, and helping to manage public functions at the White House. After the reorganization, the secretary's role changed considerably. The newly created Office of Executive Clerk inherited the ordinary desk work the secretary had previously performed; this, a White House memo pointed out, freed the secretary to take on "important political work," participate in the president's conferences, and become more heavily involved in the partisan conflicts confronting the president and his party. In addition to an increase in partisan responsibilities, the secretary's position was made more politically prominent. The secretary's social status was elevated by substantially increasing his salary, and he was also seated below cabinet officers and senators but above members of the House at official functions. Such changes, Taft hoped, would allow the president to employ "a higher class of men," equal in intellect and ability to cabinet members and congressional leaders.[10]

Essentially, Taft transformed a bureaucrat charged with relatively mundane secretarial and administrative tasks into a political aide who could advise the president on policy matters and liaise with party leaders from within the White House. This development of the presidential staff, modest as it is in comparison to the modern Executive Office of the President, was a significant step forward in the gradual process of centralizing executive control in the White House.

Admittedly, Taft's contribution was limited in that he did not always employ the most able men as his private secretaries. His first secretary, Fred Carpenter, was a disaster who, Coletta writes, lacked "political sense." Carpenter was succeeded by Charles Norton, who was more interested in politics and interacting with the press, but has ultimately been remembered for his inept attempts at political intrigue. But Hilles, Taft's third secretary, possessed impressive political skills and did yeoman service for the administration. Hilles had extensive partisan and administrative experience: before his time in the White House, he had managed Taft's election efforts in New York in 1908 and served as assistant secretary of the treasury. His background and abilities allowed him to become "de facto White House chief of staff" and to leverage his position to manage the early parts of Taft's 1912 reelection campaign.[11]

Well before Roosevelt had thrown his hat into the ring and as Wisconsin firebrand Robert La Follette's campaign floundered, Hilles began working to ensure Taft's renomination. Beginning with Taft's western swing in the fall of 1911 and continuing through the spring of 1912, Hilles secured critical support from party elites and delegates. As Taft traveled and spoke in defense of his policies, Hilles followed along, quietly probing the depth of Roosevelt's appeal in each state and working to ensure the loyalty of local party leaders. Hilles's work secured the votes of hundreds of delegates and helped Taft win multiple local conventions even before Roosevelt's entry into the campaign. Most importantly, Hilles secured the support of southern African Americans, whose backing provided Taft with 252 delegates, nearly half of the 537 needed for renomination. As the campaign continued, Hilles served as Taft's preconvention manager, doubled as campaign manager and the president's official spokesman at the convention, and finally served as chair of the RNC during the general election.[12]

Taft continued a trend begun by Roosevelt in 1904, when TR had made his personal secretary chairman of the RNC. Beyond Hilles's RNC leadership, Taft's incumbency ensured his supporters dominated the party apparatus. The president's campaign was run by Representative William B. McKinley of Illinois, who also acted as chair of the Republican Congressional Campaign Committee. Senator Elihu Root of New York, who had been secretary of war and secretary of state under Roosevelt before balking at TR's new and more radical brand of progressivism, served as temporary chairman of the Republican Convention. Finally, Taft men controlled the party's Credentials Committee. Despite Roosevelt's seven and a half years in the White House and his formidable political abilities, it was Taft and his supporters who dominated the Republican Party's internal workings throughout the nomination process.[13]

As a result, Taft and his campaign could look ahead to the Chicago convention with a great deal of confidence. By late May the president predicted hopefully, "We have already enough votes to give us considerably more than a majority in the convention." Because he had won a number of popular primaries, Roosevelt led Taft among committed delegates by a 411–201 margin, but Taft held a massive advantage among uninstructed delegates. He controlled the vast majority of the large New York delegation in addition to the 252 southern delegates. Taft's early work through Hilles ensured his victory over Roosevelt, and he was renominated on the first ballot by a margin of 561 to 107 (344 delegates, mostly Roosevelt supporters, abstained), with another 60 votes split between La Follette and Iowa's Albert Cummins.[14]

Hilles's work and Taft's incumbency had cemented the support of party regulars and guaranteed the president control over the Republican Convention and a narrow but significant delegate lead. As a result, Roosevelt was left with little choice but to contest the selection of delegates, a hopeless pursuit in light of Taft's control of the Credentials Committee. After the Credentials Committee awarded Taft 235 of the 254 delegates contested by Roosevelt's campaign, leaving the colonel with a mere 19, TR claimed he had been robbed of 72 delegates. This accusation was not entirely honest. After the election, a story circulated that, when his allies told him they believed he had been wrongfully denied only twenty-eight delegates, TR replied, "Twenty-eight! Twenty-eight! Why, if you got the whole lot, it wouldn't change the result or give you control of the Convention. You must make it at least a hundred. Contest at least a hundred seats!" It is impossible to prove the veracity of this report, which may well have been exaggerated or untrue; but the story is lent some credibility by the fact that it came from Roosevelt supporter Governor Herbert Hadley of Missouri; Hadley had denounced Taft's alleged "naked theft" of Roosevelt's delegates at the convention, but three years later admitted that Roosevelt had a fair claim to only 28 delegates, not the 254 contested by TR's campaign or the 72 TR claimed had been stolen.[15]

It is true that some corruption occurred on the Credentials Committee, yet the improprieties were less widespread than the Roosevelt campaign claimed. At least some Roosevelt delegates were wrongfully replaced by Taft supporters, and some of the Credentials Committee's decisions were rendered on partisan votes, with the thirty-nine committeemen who supported Taft awarding delegates to the incumbent, while the fourteen Roosevelt supporters protested. However, in other cases, Roosevelt's supporters united with Taft's and the committee unanimously voted to seat the Taft delegates. Period assessments and modern scholarship have estimated that the number of stolen delegates ranged from thirty to fifty. Nevertheless, two important facts suggest that TR's efforts to contest the seating of delegates were never more than a forlorn hope. First, Taft always controlled a plurality of delegates and would have led Roosevelt at least 511–501 even if TR had been awarded an additional fifty delegates. Second, the success of Taft's party organization work was augmented by the disorganization of the radical wing of the party. La Follette's lackluster candidacy had divided the insurgent vote, and the senator was unwilling to throw his own support to Roosevelt. Roosevelt's best chance for victory, therefore, would have hung on keeping Taft below a majority on the first ballot, then hoping for a mass exodus of the incumbent's supporters. But in light of Taft's campaign organization and control of party elites, it seems unlikely such a plan would have succeeded.[16]

After Roosevelt seceded from the party, Taft continued to work to maintain the Republican Party apparatus by reconciling alienated party elites. Many Republican insurgents balked at defecting to Roosevelt's Bull Moose Party because of the tremendous electoral difficulties involved in forming a new party. Hoping to capitalize on their uncertainty, Taft attempted to woo alienated Republicans and insisted that "our campaign has got to be one of conciliation instead of alienation. We must educate rather than excoriate." His efforts and the risk of failure that comes alongside any third-party bid generally deterred insurgents from bolting. George Mowry writes, "Most of the professionals remained with Taft, while Roosevelt had to depend on amateurs." Somewhat remarkably, many of the eight progressive Republican governors who had written an open letter asking Roosevelt to challenge Taft supported TR personally, but refused to declare themselves members of the Progressive Party.[17]

The president's conciliation efforts cemented his control of the party and helped him resist the most bitter of Roosevelt's assaults on the GOP. Even after walking out of the convention, Roosevelt was not willing wholly to surrender the party apparatus. TR had created his own third party, but he hoped at the same time to represent the Republican Party. To this end, Roosevelt sought to eliminate Taft electors from the ballot in the states in which insurgents dominated the local party; where he succeeded, Roosevelt electors, rather than Taft electors, were the "Republican" candidates listed on the ballot. Taft actively fought Roosevelt's scheme, even sending his temporary secretary Camri Thompson to Ohio to manage the dispute over control of his home state's ballot. The traditional Republican Party generally succeeded, but Roosevelt and his allies scored notable victories. Taft did not appear on the ballot in South Dakota or California, denying him an opportunity to compete for the two states' combined eighteen electoral votes.[18]

Taft was soundly defeated in the 1912 general election, but his management of the party apparatus in both 1908 and 1912 displays his abilities as a practitioner of party politics. He certainly did not run an impeccable, conciliatory campaign, as is vividly demonstrated by the Republican Party division and the loss of California and South Dakota. Yet faced with unprecedented difficulties, he showed his ability to manage the party's institutions, secured renomination, and defeated an exceptionally talented political opponent. Whatever his weaknesses, Taft understood how to take over the party in 1908 and keep control over it in 1912. As one careful student of the Progressive Era has pointed out, Taft understood the central truth of the 1912 campaign: an incumbent president could use his influence with party elites and his control over the party's structure to win renomination despite dim prospects in the general election.[19]

Rejection of Popular Leadership and Defeat in 1912

Because of his belief in the importance of parties, Taft made significant efforts to lead his party; the sitting president's heavy involvement during the primaries broke precedents and demonstrated his commitment to preserving the Republican Party as a bastion of constitutionalism. Taft had a clear sense of the president's institutional role as chief of the party. Yet after winning renomination in June, Taft lapsed into inactivity and all but sat out the general election in November. The motives that convinced Taft to toil sedulously for renomination but passively surrender reelection help to reveal his understanding of presidential leadership. As I show, Taft's single-minded focus on his party led him to subordinate popular leadership to party leadership, although other factors, such as his meager chances for reelection and his fatalism, also likely played a role in his decision. Consequently, after exerting every effort to protect his party, he ignored, or failed to understand, the nation's desire for more active and personal presidential leadership during the fall campaign. This failure to provide leadership for the public, in turn, ultimately undercut his ability to lead his own party and maintain its unity during the general election.

In Taft's mind, the president had an obligation to lead the nation because he was the head of a political party. Taft believed his primary partisan duty as president was to preserve his party; the broader electorate's support, he thought, would be secured through the instrumentality of the party, not through the magnetism of the president's personality. This understanding may be seen in Taft's 1908 claim that party organizations were important tools that "focus on election day the strength that is behind the party in popular opinion."[20] Thus, when Taft interacted with the public, he did so primarily as the leader of his party; he assumed that it was the GOP's organization and platform that would rally the votes of the electorate—not the personality or charisma of the party's leader. Because Taft saw party institutions as the critical and lasting means by which voters could be organized, he believed that the permanent maintenance of the party structure was more important than building a coalition of voters in any particular election. As a result, in 1912 he argued that winning renomination and protecting his party from TR was actually more important than winning the general election.

Taft's activities in 1912 consistently pointed to a single goal: to save his party from Roosevelt and preserve the constitutional values the GOP embodied. Taft repeatedly insisted that his paramount goal was to preserve the "regular organization" of the Republican Party structure as a "nucleus" around which "people who are in favor of maintaining constitutional government can gather." Winning renomination would secure the Republican Party as a vehicle for "constant progress . . . along safe and sane lines." Thus, defeating Roosevelt in Chicago was Taft's principal objective, for he believed denying TR the nomination would purge the party of "these wild-eyed populists who insist on being Republicans" and so undermine Roosevelt's appeal to the party that "it [is] impossible for him to become President. . . . He is being driven so far from the Republican party." By making the party smaller but purer,

Taft could ensure that it would be preserved from radical populism and continue to stand for "the Constitution as it is, with such amendments . . . as new conditions thoroughly understood may require." To this end, Taft determined that "I am going in to fight . . . *until the end of the Convention*"; he would fight Roosevelt during the primary canvas but not during the general election.[21]

Although he did actively oppose TR until the end of the convention, Taft did not want to campaign in 1912 even during the primaries. He held a principled belief that the president should not engage in demagogic popular rhetoric. Taft was troubled by Roosevelt's use of popular appeals to promote constitutional transformation, particularly TR's call for "pure democracy" and his endorsement of the recall of judicial decisions. Roosevelt, Taft charged, was a reckless demagogue who appealed "to discontent and class hatred," promised the people heaven on earth, and would lead the country toward "benevolent despotism." The president feared that to "descend into the ring" with Roosevelt and appeal for votes would only encourage further demagoguery and harm the dignity of his office. Taft clearly respected the rhetorical precedents set by past presidents: "I do not expect to take any part in the campaign," he wrote during the general election, "following in that respect the tradition of former Presidents." Stephen Knott is correct when he argues that Taft's sense of presidential dignity made him reluctant "to pander to public opinion and engage in presidential theatrics."[22]

This rejection of demagoguery was linked to two additional considerations. First, Taft insisted he would not "indulge in criminations and recrimination [against Roosevelt] however great the provocation," not only out of fear of lowering the dignity of his office, but because he was unwilling to attack his old friend "in view of our previous relations." Moreover, Taft insisted that he was incapable of emulating Roosevelt's populist style. Since he lacked the rhetorical skill of his predecessor, he insisted, "I cannot be spectacular." Similarly, he did not believe he could act as the educator of the people and shaper of the public consciousness: "I have not the faculty for educating the public as you [Roosevelt] had through talks with correspondents."[23] Taft therefore attached two more personal reasons—friendship and rhetorical ability—to his principled rejection of popular rhetoric.

Remarkably, these concerns did not prevent Taft from campaigning before the convention. In late April 1912, after Roosevelt won significant victories in the Illinois and Pennsylvania primaries, Taft responded by delivering an aggressive defense of his administration in Boston in advance of the Massachusetts primary. In doing so, he became the first incumbent president to enter a primary contest. Taft directly addressed a popular audience, discussed the major issues of the campaign, and accused Roosevelt of "audacious effrontery" and "particularly unfair" mischaracterizations of his administration. Despite his misgivings, Taft was willing to use popular rhetoric—and even hurl "criminations and recrimination"—to defend the Republican Party against TR's insurgency. Roosevelt, he argued, posed such a danger to constitutional government "that the ordinary rules of propriety" that typically restrained the president "must be laid aside." Taft won a narrow victory in the Massachusetts primary and continued to campaign, eventually making fifty-five speeches in Ohio alone. His entry into the primary campaign at Boston, and the resulting victory in Massachusetts, are now regarded as a critical juncture in the campaign that stymied TR's rise and helped secure Taft's renomination.[24]

Why did Taft, who hoped to maintain an elevated tone in political rhetoric and lamented "having to trail the office of the President in the mire of politics," break from tradition and engage in a primary fight? Taft swallowed his objections because he believed he had a duty to defend the Republican Party. Party loyalists, he insisted, "look to me" to respond to Roosevelt's attacks and to defend "the Republican Party whose integrity is threatened." It was necessary to respond publicly and forcefully to TR's charges, he argued, because "I represent a cause. I stand for . . . [the policies] that the Republican Party stands for. I am the titular head of that movement." Notably, Taft explained that his duties as the chief of the Republican Party, not his obligations as president of the entire country, were the basis for his active partisan role.[25]

The implications of this emphasis on presidential party leadership became clear after Taft won renomination. Having driven the "wild-eyed populists" from the party, he did not continue to fight those very same radical insurgents during the general election. Instead, he insisted that he had done enough simply by preserving the integrity of his party. Taft continued to oversee the efforts of the RNC, yet his campaign consisted of delivering his speech of acceptance and giving a single additional speech in Beverly, Massachusetts. Aside from these minimal initiatives, he also issued statements by mail and telegraph, intended merely "to meet unfounded accusations" from the Roosevelt camp, and he gave interviews. But Taft emphatically did not embrace the involved leadership role he had taken on during the primaries. In a particularly revealing letter to his wife, he refused to worry about how he was depicted by the press. He believed his subordinates would deal with such matters: "I decline to take any responsibility."[26] Taft protected his party's integrity in the primary contest, then evidently decided to abandon the party to defeat in the general election.

He ultimately provided three interconnected reasons for his decision. First, Taft believed Roosevelt was such a menace that ensuring his defeat was the single most important goal of the campaign. The president believed that Roosevelt was "the most dangerous man that we have had in this country since its origin" because TR favored "fundamental changes in our constitutional, representative government." By defeating TR at Chicago, Taft ensured it would be "very improbable that a dangerous man will come a third time to the presidency." In contrast, he thought Woodrow Wilson was relatively moderate: "I do not think he or the [Democratic] party will attempt greatly to change our fundamental law." He even admitted that "if I can not win I hope Wilson will." Having hamstrung TR's presidential hopes, Taft believed he had struck a decisive blow in defense of the Constitution.[27]

Second, Taft could comfortably accept a Democratic victory because he believed defeat would actually strengthen the Republican Party. After years of political dominance, the party had become fractured by "jealousies and factions" that had "destroyed the discipline and loyalty of its members and injured its political prestige." His party would only overcome its internal divisions after facing an electoral reckoning; "the Republican party," he insisted, "needs the discipline of defeat." Moreover, the president comforted himself by predicting that "four years of Democracy is quite sufficient to teach the people the lesson to let well enough alone for at least another decade." With the people fatigued by irresponsible Democratic policies and the GOP again "in proper condition," he hoped his party could "make a vigorous and healthy opposition to the Democrats and be ready upon their mistake to succeed again to the Government."[28] Thus, Taft's approach was at least partially strategic; he did not simply surrender out of complacency, despair, or distaste for active politics, as some commentators have suggested.[29]

Nevertheless, a certain political fatalism likely played into Taft's calculus. Certainly, the incumbent recognized that a divided Republican Party faced a stiff challenge in 1912. Although he claimed his own "chances [for reelection] are better than a good many people think," he also acknowledged that "the Colonel . . . will do us a good deal of damage." It may be that Taft stopped campaigning after the convention in part because he felt that his campaign was not worth the effort. Indeed, as president, Taft had often justified inaction by expressing his faith that the people would—eventually—judge his presidency kindly: "If the people do not approve of me or my administration after they have had time to know me, then I shall not let it worry me," since "by and by the people will see who is right and who is wrong." After his defeat, he predicted, "I must wait for years if I would be vindicated by the people." But he concluded, "I am content to wait." Taft's faith in the ultimate fairness of the American mind is somewhat touching, but coming from an incumbent president, it also suggests a willingness to excuse political defeat by naively projecting hope for the future.[30]

Taft's belief in the importance of political parties provides the best explanation for his active participation in the nomination battle and his passivity during the general election; it also ties together his trifold excuses for inaction. The danger TR posed to constitutional government and the Republican Party's integrity could be defeated most surely by denying Roosevelt the party's nomination. Similarly, since Taft believed the GOP might actually benefit from a temporary defeat and because he saw Wilson as a relatively minor threat to constitutional orthodoxy, he could justify his refusal to take responsibility during the general election. It is also noteworthy that Taft knew he had a good chance of winning the primary because of his control over the party apparatus, but recognized Wilson's likely victory in the general election. Nevertheless, Taft's focus on party leadership, and not the long odds he faced in November, was always the cornerstone principle by which he explained his actions. Because he was dedicated to preserving his party, he could justify his violation of presidential norms with his entry into the primary canvass; after securing the GOP, he could just as easily excuse his passivity during the general election.

Even if he was correct that protecting his party by denying TR the nomination was his most important strategic goal—and even if his chances of reelection were never strong—it does not automatically follow that the general election was unimportant or that the president's involvement in the campaign would have yielded no meaningful results. Particularly in light of the fact that he evidently believed Wilson's Democrats would enact harmful policies and thought they would challenge the constitutional order—albeit in a less radical way than Roosevelt[31]—the sitting president's decision to declaim responsibility seems to evince indifference to the country's future. Early in 1910, as he worried about his ability to gain reelection and defeat the insurgents and Democrats, Taft told Butt, "I am going ahead as if there were no second term." The country, he insisted, would "sooner or later" demand "its dose" of radical policies and politicians, and "I am in favor of never again using such efforts as we did in the past to stay it."[32] In the primary, he broke precedents to protect his party from TR because, as he declared, "I represent a cause." It is somewhat troubling, therefore, that he made no similar claim during the general election and made few efforts to protect his country from Wilson.

In fact, Taft's lopsided focus on party leadership over popular leadership ultimately undermined his ability to lead and protect his own party. His refusal to even try to make a compelling case to the voters handed victory to Wilson and also threatened what little unity remained within the Republican Party. A divided Republican Party was almost sure to be defeated in November, but Taft's inaction as a popular leader only exacerbated the party split. The party itself needed Taft to engage in popular leadership after Chicago; it needed a strong leader who could rally party regulars and appeal to disaffected Roosevelt voters who could be convinced to come back to the Republican fold. Taft actually recognized the importance of presidential leadership when he adopted his campaign of conciliation and sought to maintain the loyalty of political elites. Yet he made no such efforts to retain the support of rank-and-file Republicans who—partially as a result of the incumbent's noncampaign—ultimately voted for Roosevelt by a 53 to 47 percent margin.[33] Although it is unlikely that Taft could have wholly avoided a party division in 1912, a more extensive effort could have at least decreased its gravity and allowed the Republican Party to be in a stronger position to oppose the Democrats in 1914 and 1916. Taft would have been a more impressive party leader had he made a greater effort to also be a popular leader.

Taft's distaste for popular leadership also hindered his ability to articulate his constitutional principles during the general election. Although his sense of presidential dignity and his antipathy for TR's theatrics were praiseworthy, Taft went too far when he refused to address the public and failed to offer a principled form of presidential rhetoric to counter Roosevelt's demagoguery. Jeffrey Tulis's seminal

Rhetorical Presidency contrasts two rhetorical styles, that of the Founders, which was largely maintained through the end of the nineteenth century, and the new "rhetorical presidency." The older rhetoric was more often written than spoken, usually addressed to Congress rather than directly to the people, and directed at educating the people about constitutional principles; the newer presidential rhetoric is usually spoken and emphasizes public policy, presenting the president's case directly to the people and over the heads of members of Congress and potentially short-circuiting legislative deliberations. Tulis also examines President Roosevelt's 1906 campaign in support of the Hepburn Act and argues that Roosevelt demonstrated a "middle way" that presented the president's policies directly to the people while also maintaining a certain moderation and respecting Congress's role.[34]

Taft's own style, like TR's in 1906, straddled the divide. An analysis of Taft's speeches shows that he continued the older tradition by discussing the importance of constitutional government, ordered liberty, the dangers of majority tyranny, and the need to strengthen the courts to protect individual rights. At the same time, he stressed policy priorities in his speeches and messages. His minutely detailed missives to Congress, Tulis observes, made Taft "the first president to regularly build his messages around 'laundry lists' of legislative initiatives." Similarly, in addressing the public, Taft often focused on policy; a "swing" through the country allowed him to learn the views and "needs of particular sections" for "national legislation and executive action" and gave him an opportunity to explain "some of the difficulties of government and some of the problems of solution" his administration faced. Thus, Taft defended his policies directly to the voters, promising to continue the "Roosevelt Policies" as a whole, detailing his tariff revision, promoting his conservation efforts, and encouraging the public to support increased regulation of interstate railroads. Not only did he speak directly to the people on policy matters, but in some cases—Canadian reciprocity, for instance—he even took his case to the voters amidst congressional deliberation on a bill. Thus, the president often employed the tools of popular leadership in order to promote and defend his party's agenda.[35]

Moreover, Taft actually had the ability to take his case to the voters. His weaknesses as a public speaker were real, but they have too often been exaggerated. Certainly, he gave excessively lengthy public missives filled with verbose syntax, copious subordinate clauses, and repetitive phrases. Since many of his 1908 campaign speeches were actually relatively short, we may assume that he did understand the importance of brevity, yet he was often unable to control his desire to be thorough. Moreover, Taft too often focused on mundane policy details when speaking before the people. For example, when he spoke of his desire to reform labor injunctions, which could have been the basis for an appeal to the labor vote, he strayed from the issue in order to discuss the challenges of efficiency in the judicial system, the corruptions of defense attorneys, and the exorbitant expense of litigation. Similarly, he pitched his plan for postal savings banks at a state fair, but he employed language better suited to a banker's convention than a popular gathering: he detailed proposed interest rates, the geographic distribution of banks and investments, and explained comparative banking practices in the United States and Europe.[36] As a result, although he defended his party's initiatives, he often failed to appeal to the popular mind.

Yet despite these strategic errors—which were significant—Taft was neither a lazy candidate nor an incompetent speaker. During the 1904 and 1906 elections, Taft won praise for campaigning on behalf of his party, and as the Republican presidential nominee in 1908, he broke from the traditional "front porch" campaign recommended by his advisers. His 18,000-mile "swing" through the country took him to 22 states and allowed him to deliver about 400 speeches. As president, he traveled more than 150,000 miles while promoting and explaining his party's policies, causing his military aide to complain of the president's "ghoulish delight" in travel.[37] Nor was Taft a bad public speaker. Period press accounts of Taft's 1908 canvass tell of massive torchlit parades and "rousing demonstrations" in support of the Republican nominee. Some of this enthusiasm for Taft was likely caused by public excitement at meeting a presidential candidate. But although Taft lacked the fireworks and star power of his predecessor, the fact remains that he was a reasonably popular candidate.[38]

During the general election of 1912, Taft had the opportunity and the ability to display a type of presidential rhetoric that was both popular and principled. Since the election was in many ways a battle over fundamental constitutional principles, Taft could have employed dignified and moderate rhetoric while urging the people to adhere to republican principles and traditional constitutionalism. He could have used the election as an opportunity to make use of the tools of modern presidential communication while holding fast to older constitutional principles of moderate and principled presidential rhetoric, jettisoning demagogic attacks on his opponents and mere partisan proposals of policy initiatives. Instead, he retreated into the White House. Taft's fear of demagoguery cannot alone explain his inaction, as he had employed popular rhetoric during the primaries to maintain the integrity of his party. Instead, it was his misplaced prioritization of party leadership at the expense of popular leadership that led him to surrender an opportunity to use the power of presidential rhetoric to buttress his defense of the Constitution and reject Roosevelt's demagoguery. Taft's apparent inability to meld his constitutional principles to an appropriate rhetorical approach stands out as a major failure of his presidency.[39]

Ironically, *after* losing the election, Taft devoted himself to instructing the public on constitutional principles. He immediately proposed the creation of a fund to print literature and facilitate public lectures that would educate students and voters on the principles of American government. Throughout his retirement, Taft actively spoke and lectured on the Constitution, hoping thereby to defeat those "unscrupulous demagogues who . . . do not hesitate to inculcate disrespect and even contempt for the Constitution." His lectures, some of which were later printed in book form, present engaging and accessible commentary on democracy and constitutionalism (*Popular Government*, 1913), the world peace movement (*The United States and Peace*, 1914), and presidential power (*Our Chief Magistrate and His Powers*, 1915).[40]

As a result of these inconsistencies, we are left with unanswered questions when we attempt to evaluate Taft's partisan abilities. Why was he willing to violate political norms and become the first incumbent president to engage in a primary contest, but unwilling to recognize the importance of also vying for reelection during the general election? Why was he reticent to use the power of the modern rhetorical presidency to instruct the public on constitutionalism during the general election even though he had been willing to engage in partisan "criminations and recrimination" during the primary? Finally, why did the silent President Taft give way to the vocal and active Professor Taft, who used his influence as a former president to teach the public about his political and constitutional ideals? Recognizing Taft's fear of demagoguery and his belief that preserving the party from Roosevelt was of primary import helps to resolve some of these uncertainties, yet Taft's partial explanations of his actions remain unsatisfactory.

Taft the Politician

In this chapter, I have sought to provide a multidimensional view of Taft's partisan abilities, recognizing his skills as a party leader but also pointing out his significant failures as a popular leader. Taft did actually seek to provide forceful partisan leadership through various institutions, as his legislative leadership, cabinet government scheme, party leadership, and West Wing reforms show. But because he evidently viewed executive power almost exclusively through the lens of constitutional and party institutions, he was unwilling to campaign actively for reelection in the general election. The president might be the head of government and leader of his party, but Taft did not believe the president had a more personal and less formal role as leader of the people. Thus, though his conception of the president as the chief of the party led him to defend the GOP against Roosevelt and even to embrace significant aspects of modern campaigns through public appeals to the party faithful during the primary, his refusal to act as a popular leader during the general election weakened his influence with rank-and-file Republican voters and undermined his efforts to maintain the unity of his own party.

Taft has sometimes been blamed less for his own weaknesses than for not having Roosevelt's strengths. After his defeat, the *New York Times* concluded, "President TAFT has been the victim of too much ROOSEVELT." Admittedly, Taft faced difficult, if not nearly impossible, circumstances. In the lead-up to the 1912 elections, the Republican Party was brewing for an internal revolt. Roosevelt had held the party together for the seven and a half years of his presidency, but he had also undercut its cohesiveness by playing the insurgents and old guard off each other. By 1909, he had failed to re-create the GOP as an unambiguously progressive party, but he had given enough legitimacy to the insurgents that they were no longer satisfied with being a minority wing of the party. Taft inherited a party on the brink of civil war and was also confronted with the unprecedented problem of facing down a challenge from his mentor and immediate predecessor.[41]

Nevertheless, even if the party split in 1912 was not wholly Taft's fault, his approach to leadership only exacerbated the problem. It was Taft, not Roosevelt, who stood at the helm of the Republican Party in 1912, and it is obvious that Taft could have been more active. As his Boston speech showed, Taft could connect with the public when he exerted himself. Whatever his rhetorical weaknesses, the public did generally like "Big Bill" Taft and was willing to hear him present his case. Yet Taft squandered the opportunity to offer a moderate, reasonable, and dignified rhetorical alternative to TR's demagoguery. Although many of the scholarly accounts of Taft's supposed apolitical "judicial temperament" are overstated, as Taft's astute party leadership shows, these analyses clearly do have some foundation in fact: in the general election campaign of 1912, Taft gave up the political ghost and convinced himself that the sitting president could conscientiously shrug off partisan politics.

Taft was mistaken in believing that he could rest presidential influence on institutional and party structures and keep the president at arm's length from the average voter. His predecessor erred in unmooring presidential power from its constitutional and institutional foundations and insisting that the people's approbation was the basis for executive power, claiming, "Whatever I did as president I was able to do only because I had the backing of the people. When on any point I did not have that backing . . . my power vanished."[42] Taft, in sharp contrast, saw too little room for the president to function outside of governmental and party institutions. The irony of Taft's failure is that he did often see that the government and the presidency needed to develop to meet the changing needs of politics and society. He had envisioned innovative ways to expand presidential influence over Congress and his party, yet he was singularly uninventive in his view of presidential leadership outside the institutional structures of government and party. He recognized that the presidency must adapt under the Constitution, but he failed to acknowledge that there might exist a need for the president himself— for William Howard Taft—to develop and change his own approach in order to provide the public with the leadership it demanded.

5 | The Professor on the Presidency
Our Chief Magistrate and His Powers

Once close friends, Taft and Roosevelt had broken their friendship and their political alliance for personal as well as partisan reasons. Taft had removed some of TR's close friends from office, initiated the U.S. Steel suit, and implicitly critiqued Roosevelt's approach to reform by legalizing many of TR's progressive initiatives. However, their most significant disagreement arose over their differing conceptions of the president's constitutional powers and his role in American political life. Their dispute was immortalized in Roosevelt's 1913 *Autobiography*, which famously laid out his "stewardship" theory of the presidency and attacked what TR termed the "Buchanan–Taft" school of presidential power.[1]

In his *Autobiography*, Roosevelt accused Taft of embracing a rigid formalism that radically limited the president's capacity to lead the nation and hamstrung the nation's ability to modernize and develop. Taft, TR claimed, believed that "the President should solve every doubt in favor of inaction . . . [and] construe strictly and narrowly the Constitutional grant of powers both to the National Government, and to the President." According to Roosevelt, rather than striving "actively and affirmatively to do all he could" to serve the people, Taft had "content[ed] himself with the negative merit of keeping his talents undamaged in a napkin."[2] Roosevelt was not the first to criticize Taft's understanding of presidential power or political leadership, but his *Autobiography* had a tremendous influence and modern scholarship has almost unanimously agreed with his assessment.[3]

During his time teaching law at Yale, Taft responded to TR's charges in a series of public lectures later published together as *Our Chief Magistrate and His Powers* (1915). Roosevelt's *Autobiography* made a political case for expansive presidential power, citing specific crises during his tenure to drive home the necessity of his broad interpretation of executive power. In contrast, Taft presented a legal defense of the powers of the executive under the Constitution. Taft's book, the only work by a former president to offer a comprehensive examination of Article II, addresses the president's powers clause by constitutional clause and evaluates the president's role in American politics. This chapter considers Taft's analysis of the constitutional presidency in *Our Chief Magistrate* and, by comparing his argument to TR's, shows that Taft both avoided legal formalism and presented a viable alternative to the "stewardship" theory.

➤ Taft's and Roosevelt's competing theories of the presidency are frequently contrasted as representatives of "formalist" and "functionalist" views, respectively, of executive power. Taft looked to the Constitution as the source of the president's powers and insisted that the chief executive wields "wide powers, not rigidly limited" but "can exercise no power which cannot be fairly and reasonably traced to some specific grant of power or justly implied and included within such express grant." Roosevelt, in contrast, de-emphasized the Constitution to focus on functional power: "I did not care a rap for the mere form and show of power; I cared immensely for the use that could be made of the substance." Roosevelt believed the president should have the right to do anything to promote the public good unless his actions were expressly forbidden "by direct constitutional or legislative prohibition." His argument paid lip service to the Constitution, but TR ultimately unmoored the presidency from the fundamental law and chose to ground executive power on popular support rather than Article II. Roosevelt himself acknowledged this; in one extreme case, he even admitted that his planned actions were potentially impeachable, but then he justified them by claiming that they would have served the public.[4]

Ultimately, the disagreement between Taft and Roosevelt points to the tension between law and necessity. Roosevelt was willing to bend legal limitations because he believed a Constitution that rigidly restrained executive power would prevent the nation from responding to emergencies or rapidly changing circumstances. In many ways, his argument is compelling. Unless the Constitution grants the president such vast powers, does it not prohibit the executive from doing what is necessary to lead the nation and become what TR called "a straitjacket cunningly fashioned to strangle growth"? On the other hand, Roosevelt's case raises serious questions for constitutionalism. If he was correct and the president holds such extensive prerogative powers that he may do anything necessary in an emergency, does this not institutionalize a dangerous and illimitable executive power that may easily harm the nation?[5]

In rebutting Roosevelt, Taft offered a workable solution by showing that the Constitution may impose real limits on government without depriving it of the powers necessary to protect itself and its citizens. Through his examination of the constitutional basis of executive power, Taft provided a legal solution to the problem of prerogative by showing that the Constitution may empower the president to defend the nation during an emergency while also limiting his power and protecting the nation against the president. Thus, by delineating an impressively broad framework for executive power under the Constitution, Taft managed to ground the executive's authority in the fundamental law without embracing legal formalism or crippling the president's ability to act.

Furthermore, although this chapter emphasizes Taft's understanding of emergency executive power, the dispute over prerogative may serve as a stand-in for a larger conflict over the Constitution's flexibility and ability to survive in the twentieth century. As Lance Robinson points out, the traditional scholarly assessment of the dispute between Taft and TR assumes Taft was a formalist whose understanding of executive power was "insufficient to meet the challenges of twentieth-century America."[6] The stakes were higher than a mere disagreement over executive power. If TR was correct that a legal, rather than pragmatic, understanding of the Constitution would prevent growth and turn the fundamental law into a "straightjacket," it follows that the Constitution and its limitations needed to be altered or reformed in order to allow the nation to confront the challenges of the Progressive Era. On the other hand, if Taft was correct that the Constitution could empower the government to act and at the same time maintain basic limitations on government power, then his understanding of constitutional progressivism provides a viable legal alternative to Roosevelt's argument for virtually unlimited government power.

The President under the Constitution

In *Our Chief Magistrate*, Taft contended that the Constitution simultaneously confers upon the president duties and the corresponding powers necessary to carry them out. According to his understanding of Article II, the oath of office and take care clauses impose extensive responsibilities on the president, but also provide him with the powers necessary to carry out those duties. Taft argued that the president has sufficient means to execute his obligations but that his powers are ultimately limited by the Constitution. Essentially, he offered a theory of unlimited executive means to attain limited constitutional ends.

Taft was responding immediately to Roosevelt and his "Hamiltonian" approach to the presidency, but his argument also offered a useful critique of the "Jeffersonian" theory of executive power. According to the Jeffersonian school, the executive's powers are clearly and stringently limited by the Constitution, but—in certain circumstances—the president may violate the law to preserve the nation. Thomas Jefferson himself relied heavily on John Locke's understanding of prerogative power: the power to act "where the law was silent, and sometimes too against the direct letter of the law, for the public good." Jefferson argued that "strict observance of the written laws is doubtless *one* of the high duties of a good citizen," but the "laws of necessity . . . are of higher obligation." Jefferson here speaks of necessity, but remarkably, as Jeremy Bailey points out, Jefferson also argued that a president could justifiably go beyond the law not only to preserve the nation in a time of crisis but even to secure some important advantage for the public. Jefferson and his followers therefore justify extralegal executive actions, but insist— again following Locke—that the executive must submit his actions to the judgment of the legislature and ask that body to ratify them after the fact.[7]

For Hamiltonians such as Roosevelt, prerogative may be legalized in a certain sense. Hamiltonians see prerogative as a "*supplement* to law," which may require the executive to act outside of the law, yet is justified so long as he acts only in the service of "the fundamental principles of our regime." In contrast to the Jeffersonians, who argue that prerogative power is illegal and unconstitutional, the Hamiltonians seek to legitimize prerogative by claiming that it can be *both* extralegal *and* constitutional.[8] If Jeffersonians permit the executive to act outside the law but demand he later seek legislative ratification, the Hamiltonians remove the need for ex post facto approval by Congress. Both, in the end, allow the president to avoid the limitations of the Constitution in an emergency.[9]

Taft's own views differed substantially from both schools, for he refused to endorse the idea that the executive may violate the law and the Constitution in order to serve the nation. Because of his strong reliance on the Constitution, Taft's theory of executive power has traditionally been cast as a weak response to Roosevelt's "stewardship" theory. Yet Taft actually presented an argument for a vigorous executive. His insistence that the president has only those powers arising from "some specific grant of power or justly implied and included within such express grant" did not prevent him from also recognizing that the president holds "wide powers." For Taft, the president's broadest powers are implied by his duty to "take Care that the Laws be faithfully executed" and his oath to "preserve, protect and defend the Constitution of the United States." Out of these clauses springs the president's responsibility to act upon "any obligation inferable from the Constitution, or . . . derived from the general code of his duties under the laws of the United States." These two clauses, taken together, enjoin upon the president the "widest power and the broadest duty" and at the same time point to the limits of presidential power.[10]

Taft argued that the executive must have the appropriate powers to fulfil his legal duties: the existence of a presidential duty implies a corresponding power to carry it out. Having been tasked with specific obligations, the president is given the powers "proper and necessary" to execute his duties. As Louis Fisher has observed, rather than providing a rigid understanding of executive power, Taft actually "adds to the Constitution a 'necessary and proper' clause for the President." Taft did not embrace a formalist conception of Article II. Instead, he provided the same argument for executive power under the take care and oath of office clauses that Alexander Hamilton and John Marshall provided for the legislative power under the necessary and proper clause. By distinguishing between a president's powers and his duties, Taft showed that the Constitution created a strong yet limited executive; although the president may employ the powers necessary to carry out his duties, his duties are finite, defined and circumscribed by the Constitution.[11]

As a result, the president may use any means necessary and proper to carrying out his duties, but he lacks untrammeled power. Indeed, not only is the president controlled by the Constitution, but Congress may alter or expand his obligations by statute. Congress "by its legislation . . . often creates a duty in the Executive which did not before exist." The legislature may impose ministerial duties on the executive branch and even limit the discretion of the officer tasked with carrying them out. Congress has wide power to impose ministerial duties on executive officers, "definitely limiting their discretion and commanding a certain course by [subordinate officers] which it is not within the power of the [Chief] Executive to vary." Thus, when the legislature directs an executive officer to perform a task that "does not involve and was not intended by Congress to involve discretion," the chief executive has virtually no direct control over his subordinate in the execution of that task.[12]

Despite these concessions to legislative authority, Taft insisted that the president was not a mere minister of Congress. He has an obligation to execute the Constitution and laws passed by Congress, but nevertheless he wields substantial discretionary power in doing so. He must both interpret his duties under the law and determine how best to carry them out. Primarily, the president's discretion comes about because he is bound by his oath of office to interpret the laws he must execute. Because universal laws passed by Congress are necessarily general and cannot define the specific manner in which they will be applied in various circumstances, this power to interpret the law is "practically one of the greatest of executive powers." Moreover, the nature of the executive power is "perhaps less subject to judicial interpretation than that of Congress." Unless executive action directly infringes upon individual rights, Taft argued, the president's interpretation of a law cannot usually be appealed to any court. As a result, in the vast majority of instances, the president is not only the first but the final judge of his own constitutional authority. Thus, by pointing out the tremendous discretion bestowed upon the president, Taft shows that the president may serve Congress by enforcing its laws, but that he does so as an executive officer with wide political discretion, not as a mere ministerial officer whose tasks are clearly defined and controlled by legislation.[13]

Taft believed that Congress could not restrict the president's power to control the executive branch in performing discretionary tasks, particularly with respect to the duties and powers directly conferred upon the president by the Constitution. The legislature "may not prevent or obstruct the use of means given [the president] by the Constitution for the exercise of those [executive] powers." For example, as commander in chief, the president "can order the army and navy anywhere he will, if the appropriations furnish the means of transportation" without fear of legislative interference. Congress may impose responsibilities on the executive and determine the instruments at his disposal to carry out those duties, yet its ability to control the method by which he employs those forces is limited. Ultimately, Taft believed that the president bears primary responsibility for determining what actions are "proper and necessary" as a means to carry out his duties.[14]

Thus, Taft laid out an expansive understanding of Article II, showing that the president both serves the legislature by enforcing the law and acts as an independent political entity, wielding powers derived directly from the Constitution. Although the president's broadest powers were created to allow him to carry out his duties under the Constitution and laws of the union, nevertheless he is not a mere functionary, but maintains vast discretion and remains largely independent of the legislature. Taft showed that the president is limited by legal restrictions, but he also argued that the Constitution and laws of the United States provide the chief executive power to exercise his duties largely according to his own discretion.

Additionally, the duties imposed on the executive are extremely broad and diverse and cannot be laid out in explicit detail; as a result, Taft contended that the president had many obligations that grow out of, but are not expressly defined by, the Constitution or statutes. The broadest of these responsibilities, which permits the president to wield a wide legal prerogative power, is his duty under the oath of office and take care clauses to defend the "peace of the United States." Citing *In Re Debs*, Taft contended that the president has an obligation to maintain the "peace of the United States" in "every foot of land within the jurisdiction of the United States" by enforcing the national law. Thus, the president has the authority to use "all the forces which he has at his lawful command" to prevent the violation of national laws and to respond to any attempt to hinder their execution. The president, for example, may use the forces at his disposal to guard federal officers in the performance of their duties or to remove obstructions to the delivery of the federal mails, even without express statutory authorization.[15]

In certain circumstances, this power could balloon to tremendous proportions. For instance, if the United States gained territory during a war, Taft believed the president had both the right and the duty to enforce the law and maintain the peace in that territory. Indeed, should Congress fail to enact a comprehensive system of law, Taft argued that the president had the power to exercise not only executive but even legislative and judicial power. For example, in 1904, Congress temporarily gave the president all "'military, civil, and judicial powers'" and also power to stipulate the "'rules and regulations necessary'" to govern the Panama Canal Zone. Although this authority was intended to be transitional, Congress made no further provision for the governance of the Canal Zone before that temporary authorization expired. As secretary of war, Taft had advised President Roosevelt that he had the power to maintain the status quo. Despite the legislature's irresponsible inaction, the president had an obligation to enforce the law and maintain the peace using the necessary and proper means available to him; because Congress had failed to act, the president was left with no choice but to maintain the peace using the means already at his disposal.[16]

Further, according to Taft, the "peace of the United States" extended not simply to enforcing the law and keeping the peace within the continental United States and in American possessions, but even to protecting American citizens abroad. Taft acknowledged that Congress alone could declare war, but he also argued that "war as a legal fact" exists whenever a foreign nation commits an act of aggression against the United States. The commander in chief had a duty to intervene, potentially utilizing the full power of the army and navy, as soon as violence threatened either American citizens or their rights. As an example, Taft cited William McKinley's intervention in China to protect American diplomats in Beijing during the Boxer Rebellion. Despite the fact that McKinley essentially declared a limited war, initiating military action in a foreign nation "without express Congressional authority," Taft insisted that the president had an obligation to protect the diplomatic legation and could use the military as necessary to fulfill that duty.[17]

In short, Taft's understanding of presidential authority presents an argument for a powerful and vigorous executive who nevertheless remains limited by the Constitution through the duties prescribed by Article II. Taft's *Chief Magistrate*, Robinson points out, "illuminates the potential for executive power to be exercised for the good of the republic on explicitly constitutional grounds."[18] Taft relied on the text of the Constitution as the basis for presidential power, but he also knew that executive power is, by its nature, incapable of precise definition. He understood that Article II grants the president certain implied or inferred powers but limited these powers by linking them to the president's duties. Thus, by attaching executive authority to presidential duties, Taft preserved sufficient presidential power to enforce the peace of the United States and respond to many national exigencies while also defending the Constitution against untrammeled executive action.

Theory and Practice during Taft's Presidency

Despite the numerous criticisms of Taft's alleged formalism, a careful analysis of his four years in office shows that he was willing to make robust use of presidential power. By considering Taft's use of executive power in light of *Our Chief Magistrate*'s theoretical understanding of that power, I will show that his theory of executive prerogative permitted energetic use of executive power to address both domestic and foreign crises. As president, Taft's actions generally adhered to the theory he outlined in *Our Chief Magistrate*, although it is true that on at least one occasion he was unfaithful to his own understanding of the Constitution. As we will see, much of Taft's argument for unlimited executive means to achieve limited constitutional ends resembles Abraham Lincoln's understanding of prerogative as he explained it in his defense of the Emancipation Proclamation.

Taft's claim that the president could use the forces at his disposal to defend "the peace of the United States" points to the president's power to respond to a variety of domestic crises. In *Our Chief Magistrate*, Taft applauded Grover Cleveland's use of troops to break the 1894 Pullman Strike in order to "remove the obstruction to the passage of the mails."[19] For Taft, Cleveland had the power to remove obstructions to the delivery of the federal mails, even if doing so involved breaking the strike as a means to that end. Cleveland had intervened in a local strike, but Taft claimed that Cleveland intervened only in order to meet his constitutional obligation to enforce the law and protect the operations of the federal government.

During his own presidency, Taft was similarly prepared to use federal troops to break a railroad strike in Georgia. In 1909, race-based union conflict among railroad workers led to an extended strike in Georgia, interfering with interstate commerce and the delivery of federal mails. In the face of this threat, Taft was ready to issue "the order to patrol the line from Atlanta to Augusta with federal troops." This proposed use of federal troops was justified in a memorandum from the Department of Commerce and Labor pointing out that the strike obstructed the delivery of the mails and that violence during the strike had sometimes endangered property in the flow of interstate commerce. As a result, the government would have a right to use federal forces to break the strike and take any other actions that might become necessary; as Taft claimed, "The law on the subject is so clear and my duty was so manifest that I should not have hesitated a minute had the strike not ended when it did." Ultimately, the dispute was settled without the use of federal troops. Nevertheless, this incident shows that Taft, like Cleveland during the Pullman Strike, was willing to use federal troops for federal purposes, and saw justification for employing national power when a local dispute interfered with the enforcement of national laws.[20]

It is useful to consider Taft's threat to exercise presidential power alongside a similar threat made by Roosevelt. Roosevelt too had come close to intervening in a domestic labor strike in the winter of 1902, but, unlike Taft, he had not defended his proposed actions on constitutional grounds. Roosevelt's "stewardship" theory taught that it was "not only [the president's] right but his duty to do anything" that was "imperatively necessary" for the general welfare. Moreover, he believed "the executive power was limited only by specific restrictions and prohibitions" imposed by the Constitution or laws. This theory, when applied to the 1902 strike, shows that Roosevelt adopted an essentially Hamiltonian position and insisted that the president had the power to do anything for the common good unless the Constitution or laws explicitly forbade that action. In so doing, Roosevelt undermined any real limits on presidential power by basing his argument for prerogative on a moral appeal to the nation's needs, not on the president's legal authority under the Constitution.[21]

Roosevelt argued that the "public interest" in the outcome of the Pennsylvania Coal Strike of 1902 was so great that he had the power to seize private coal mines and operate them under the command of "some first-rate general." TR never explained how the public interest in ending "the coal famine" could be tied to any presidential power or duty. He did vaguely reference the republican guarantee clause, claiming he would ask the governor of Pennsylvania to request federal aid against domestic violence. Yet even if the president has a responsibility to intervene when internal turmoil threatens the existence of a state government, he has no duty to provide the public with coal by seizing private property and placing the military in command of privately owned coal mines. Ultimately, Roosevelt made no meaningful argument that the operation of coal mines in Pennsylvania was in any way attached to his powers under Article II. Instead, he based his argument on popular support, insisting that the nation's "wave of indignation" would have authorized him to act with powers appropriate to wartime. Public opinion, not the Constitution, was the source of his authority, for "with the [coal] famine upon them the people would not have tolerated any conduct that would have thwarted what I was doing."[22]

Roosevelt's arguments in 1902 show the potential danger of the Hamiltonian argument, for ultimately TR was willing to flatly reject constitutional constraints. He ignored Article II and turned to public indignation as a foundation for presidential power. Moreover, rather than making a convincing legal argument to justify his proposed actions, Roosevelt strongly suggested that his plan violated constitutional and legal norms and could have justified impeachment and removal. He admitted that Congress could have tried to impeach him for his proposed actions, but he insisted that his intervention would have been so popular that Congress "would not have ventured to try" to remove him from office.[23]

In contrast to Taft, who insisted on a constitutional basis for his actions, Roosevelt saw an opportunity for the executive to act wherever and whenever the public would support his actions. By unmooring presidential power from the Constitution, he ultimately undermined the Constitution's safeguards. Essentially, Roosevelt sought to defeat the constitutional system of separation of powers by basing his powers not on Article II, but on popular approval. And although he evidently knew that his actions would have violated the law, he reassured himself that Congress would never impeach him so long as he was supported by the public. Taft, in contrast, understood that the Constitution empowers the president to take dramatic actions in some circumstances, but also recognized that the president's powers were limited by law and that he could be held accountable by both the judiciary and Congress if he sought to exercise extraconstitutional powers.

Taft was willing to take similarly strong, but legal, action in the realm of foreign policy. In *Our Chief Magistrate*, he argued that the "peace of the United States" guaranteed the safety of every American citizen, even those living abroad, and cited McKinley's use of troops to protect American diplomats in Beijing as a legitimate use of executive power. As president, Taft showed himself ready to use the armed forces to protect the lives and property of US citizens living abroad. For much of Taft's term, the regime of Mexican president Porfirio Díaz was ravaged by tremendous civil unrest. During this period of turmoil, the Mexican government proved incapable of maintaining order, leaving the lives and property of US citizens to be destroyed during riots and threatened by roving bands of brigands. In order to protect thousands of American citizens and $2 billion in American-owned property and investments in Mexico, Taft mobilized 20,000 troops along the Mexican border.[24]

Notably, he did not actually make war with the troops at his disposal. His duty was not to invade Mexico, but to protect the American lives and property endangered by the rebellion. He had little interest in sending troops across the border, for he realized doing so would force the United States into a conflict with a bordering nation already gripped by civil war and internal strife. Indeed, he believed intervention might actually increase "the possibility of resistance and greater bloodshed," endangering more lives than it would save. Taft determined that if he could protect American lives by the threat of force—or as he put it, by convincing the Mexican government and the rebels that "there is a God in Israel and he is on duty"—it would be sufficient.[25]

Indeed, Taft went to great lengths to insist that he would not—even could not—make war without a declaration of war from Congress. In a letter to commanding general Leonard Wood, the president insisted, "I seriously doubt whether I have such authority [to invade Mexico] under any circumstances, and if I had, I would not exercise it without express Congressional approval." This letter seems to provide evidence of his formalistic view of the presidency, for it suggests that Taft believed he could not defend the lives of US citizens unless Congress had issued a formal declaration of war. However, Taft's letter seems to have been a political ploy rather than a clear statement of his view of executive power. Having specified that his letter to Wood was confidential, the president personally leaked it to at least nine journalists, thereby telegraphing to the nation his own reticence to intervene with military force. Taft, as events showed, did not actually doubt his own power to act; in fact, in 1912, he sent 2,700 marines to Nicaragua without a declaration of war in order to defend American lives and property. However, whatever his understanding of his own power, he did recognize that prudence dictated a public statement of presidential reluctance in order to avoid rousing the nation to war fever.[26]

In 1911, Taft was actually willing to take strong action against Mexico even without congressional authorization. He insisted to the press that the troops on the border were merely out for training maneuvers, but he made it clear to the Mexican government and the insurgents that the lives of US citizens must be respected. He took prompt action when firefights between Mexican regulars and insurgents sent bullets across the Arizona border and wounded American citizens. In response, he warned the Mexican government that any further action that endangered American lives would result in the use of force. He wrote to Arizona governor Richard E. Sloan, "The situation might justify me in ordering our troops to cross the border and attempt to stop the fighting, or to fire upon both combatants [the Mexican army and the insurgents] from the American side."[27] Notably, Taft only argued that the president could wield the powers necessary to protect American lives. He saw that he could eliminate a threat to American citizens—even if that entailed unilaterally declaring a very limited war—but he did not argue that he had the power to conquer and hold Mexican territory. Taft's warnings prevailed, and future loss of life was prevented.

These examples show the extent to which President Taft's actions aligned with the theory Professor Taft delineated in *Our Chief Magistrate*. However, actions taken by Taft in 1912 point to the limitations of his theory of presidential power. When faced with a serious flood in the Mississippi valley in 1912, Taft permitted the military to provide emergency supplies to the crisis zone without express legislative authorization for the expenditures. In a letter to Stimson, he admitted that he was acting "without legal authority . . . and depend[ing] upon the action of Congress to ratify what we have done." Notably, he did not act until after he had met with the House Appropriations Committee and had gained assurance that Congress would quickly ratify his extralegal expenditures.[28]

Taft could reasonably claim that his actions, illegal as they may have been, were not particularly radical or dangerous. He faced a genuine emergency and he did actually seek and secure legislative promises to promptly legalize his deeds. Yet his behavior clearly does not align with his theory of presidential prerogative and shows that, on at least one occasion during his presidency, his actions diverged from his constitutional theory. His willingness to seek informal congressional approval prior to acting does separate Taft from a Hamiltonian approach, which would have seen little need to gain legislative support. Likewise, although Taft's actions are similar to a Jeffersonian understanding of prerogative, the fact that he sought and gained informal congressional approval *before* acting does differentiate him from the standard Jeffersonian approach: he did not act unilaterally then present the legislature with a fait accompli to be ratified. Instead, Taft effectively secured de facto legislative approval for his expenditures, but acted before he had technically received de jure support. None of these caveats, however, permit us to ignore Taft's own admission that he acted "without legal authority."

Taft's actions in 1912 demonstrate both his pragmatism and the limits of his understanding of presidential power. According to his argument in *Our Chief Magistrate*, the Constitution permitted unlimited executive means to achieve limited constitutional ends. This theory simply does not address emergency expenditures, since the power of the purse belongs to Congress, and cannot be considered an executive power or an executive means. In addition, the end—providing aid to citizens after a natural disaster—is not one of the president's constitutional duties. His theory of constitutional prerogative power was actually quite effective at showing legal means for the executive to enforce the law and defend the peace of the United States against lawless actions by criminals, but it provided no answer to what the president might do to combat the forces of nature and respond to acts of God. Moreover, although Taft's willingness to seek the support of congressional leaders may evince his respect for the legislature's role, his actions in this case are closer to Jeffersonian prerogative than to the theory Taft laid out, a fact that becomes only more notable when we recall that the ex-president wholly avoided discussing his extraconstitutional expenditures in his book. Taft, evidently, was pragmatic enough to compromise some aspects of his constitutional principles in emergencies, but honest enough not to pretend he could defend his actions on constitutional grounds.

For all this, Taft's contribution in *Our Chief Magistrate* remains significant and is useful for explaining and understanding executive power in many emergency situations. Neither Taft's theory nor his practice was perfect, yet one example of inconsistency during four years in office should not lead us to discount his understanding of presidential power. Moreover, the fact that Taft's theory could not be applied to emergency expenditures and acts of God does not alter the fact that his understanding of Article II justified robust and legal executive action to respond to the vast majority of national crises. Indeed, as we will see, his theory was so robust that it actually has much in common with Lincoln's defense of the Emancipation Proclamation.

Roosevelt enjoyed referring to Taft's constitutionalism as the "Buchanan–Taft" school of thought and associating his own "stewardship" theory with what he called the "Lincoln–Jackson" school. Yet Taft actually made a strong appeal to Lincoln to justify his own understanding of presidential power. He praised Lincoln for making a constitutional argument for the drastic actions he took during the Civil War. Taft acknowledged that Lincoln sometimes acted in ways that raised serious constitutional questions, but defended him by observing he had "always pointed out the source of the authority which in his opinion justified his acts." Indeed, Lincoln's argument for the Emancipation Proclamation aligns closely with Taft's understanding of Article II powers.[29]

Perhaps unsurprisingly, Lincoln's emergency actions during the

Civil War have been cited with approval by both Hamiltonians and Jeffersonians.[30] In his July 4, 1861, Message to Congress, Lincoln set out a defense of his actions that lends itself to a variety of interpretations. Having expended funds without congressional appropriation, he asserted that his actions, "whether strictly legal or not," were justifiable because of the necessities posed by the emergency; he also stated that "nothing has been done [by the executive] beyond the constitutional competency of *Congress*," which suggests a recognition that the president had infringed on legislative powers by spending unappropriated money. He did not explicitly ask for congressional action, but he seems to have desired it, "trusting . . . that Congress would readily ratify" his expenditures. However, he presented a more vigorous defense of his suspension of the writ of habeas corpus. It is true that Lincoln may have acknowledged a willingness to bend the law when he asked, "Are all the laws, *but one*, to go unexecuted, and the government itself go to pieces, lest that one be violated?" Yet he then argued that, nevertheless, "it was not believed that any law was violated." Moreover, his comments on the importance of congressional action are telling. He had trusted that Congress would ratify his expenditures, but Lincoln seemed far more certain of his power to suspend the writ and observed only that the question of ratifying his suspension "is submitted entirely to the better judgment of Congress."[31]

Two years later, when explaining his Emancipation Proclamation, Lincoln offered a clearer and more forceful defense of his actions. Lincoln actually could have relied on statutory powers in issuing the proclamation, since Congress had passed two confiscation acts providing him with authority to free the slaves of those engaged in open rebellion against the United States. Lincoln even cited the 1862 Confiscation Act in the first two drafts of the Emancipation Proclamation. Yet neither his third draft nor the final version of the proclamation even referenced the confiscation acts. Instead of relying on legislative authorization, Lincoln insisted that he had power to free the slaves held in rebelling states simply by the merit of his constitutional power as commander in chief.[32]

The final proclamation, employing arguments strikingly similar to Taft's, insisted that as president and commander in chief, Lincoln had the "right to take any measure" that was "fit and necessary" to suppress the Southern rebellion. In his later defenses of the Emancipation Proclamation, Lincoln argued that it was a suitable means to fulfilling the duties imposed on him by his oath of office. As he wrote in 1864,

It was in the oath I took that I would, to the best of my ability, preserve, protect, and defend the Constitution of the United States. . . . I did understand however, that my oath to preserve the constitution to the best of my ability, imposed upon me the duty of preserving, by every indispensable means, that government—that nation—of which that constitution was the organic law. . . . I felt that measures, otherwise unconstitutional, might become lawful, by becoming indispensable to the preservation of the constitution, through the preservation of the nation. . . . I was, in my best judgment, driven to the alternative of either surrendering the Union, and with it, the Constitution, or of laying strong hand upon the colored element.

He believed that emancipation became a necessary war measure because it was a means by which to preserve the Union. More specifically, he expected it to gain the sympathy of Europe, boost Union morale, increase the number of volunteers, and encourage slaves to flee to the North, thereby both depriving the Confederacy of slave labor and providing the Union with a new supply of troops and manpower. Lincoln believed emancipation improved Union relations with Europe and credited it with providing the North with 130,000 extra soldiers, sailors, and laborers.[33]

In short, Lincoln did not emancipate the slaves as an end in itself, but as a necessary means for fulfilling his constitutional duties. He did not adopt a Hamiltonian or "stewardship" theory and claim that he could emancipate the slaves because such action was necessary for the public good and served the fundamental principles of the American regime. Instead, emancipation was a means by which to carry out his obligation to preserve, protect, and defend the Constitution and the Union. Like Taft in *Our Chief Magistrate*, he indicated that the Constitution gives the president unlimited executive means to achieve limited ends, since he argued that the president had the powers necessary to carry out his constitutionally prescribed duties.

The Constitution, the Presidency, and Progress

Our Chief Magistrate provides a valuable insight into the nature of executive power. Taft offered his readers a theory that both takes seriously the constitutional limits to presidential prerogative and provides the executive with sufficient powers to carry out his prescribed duties. Taft acknowledged the necessarily broad language of Article II, but rejected a large part of the traditional understanding of Lockean prerogative. In contrast to the Lockean argument, which permits an executive to perform extralegal or illegal actions for the common good, Taft argued that the president should act in accord with the nation's fundamental law. In this way, his theory both empowered and limited the president, showing that "the President's powers are broad," but also that "the lines of his jurisdiction are as fixed as a written constitution can properly make them."[34]

On the one hand, Taft's understanding of Article II grants the president broad emergency powers. In contrast to the Jeffersonian conception of executive prerogative, Taft's argument strengthens the president by showing that he must act in accord with the Constitution rather than outside the law. Under Taft's theory, the Constitution empowers the president to take dramatic action during times of crisis or emergency. As a result, the president has extensive powers to respond to difficult and rapidly developing events within the constitutional structure and without seizing extralegal or unconstitutional powers. Because the president does not act outside the Constitution, he need not later rely on the legislature to excuse his violation of the laws. In this way, Taft showed the potential for lawful prerogative under the Constitution and based on institutional powers.

On the other hand, by distinguishing between powers and duties, Taft separated means and ends. Although the president's duties, or ends, are limited by the Constitution, the use of his powers, the means, are far more indefinite and flexible. Hamiltonians would permit the executive to act in an extralegal manner, citing the necessity of the moment, but Taft argued that the president should act in accord with, rather than in opposition to, the Constitution. The Hamiltonians ultimately fail to see any real limit to executive prerogative; so long as the president acts for a good end, his actions are legitimate. In contrast, Taft argued that the president's ends are limited, but his means are far broader. The president may use whatever means are "proper and necessary" for the fulfillment of his constitutionally defined duties, but he should not invent new obligations for himself by claiming that they are necessary for the common good. Because he recognized that the president's duties are limited by the Constitution, Taft tried to ensure that the president could appeal to necessity only in defending the means he used to achieve his constitutional ends, not in defending extraconstitutional ends.

By requiring the president to limit his actions to those duties mandated by the Constitution, Taft's theory proscribed the broad appeals to necessity that may be used to justify unlimited executive action. It is true that many presidents have made such appeals in order to defend beneficial policies, as Jefferson did to excuse the Louisiana Purchase. But others have argued that it was necessary to seize private coal mines (as TR threatened to do in 1902) or to seize steel mills (as Harry Truman actually did in 1952); most notoriously, Franklin Delano Roosevelt appealed to necessity to justify the mass internment of Japanese Americans at the beginning of World War II. Appeals to necessity therefore leave open the prospect that presidents will regularly undermine the Constitution and the rule of law during times of danger.

Taft laid out a detailed theory that shows how a president may judge the constitutionality of his own actions and provided a thorough argument to explain when and how he may act in an emergency. In this way, by careful attention to the constitutional executive power, he required the president to understand his powers under Article II and present a constitutional argument for his actions. Yet, he did not simply assume that the chief magistrate would always be prudent and restrained. Taft not only offered the president a theory by which to understand his powers and duties, he also provided the other branches and the American people with a constitutional guide by which to measure executive action. If Article II fails to limit the president sufficiently—if a president repeatedly interprets his duties and powers in unconstitutional ways— Taft recognized the numerous checks provided by the constitutional system. First, the judiciary may intervene in disputes involving private rights or disagreements over the separation of powers; second, he knew that Congress may check the executive with its own powers, including impeachment and removal; and finally, Taft pointed out, the president must answer to "the political determination of the people," who are "the ultimate sovereign."[35]

Roosevelt's critique of Taft's alleged formalism ultimately implies that Article II and the Constitution as a whole are simply too rigid and constrictive to permit the executive to respond to crises energetically. Taken to its logical extreme—as exemplified by the arguments of both Hamiltonian and Jeffersonian scholars—this argument suggests that the Constitution fails to provide the government with a legal means of responding to emergencies. Taft, in response, sought to show that the Constitution not only provides the president with ample powers but also manages to limit him "so far as it is possible to limit such a power consistent with that discretion and promptness of action that are essential to preserve the interests of the public in times of emergency."[36] Ultimately, Taft's theory provided a counter to TR by showing the extent to which law and necessity may be reconciled and by offering a means by which the president may serve and protect the nation without undermining its fundamental law.

Although the dispute between Taft and Roosevelt focused on the authority of the chief executive, the implications were far broader, for TR charged Taft with unduly restricting not only the authority of the president but also the power of the entire national government. Roosevelt believed Taft's attachment to the Constitution prevented the government from adapting and addressing the country's needs in the twentieth century. As a result, *Our Chief Magistrate* addressed the narrow issue of executive power within the context of a far more extensive critique of the Constitution. Thus far, I have primarily considered Taft's understanding of the potential for constitutional government action in terms of public policy, institutional developments, and presidential leadership. However, Taft's understanding of executive power in *Our Chief Magistrate* displays another facet of his constitutionalism. Taft believed the Constitution had created a strong government capable of surviving and adapting to rapid social and economic developments and to crises at home and abroad.

Thus, the disagreement between Taft and Roosevelt over presidential prerogative power is a vital aspect of Taft's constitutional progressivism and is tied up with other disputes over the possibility of energetic government action. More broadly, this dispute requires us to consider the tension between necessity and law and to contemplate the Constitution's viability during times of crisis and stress. Just as the constitutional executive power is flexible enough to meet emergencies, so too Taft believed the powers of the government as a whole were not rigidly limited but were instead sufficiently broad and elastic to modernize and adapt to the challenges of the Progressive Era. In response to a call for virtually unlimited power from Roosevelt, Taft explained the extensive legal powers wielded by the president and showed that his constitutionalism may be coupled with dramatic governmental action. In the end, by arguing that the Constitution confers broad powers on the government's chief magistrate, Taft suggested that our fundamental law actually empowers the government more than it limits it, providing the basis and foundation for a robust national policy rather than simply fettering progressive reform.

6 | The Chief Justice on the Presidency
Myers v. United States and the Removal Power

In *Our Chief Magistrate*, Taft argued that the First Congress settled the removal controversy in 1789 when it determined that the president possessed "absolute power" to terminate executive officers "without consulting the Senate." Although he acknowledged that the Decision of 1789 had not always been respected, he predicted that the Supreme Court, if given the chance, would likely endorse that precedent. A decade after Professor Taft published *Our Chief Magistrate*, Chief Justice Taft had an opportunity to rule on presidential removal power. In *Myers v. United States* (1926), Taft laid out an extensive theory of the president's power over the executive branch and defended his right to remove subordinate officers.[1]

Modern scholarship has recognized the importance of the Decision of 1789 in Taft's opinion and has generally seen his *Myers* decision as an endorsement of absolute presidential power to remove executive officials.[2] However, Taft's defense of executive removal power is far more nuanced than has traditionally been recognized.[3] He did believe that the president had power to remove any official he had personally appointed to office, yet Taft also recognized that Congress could circumvent the president's power to appoint and remove by vesting the appointment of inferior officers in department heads and then protecting those officers from removal through civil service laws. Taft both defended the president's removal power and pointed out how Congress could constitutionally limit the chief executive's authority.[4]

After analyzing Taft's argument in *Myers*, this chapter will show that his understanding of Congress's constitutional authority to protect administrators from partisan removals left room for civil service reform. Moreover, his legal arguments provided a viable alternative to two contemporaneous progressive theories of civil service reform offered by Woodrow Wilson and Herbert Croly. Wilson's "Study of Administration" made a strong case for scientific administration, but he seemed relatively unconcerned with the means by which bureaucrats would be held accountable to the voting public; his desire for expert administration was far stronger than his interest in popular government. Croly, on the other hand, saw clearly the need to maintain political accountability in administration, but hoped to ensure that accountability by centralizing power in the executive and all but destroying the power of the legislature. In contrast, Taft's *Myers* opinion sought to maintain both responsible administration and separation of powers, thereby acknowledging the importance of executive responsibility but also showing that Congress could promote civil service reform in the executive branch.

Executive Power: *Myers* and the Unitary Executive

In *Myers*, the Supreme Court addressed a claim brought against the government by a first-class postmaster. Frank S. Myers was appointed postmaster for Portland, Oregon, in 1917 and removed by Postmaster General Albert S. Burleson two and a half years later. The constitutional issue revolved around the method of terminating Myers. Burleson had removed him without consulting the Senate, in violation of a statutory mandate that first-class postmasters could be removed by the president only "by and with the advice and consent of the Senate."[5] Since Myers believed he had been removed illegally, he brought suit against the government.

The Court ruled for the government 6 to 3. Taft's majority opinion clearly relied on the Decision of 1789; as he explained in a letter to Justice Pierce Butler, that decision had laid down "a long established constitutional construction" that was due a great deal of deference since the First Congress "was almost a part of the Constitutional Convention."[6] The structure and logic of Taft's opinion reveals his nuanced and intricate understanding of the nature of executive power under the Constitution. Taft's ruling presented four essential arguments to defend presidential removal power. First, the chief justice contended that removal is by its nature an executive function; second, the text of the Constitution indicates that the removal power is vested in the president alone; third, although Congress retains a great deal of power to regulate the executive branch, it may not control its essential functioning; and fourth, the president must maintain control over his subordinates in order to carry out his duties and be held responsible by the people for the actions of his administration.

Taft's first and most important argument held that the structure of the Constitution treats removal as an executive action in its very nature. Quoting James Madison's insistence that the system of separation of powers is the most "sacred" principle contained in the Constitution, Taft observed that the Constitution created a strong and independent executive "so as to avoid the humiliating weakness of the Congress . . . under the Articles of Confederation." Because the executive power is "essentially a grant of the power to execute the laws," the president must have the authority to control the subordinates who aid him in this task. Notably, this claim expanded upon the well-known functionalist argument that the president must control his subordinates if he is to execute the law, for Taft argued that the control of subordinates within the executive branch is an inherently executive function. To his mind, the Article II vesting clause granted the president all "executive Power," including within the "natural meaning" of that phrase the power to remove subordinates. Moreover, he insisted removal power could not naturally belong to any other branch: "If such appointments and removals were not an exercise of the executive power, what were they? They certainly were not the exercise of legislative or judicial power in government as usually understood." Since appointing and removing executive officers is fundamentally an executive action, Taft believed the president would have power to appoint and remove his subordinates "even in the absence of express words" granting him that authority.[7]

Second, the chief justice grounded the president's power in the text of the Constitution. Taft argued that Article II's "express recognition" of the president's power to appoint officers indicates that the removal power was "incident to the power of appointment." Though Article II does give the Senate the authority to advise and consent to presidential appointments, the Senate's authority simply constitutes an exception to the general executive power and is functionally different than the president's power to appoint. Oliver Ellsworth, later the third chief justice of the United States, argued in the First Congress that "the advice of the Senate does not make the appointment. The President appoints." The Senate's power, Taft argued, permitted it merely to *consent* to an appointment, not actually to *appoint*. Its authority is limited to a single moment during the appointment process, whereas the president's role is continuous, since he not only nominates and appoints officers, but also oversees and directs officials in carrying out executive duties after appointment. As a result, though the president's appointment power carries with it removal power, the Senate's power is strictly circumscribed. The power to consent to an appointment, the chief justice insisted, was nothing more than a limited exception to a general executive power, and any blending of executive and legislative powers by such exceptions should be interpreted as narrowly as possible, and "should not be extended beyond its express application."[8]

Third, in evaluating the power of the legislature, Taft acknowledged that Congress as a whole has broad power to regulate the appointment and removal of inferior officers, but he warned that this power did not allow Congress to control the functioning of the executive branch. Under Article II, the president has the power, with the advice and consent of the Senate, to appoint "Officers of the United States," but "Congress may by Law vest the appointment of such inferior Officers, as they think proper" in the president or heads of executive departments.[9] The Constitution thus dictates that superior executive officers, such as department heads and other political officials, must always be appointed by the president with the consent of the Senate. Congress may simplify the appointment process for "inferior Officers," likely those whose duties are administrative and ministerial, by giving the president or a cabinet officer the sole power of appointment. However, barring any affirmative action by Congress, all executive officers will be appointed by the president with the advice and consent of the Senate.

Here, Taft recognized that the Constitution had created a second exception to the executive power of appointment. In addition to the Senate's authority to consent to appointments, Congress's power to regulate the mode of appointment of inferior officers provides a further limit on presidential power. Critically, because Congress is given authority to transfer the power to appoint inferior officers from the president to department heads, it may also regulate the removal of such officers. Congress's power to vest the appointing power in a department head carries with it "authority incidentally to invest the heads of departments with power to remove . . . [and Congress] may prescribe incidental regulations controlling and restricting the latter in the exercise of the power of removal."[10] Congress may not regulate the removal of all executive officers, for denying the president power to remove his chief subordinates would unduly hinder his control of the executive branch. Yet Taft nevertheless acknowledged the legislature's constitutional power to regulate the removal of inferior officers appointed by department heads.

Fourth, Taft explained that the Constitution maintained the separation of powers in order to guarantee presidential responsibility for the actions of his administration. Despite the Senate's authority to consent to appointments and Congress's power over subordinate officers, the president cannot be denied power to oversee the essential functioning of the executive branch. Because the president is "made responsible under the Constitution for the effective enforcement of the law," he must have the power to remove his subordinates and maintain a "disciplinary influence upon those who act under him." The president has a particular need to control his chief subordinates, "Officers of the United States," when they carry out political and discretionary duties, for in these cases his subordinates act as his "alter ego," and he "must have the power to remove [such officers] without delay" should he lose confidence in them. The president is responsible for the enforcement of law and must have the power to discipline and remove officials who hinder the execution of the law, for without this authority he cannot "discharge his own constitutional duty of seeing that the laws be faithfully executed."[11]

This claim, to Taft, proved that presidential removal power was necessary for the maintenance of responsible government, since a president who lacks the power to control his subordinates can hardly be held responsible by the voters for his administration's actions. Ultimately, removal power is critical to maintaining political accountability, for this is the only way that "the chain of dependence [can] be preserved, the lowest officers, the middle grade, and the highest, will depend, as they ought, on the President, and the President on the community."[12] Modern democracies, Taft suggests, would demand increasingly extensive services from the government, which will lead to the creation of a large bureaucracy. But how can the democratic voter hold an expansive bureaucracy accountable? For Taft, the solution was presidential removal power. In the final analysis, he argued that presidential control over subordinate officials was necessary if the nation intended to maintain responsible popular government while also expanding the federal bureaucracy.

Congressional Power: Inferior Officers and Civil Service Reform

Taft defended executive power so expansively that *Myers* initially seems to preclude any possibility for civil service reform. If the president's removal power is so vast, is there any possibility of protecting career civil servants and preventing them from being removed for political reasons? This, indeed, was a major concern of both Justice Louis Brandeis's dissent and the 1927 monograph Edward Corwin authored in response to *Myers*. Taft recognized that some critics feared his opinion would "open the door to a reintroduction of the spoils system" and therefore sought to ameliorate these fears by emphasizing the extent of Congress's power to protect inferior officers from arbitrary removal.[13]

The chief justice did acknowledge Congress's extensive authority to create offices and, in the case of inferior officers, dictate the manner of appointment to them, but he also insisted that the overall system of separation of powers must be maintained. Quoting Madison, Taft distinguished between legislative and executive functions: "The powers relative to offices are partly Legislative and partly Executive. The Legislature creates the office, defines the powers, limits its duration, and annexes a compensation. This done, the Legislative power ceases. They ought to have nothing to do with designating the man to fill the office. That I conceive to be of an Executive nature."[14] Creating and defining the powers of an office is a legislative function, but filling that office and overseeing the appointed official's execution of that office are executive functions. Taft argued that the Constitution created interreliance and dependency between the legislative and executive branches, but it did not wholly blend the two powers in the matter of appointment and removal. In the same way that Congress can legislate but cannot enforce its own laws, the executive is tasked with carrying out the law, but he is incapable of acting unless the legislature provides him with the officers necessary to take care that the laws are faithfully executed. This codependence was a feature, not a flaw, of the Constitution's system of separation of powers.

However, Taft also recognized that the second exception to executive appointment power—Congress's power to vest the appointment of inferior officers in the president alone or in heads of departments—empowered Congress to regulate some removals. The *Myers* majority recognized three categories of executive officers. First are those executive officers—typically superior "Officers of the United States"—whose appointment has been left, as the Constitution placed it, with the president subject to the advice and consent of the Senate. Second are inferior officers whose appointment Congress chooses to bestow on the president alone. Finally, there are inferior officers whose appointment the legislature vests in department heads. In this third category Taft saw room to initiate civil service reform and guard officials from arbitrary partisan removals.

Taft unhesitatingly defended the president's power to remove officials in either of the first two categories. Because Myers himself had been appointed after senatorial consent, he fell into the first group, and the majority of Taft's opinion addresses the president's authority over this class of officials. However, Taft also briefly, in dicta, defended the president's power to remove officials he had appointed without the consent of the Senate. Since he believed that the power of appointment was naturally a part of the chief executive's constitutional power and moreover that it carried with it the power of removal, the chief justice insisted that any officials appointed by the president were subject to removal at the president's sole discretion.[15] Put simply, if an official is appointed by the president—with or without the advice and consent of the Senate—then that official is removable by the president alone. As a result, Taft defended absolute presidential removal power to the extent that he acknowledged no legislative limits on the president's discretion to terminate "his appointees," officers he had himself appointed.[16]

However, as aforementioned, Congress could vest the power to appoint inferior officers in a department head. When Congress did so, it could also deny the president power to remove those inferior officers. Taft argued that the president holds absolute power to remove any official he has appointed because the power to appoint carried with it an incidental power to remove. But by linking the removal power to the authority to appoint, the chief justice also showed that Congress's power to vest the appointment of inferior officers in department heads permitted the legislature to limit not only the president's appointment power but also his removal power. Taft freely admitted that the power to give appointments to a department head gave Congress power "incidentally" to vest department heads with removal power. By taking the appointment power away from the president and giving it to a department head, Congress also deprived the president of the removal power.[17]

Moreover, the chief justice recognized that Congress's authority to give department heads removal power permits it additionally to "prescribe incidental regulations" to limit department heads "in the exercise of the power of removal." He seems to have based his understanding of legislative power to regulate removals on Solicitor General James M. Beck's argument at bar. Beck claimed that "Congress has control over those [department heads] upon whom it confers the mere *statutory* power of appointment" and could therefore regulate removals; on the other hand, Congress "has no [similar] power as against the president . . . [whose appointment power] is *constitutional.*" Because the president's appointment power was constitutional, Congress was not able to protect a presidential appointee from removal. But because a department head's appointment power was merely statutory, Congress could determine that inferior officers appointed by department heads could be fired only for inefficiency, neglect of duty, or malfeasance, thereby prohibiting the partisan removal of such officials. Taft actually recognized a broad swathe of legislative power over appointments and removals and a significant exception to the president's constitutional authority; *Myers* points toward the possibility of civil service reform.[18]

Despite his ostensibly rigid defense of the president's removal power, Taft defended the constitutionality of civil service reforms that limited the removal power of department heads. Simply put, Congress could not directly limit the president's power to remove: any official the president appointed could be removed by the chief executive's sole fiat. Yet Congress could limit the president's power indirectly, by denying him the power to appoint inferior officers and therefore also denying him power to remove them. Additionally, Congress could enact civil service reform to protect inferior officers appointed by department heads, since a department head's statutory authority to appoint and remove such officers could be regulated. Taft's concession to legislative power is critical, but it has been little noted.[19]

In light of this critical caveat in *Myers*, Taft's ostensibly absolutist defense of presidential removal power must be reconsidered. The chief justice believed that congressional refusal to act, and not the president's constitutional removal power, was to blame for the fact that Myers and other similarly situated officers were not protected under the civil service system. Had Myers's appointment been vested in the postmaster general alone, Congress could have defended him against politically motivated removal. As Taft argued, Congress could at any time protect such inferior officers; in order to do so, the legislature must "determine first that the office is inferior, and second that it is willing that the office shall be filled by appointment by some other authority than the President with the consent of the Senate." But so long as Congress left the appointment of first-class postmasters with the president and the Senate, it lacked power to restrict removals. Additionally, Taft pointed out that Congress had actually prevented the classification of first-class postmasters, since the Pendleton Act forbade the classification of officials appointed with the consent of the Senate unless the Senate explicitly agreed to that classification. Thus, according to Taft, Congress itself was responsible that first-class postmasters had not been protected under civil service laws.[20]

Robert Post, a prominent critic of Taft's *Myers* opinion, believes the chief justice's bow to civil service reform rendered his opinion inconsistent. Post points out that Taft claimed the president held "all executive power" and "that discretionary authority to remove executive officials was an executive power necessary to ensure that the laws be faithfully executed." How then could Taft also defend civil service reform, "ceding to Congress" power to determine when the president could and could not remove an inferior officer? Is not Taft's defense of civil service reform radically at odds with his stance on executive power and executive responsibility? The *Myers* opinion, Post determines, "can only be described as schizophrenic."[21] Post's concerns raise two questions immediately relevant to our analysis.

First, did *Myers* impose any limits on Congress's power to implement civil service reform, or did it cede so much power to the legislature that it undermined Taft's argument for presidential removal power? *Myers* actually did point to limits on legislative power, for the logic of Taft's decision shows that civil service laws not only limit the president's removal power but also impose a significant cost on the Senate. Under *Myers*, Congress may be involved in appointments of officers through the Senate's consenting function, or it could oversee removals of officers through Congress's power to regulate the manner of removal for inferior officers. This limit—which permits legislative involvement in either appointment or removal, but not both—actually keeps the political branches honest with regard to civil service reform. Congress could not, for instance, determine that an officer be appointed by the president with the consent of the Senate—thereby maintaining the

Senate's patronage privileges—while at the same time classifying that office and restricting the executive's power to remove the official—thereby shielding members' political allies from removal.

This logic limits congressional power by imposing a cost on the Senate when the legislature implements civil service reform. Practically speaking, this protects the president's authority by guaranteeing that both the president and the Senate have an incentive to prevent the classification of important executive officers: the president in order to ensure his complete control over them, the Senate in order to retain its authority to consent to their appointments. It is true that *Myers* did not clearly explain which officers could and could not be classified. Rather than attempting to articulate a bright line distinction between superior and inferior officers—a difficult task, in light of the Constitution's silence on the issue—Taft offered a more pragmatic solution, relying on separation of powers and the competing ambitions of the president, the Senate, and the House. Taft's argument rests on the assumption, made explicit in *Our Chief Magistrate*, that "the Senate is never likely to consent to waive" its right to approve appointments for the most important executive officers.[22] Thus, even if the House sought to limit presidential removal power by classifying high-ranking executive officials, the Senate's ambition (not to mention the president's veto) would likely protect the president.

Second, Post's objections force us to ask whether the president can actually be held responsible for ensuring the laws are faithfully executed if Congress can limit presidential removal power through civil service reform. Although civil service laws do prevent the president from removing classified officers for political reasons, they nevertheless allow the president to order an official's removal for cause: typically for inefficiency, neglect of duty, or malfeasance. As one scholar has shown, President Taft initiated "the first presidential for-cause removal" in 1912, and his administration interpreted "neglect of duty" and "malfeasance" broadly, ruling that the president could fire a classified official who was "simply not good at his job."[23] Taft made a similar argument in *Myers*, recognizing limits on presidential power to fire officers for political reasons, while defending presidential power to remove officers for legitimate administrative reasons. He insisted that the president had a general supervisory power over the executive branch and could fire a "negligent and inefficient" officer who "on the whole" failed to carry out his duties "intelligently or wisely." Without this supervisory power, the president "does not discharge his own constitutional duty of seeing that the laws be faithfully executed."[24]

As a result, because the president retains significant, albeit not unlimited, supervisory authority over all executive branch officials, he remains responsible for the actions of the executive branch. Taft's defense of civil service reform did not undermine his argument for presidential responsibility, since a president who failed to remove incompetent or corrupt civil servants—even those protected by the merit system— could justly be punished at the polls for his administration's failure to efficiently and honestly execute the law. In this way, the "chain of dependence" stretching from the people to the president down through department heads to lower ranking administrators was maintained.

The *Myers* opinion is famous for its sweeping defense of executive power, but a nuanced understanding of Taft's argument suggests a more modest approach. Taft made a detailed case for congressional regulation, albeit not congressional control, of the removal of inferior officers. He believed that the president could not be held responsible for his subordinates unless the chief executive could remove at least superior officers, but he also recognized that Congress's power to create and fund administrative posts allowed the legislature to regulate and limit the removal of inferior officers, preventing partisan removals while leaving untouched executive power to remove officers who were so inefficient or corrupt that they hindered the execution of the law. By considering both the text and the theory of the Constitution, Taft sought to protect the independence of the executive and also explain the legitimate powers of Congress to advance civil service reform and depoliticize administration at the lower levels.

Scientific Administration and Popular Sovereignty

It is striking that Taft emphasized the possibility of civil service reform in *Myers*. He explicitly raised the issue of spoils and patronage twice and pointed out that the Court's holding would not interfere with the expansion of the merit system.[25] His claim that civil service reform can be brought about within the constitutional system and occur without undermining the president's power to remove subordinate officers sharply contrasts with the views of two contemporary progressives,

Woodrow Wilson and Herbert Croly. Both Wilson and Croly offered alternative but ultimately problematic proposals for modernizing the government and advancing administrative reforms.

As a general matter, Wilson, Croly, and Taft shared similar concerns about administrative reforms. All desired efficiency and expertise in the civil service and rejected the spoils system for its tendency to create incompetence and corruption at the expense of the public interest. Taft, like Wilson, desired to promote expert, scientific administration; additionally, his strong defense of executive power aligned with parts of Croly's proposal for governmental reorganization at the state level. Thus, Taft's understanding of the need for a modern, apolitical civil service headed by a unitary executive placed him in the mainstream of contemporary progressive thought.

However, Taft's argument was far less radical than the proposals put forward by Wilson and Croly and was better suited to promoting administrative reform while also maintaining popular government and the separation of powers. Wilson's "Study of Administration" did not simply support civil service reform; it also subtly suggested that the unpredictable character of free government might require democratic rule to be limited by unelected administrators. Croly, for his part, proposed a system that was fully democratic, but he hoped to achieve efficiency in government by centering political power in the executive alone, thereby relegating the legislative branch to an advisory board and curtailing the separation of powers. Taft's reading of Article II in *Myers*, in contrast, showed that progressive administrative reforms may increase efficiency in government and guarantee political accountability to the voters, while at the same time maintaining the traditional system of separation of powers.

When confronted with the task of civil service reform, many progressives were faced with a serious dilemma. They believed in a purer form of democracy and therefore endorsed the referendum, recall, and initiative, but they also embraced the turn to scientific government and the administrative state. Ironically, because politically insulated administrators wield significant powers, the expansion of the administrative state raises the risk of undermining popular government. Wilson's "Study of Administration" acknowledged this problem but provided no satisfactory solution. What is more troubling, Wilson's work suggests that efficient administration may be more important than popular government and indicates a disconcerting willingness to permit administrators to manipulate republican government without themselves being answerable to the voters.

Wilson did, it is true, insist that administrators must serve the sovereign people. Indeed, he concluded his essay by stressing that each administrator must serve the community "with the best efforts of his talents and the soberest service of his conscience." Nevertheless, Wilson also pointed out that popular sovereignty could undermine or threaten efficient administration. He bluntly observed that although dictatorship resulted in a simple and streamlined form of administration, modern bureaucrats find their work complicated by the fact that they must answer not to a single monarch, but to the voting public. Because popular sovereignty was decentralized and unstable, fluctuations in popular opinion could hinder the consistent administration of government. It was, Wilson declared, "principally, popular sovereignty" that had thus far prevented the United States from adopting modern administrative techniques. Because most voters are "selfish, ignorant, timid, stubborn or foolish," they do not understand the importance of scientific administration. Wilson went on to complain that Americans represented the "unphilosophical bulk of mankind" and bemoaned the difficulty of enlightening a citizenry made up "not of Americans of the older stocks only, but also of Irishmen, of Germans, of negroes"; all of these groups, he feared, had "inherit[ed] every bias of environment, [and were] warped by the histories of a score of different nations." In the end, Wilson doubted whether "the people who go to their work very early in the morning" could adequately direct their administrators toward a truly constructive public policy.[26]

In light of his trust in experts and distrust of the people, it is unsurprising that Wilson repeatedly admitted that administrators would play a significant role in government, a role which involved not only administration but also politics. Although Wilson did claim that administration should be apolitical and simply administer policies enacted by the public, he also suggested that bureaucrats would in practice set policy, not merely administer it. First, administrators need to teach the people "what sort of administration to desire and demand." To do this, a reformer "must first educate his fellow-citizens to want *some* change" and next "persuade them to want the particular change he wants"; administrators should have a robust role in educating the sovereign people and informing their desires. Second, Wilson admitted that administrators are not mere "passive instruments" of the sovereign, but exercise a will of their own. Because he concedes that administrators are humans with their own interests and preferences—not faithful machines who simply attend to practical and methodological problems—it becomes difficult to see how they would not affect policy while implementing it. Finally, Wilson argued that administrators must improve the Constitution itself; they should study constitution-making and understand how best to divide power without hampering it.[27] Thus, he concedes that administrators will affect *what* government does, not simply determine *how* government acts; administration and politics, it seems, were not actually wholly separated in Wilson's mind.

Although Wilson did insist that administrators should be answerable to the public, he was surprisingly vague about how bureaucrats would be rendered politically responsible. He argued that administrators should only serve so long as they give "hearty allegiance to the policy of the government," but he never showed how this allegiance would be judged or who could remove disloyal administrators. Similarly, he had some notion of centering responsibility in heads of departments, but he did not discuss how these officials could be held accountable by the people. Ultimately, his essay fails to provide any actual solution to this all-important problem. In light of his disparaging comments about the intelligence of voters, one might reasonably wonder just how much political accountability Wilson actually considered necessary.[28]

In stark contradistinction, Taft's *Myers* opinion sought to promote both popular government and advances in scientific administration. By defending executive removal power, he showed that the Constitution linked low-level administrators, political appointees, and even the president to the electorate through a "chain of dependence," which ensured political accountability. Taft's defense of the unitary executive and the removal power did entail his defense of a strong president, but it also incorporated a meaningful argument for responsible administration. Taft therefore separated himself from a more radical and antidemocratic type of administrative reformer. It is worth remembering that Wilson was not alone in his belief that expertise in administration might need to come at the cost of political responsibility. Corwin voiced a similar sentiment: "It must be frankly recognized that when the issue is put today of 'Bureaucracy' verses 'Political Responsibility,' the verdict of thoughtful students of government will by no means be given unqualifiedly in favor of the latter alternative."[29] Taft's argument shows that expert bureaucrats may administer the law scientifically while at the same time the administration as a whole may be answerable to the voters.

If Wilson promoted civil service reform but seemingly failed to grasp the importance of making administrators responsible to the sovereign people, Croly recommended a means of advancing civil service reform that would have guaranteed political accountability to the voters. In his *The Promise of American Life* (1909), Croly proposed broad structural reforms for state governments, reforms he evidently hoped would eventually be implemented at the national level.[30] This new system ensured political accountability by guaranteeing the executive's control of the administration and his power to remove subordinates, but did so at the cost of destroying the system of separation of powers.

Because Croly distrusted the influence wielded by political "bosses," who could control parties without holding public office, he sought to implement an executive-centric system of government in which a governor would be held accountable for all his administration's actions. Under Croly's system, a gubernatorial candidate would run for office on an extensive platform, which would become the basis for his term in office. Additionally, Croly warned that separation of powers entailed a convoluted "division of responsibility" among the three branches of government and argued that institutions should be simplified. The governor, he believed, should become the single "dominant authority" and be given "substantially complete responsibility for the public welfare." Having been elected by the people to enact a specific, well-publicized platform, the executive could be called to account for the successes or failures of his administration; such an executive, Croly hoped, would not be controlled by bosses, nor could he evade responsibility for his failures by blaming an uncooperative legislature.[31]

In order justly to hold the governor responsible for the actions of his administration, it was necessary to guarantee him truly dominant authority, including power to control his subordinates. Thus, under Croly's plan, the governor would have power to appoint the members of his cabinet, who would be served by "permanent departmental chiefs" at the head of each administrative division. These department chiefs, Croly indicated, would play a key role in ensuring the efficiency and honesty of the civil service; their long tenure would promote professionalism, and, although they would have absolute power to promote or degrade their own subordinates, their power to remove inferior officers would be contingent on the approval of an inspection board. Yet Croly filled his prescriptions with caveats. These "permanent" department chiefs would not, he conceded, be "*absolutely* permanent"; instead, "they would be just as permanent or as transient as the good of the service demanded." Ultimately, Croly admitted that all executive and administrative officers would serve at the pleasure of the governor, for, as he explained in his 1914 *Progressive Democracy*, unless an executive may appoint and remove the members of his administration, he would be "deprived of any effective authority over his subordinates" and therefore would have "ceased to be the responsible head of the administration." Thus, Croly insisted that the governor must wield "the power of removing any administrative official in the employ of the state and of appointing a successor." His system, much like Taft's, promoted responsibility through strong executive control of the administration.[32]

Yet Croly's system, even if it promoted administrative responsibility in a way Wilson's would not, ultimately undermined the legislature's role in governance and destroyed the system of separation of powers. He bluntly admitted his plan entailed "subordinating the legislature to the executive." The legislature, he believed, could be transformed from a coequal branch into an elected "body of legal, administrative, and financial experts" who served as little more than a "technical advisory commission" to the governor. This commission's work "would not be in any real sense legislative"; instead, it would handle some financial and administrative matters and provide a "severe technical criticism" of the governor's legislative agenda. Lest we think this check would be an effective political hindrance to executive power, Croly reminded his readers that the governor would not only have power to draw up legislation, but could introduce it into the legislature and—should the legislative branch failed to adopt his plans—he would also be able to appeal directly to the people over the heads of the legislature and enact his legislation via popular referendum. In an effort to promote democracy and accountability, Croly would have transformed the executive into the single, unitary representative of the people and all but eliminated the legislature's political power.[33]

Thus, Taft and Croly generally agreed on the importance of executive responsibility. Yet where Croly's plan strengthened the executive and the administration at the expense of the legislature, Taft saw a need to both defend executive power and maintain a substantial role for Congress. Taft's argument for presidential power sought to promote political accountability without undermining the separation of powers. He agreed with Croly that administrators must ultimately be responsible to the people and that executive removal power helped to ensure that accountability, but he diverged from Croly insofar as he believed that the legislature should retain its power to legislate and recognized that Congress had authority to limit and check executive power. Where Croly believed that extensive civil service reforms necessitated a constitutional transformation that sidelined the legislature in favor of executive-centric government, *Myers* showed that the Constitution could permit civil service reform and that the system of separation of powers could also be maintained intact.

Thus, Taft presents us with a compelling alternative to Wilson's and Croly's proposals, which proposals might have allowed for more radical and broader administrative reforms but would also have undermined both popular sovereignty and the separation of powers. Taft argued forcefully for a unitary executive in *Myers*, yet what is most notable about his opinion is the extent to which he believed a strong executive could coexist with both popular government and a strong legislature capable of implementing civil service reform. His constitutional argument allowed extensive classification of federal officials and also avoided the more problematic elements of Wilson's and Croly's proposals.

Afterword: *Humphrey's Executor* and Independent Administration

Although *Myers* was the first Supreme Court case to address the issue of presidential removal power comprehensively, Taft believed it settled a historic dispute between the president and Congress by reaffirming the Decision of 1789. This victory for executive power, however, was short-lived. Nine years after the Court decided *Myers*, it significantly narrowed that precedent in *Humphrey's Executor v. United States* (1935). William Humphrey was a commissioner of the Federal Trade Commission (FTC) nominated by President Herbert Hoover and confirmed by the Senate in 1931. In 1933, President Franklin D. Roosevelt removed him from office because, as Roosevelt explained, Humphrey differed from the administration as to "the policies [and] the administering of the Federal Trade Commission." Humphrey appealed, pointing out that the Federal Trade Commission Act allowed the president to remove commissioners solely on the grounds of "inefficiency, neglect of duty, or malfeasance in office." The Supreme Court ruled in Humphrey's favor in a unanimous decision authored by Justice George Sutherland.[34]

Had Sutherland relied on *Myers*, the decision would have been relatively straightforward and the Court would have sided with the president. Humphrey was an officer who served in the executive branch and his duties were of sufficient political import that Congress had determined to treat him as a superior officer. He was appointed through a political process, by the president with the advice and consent of the Senate, and therefore should also have been removable by the president for political reasons. As a result, under *Myers*, FDR would have had power to remove Humphrey if the commissioner hindered the president's policies and his administration of government.

However, in his *Humphrey's* opinion, Sutherland eschewed the distinctions Taft laid out in *Myers*. Rather than considering whether Humphrey was a superior or inferior officer or considering the method of appointing him, Sutherland focused on the nature of the commissioner's duties. The Court narrowed *Myers* by ruling that the president had removal power over only "purely executive" officers and not over the members of an independent regulatory commission (IRC). The FTC, Sutherland wrote, was not truly an executive body; instead, it was "an administrative body created by Congress to carry into effect legislative policies." The commission's task to "carry" legislation "into effect" would seem to be executive in nature, but the Court insisted instead that "its duties are neither political nor executive, but predominantly *quasi*-judicial and *quasi*-legislative." Thus, according to Sutherland, *Myers* was inapplicable, since Humphrey was not an executive officer at all, but a member of some undefined fourth branch of government. Sutherland tried to narrow *Myers*, but in doing so he created a legal void.[35]

The *Humphrey's* Court ruled that since the FTC commissioners wielded "*quasi*-judicial and *quasi*-legislative" powers, they did not fall neatly within any branch of government, and therefore should not be answerable to any branch of government. Quoting congressional debates about the creation of the FTC, the Court pointed out that the commission was created as a body "separate and apart from any existing department of the government"; as such, it was "independent of any department" and not "subject to anybody in the government."[36] The Court's historical analysis of the commission's purpose may have been flawed, since it is extremely improbable that IRCs were ever intended to be truly independent. There is substantial evidence that both political branches hoped to control them: "Congress was most emphatic about the 'independence' of regulatory commissions only when challenging the president's claim over the administration. Members of Congress in the twentieth century wanted IRCs to function as legislative adjuncts. . . . Presidents, by contrast, believed that the regulatory commissions should aid the president in executing the law." Thus, it is probable that Congress had created the FTC with the intention that it would become an instrument of the legislative branch, and the president probably signed the FTC Act into law believing that he would be able to control the commissioners under the precedent set by *Myers*.[37]

Regardless of legislative history, the larger question is whether an IRC can be both "independent of any department" and politically accountable in a popular government. Having insisted that the FTC should not be a pawn of either political branch, the *Humphrey's* Court proceeded to quote the congressional debate to insist that the commissioners would be answerable "only to the people of the United States."[38] As a result, although the FTC had sufficient political power to frustrate FDR's administration, commissioners could not be removed by the president for political reasons. As an "independent" commission, Sutherland argued, they were answerable only to the people for their actions in office. But how would the people hold commissioners to account? If a commissioner, like Humphrey, chose to hinder the actions of the elected branches, the law provided no option for the people to discharge him. Even the American people, whom Sutherland claimed would possess sole power over IRCs, would have no real recourse for correcting the policies of their commissioners.

The *Humphrey's* decision may have been a good faith attempt to protect expert administrators from undue political influence. But by recognizing a wholly new branch of government, the Court ruled that the FTC was politically unaccountable. The Court ultimately adopted an extreme form of Wilson's argument in "The Study of Administration." It recognized an autonomous regulatory agency that was free not only from the interference of the political branches of government, but also from those troublesome "people who go to their work very early in the morning." The argument that the FTC was tasked with duties that were somehow apolitical and purely administrative—duties "neither political nor executive"—ultimately led the Court to destroy the commission's political accountability.

Myers is not without its critics, but it has a virtue lacking in *Humphrey's*, for it guaranteed that the growth of the administrative state would not lead to a loss of political responsibility. *Myers* provided a workable option by which the United States could both create the large administration necessary to provide the social services typically expected in a modern democracy and simultaneously maintain popular rule by ensuring political accountability to the voters. Taft's defense of the executive power has often been viewed as inherently conservative because of his originalist concern for the Decision of 1789. But his opinion displays his constitutional progressivism by its adherence to originalism, protection of separation of powers, and maintenance of republican government alongside his progressive interest in civil service reform.

7 | Jurisprudence
Commerce, Regulation, and Labor

If President Taft has often been seen as a conservative, Chief Justice Taft has typically been portrayed as a staunch originalist, conservative to the point of rigidity. The major commentators on Taft and his Court have criticized Taft's jurisprudence, seeing it as ultraconservative and reactionary. Alpheus Thomas Mason's *William Howard Taft: Chief Justice*, for example, asserts that Taft used the courts "as a brake on democracy" and claims that his "scrupulous respect for property rights" prevented him from acknowledging the government's power to engage in "social and economic experimentation." Similarly, Robert McCloskey's classic study of the Supreme Court argues that the Taft Court was "infect[ed]" by conservativism and views Taft and the other Republican appointees on the Court as "foes of the welfare state" who "defended laissez faire." Jonathan Lurie, one of Taft's most evenhanded critics, acknowledges that the chief justice displayed some progressive sympathies, but ultimately concludes that he and his allies on the Court suffered from a conservative "judicial rigidity," which ensured that "too often the Taft Court . . . pointed to the past."[1] According to this common view, Taft's attachment to the written Constitution sapped the powers of the national government and weakened the reform movement.

Notably, however, a few scholars have begun to challenge these claims by emphasizing Taft's nationalism and reconsidering his purportedly extreme defense of property rights. Robert Post, for instance, offers a compelling assessment of Taft's federalism jurisprudence and shows that the chief justice often defended national power to protect interstate commerce. Yet in the end, Post concludes that Taft's belief in strong government was restricted by his robust defense of property rights and finds the Taft Court ambivalently recognized "the virtues of national regulation" over interstate commerce and also "grieved for the loss of earlier ideals of local self-government." Allen Ragan and Jeffrey Rosen similarly recognize Taft's respect for property rights, but emphasize his frequent willingness to sustain laws that regulated economic activities.[2]

In this chapter, I will evaluate Taft's jurisprudence, first with respect to Congress's power to control interstate commerce and second with regard to the government's power to regulate business in order to protect labor. Building particularly on the work of Post and Ragan, I argue that Taft's opinions on the interstate commerce clause reveal his belief in expansive federal regulatory power and present a forceful defense of Congress's power to oversee and protect interstate commerce. Moreover, several of Taft's key labor decisions show that the chief justice was willing to uphold economic regulations that sought to protect labor, even when those regulations limited property rights. A study of these two classes of cases permits us to recognize that Taft broke significantly from traditional *Lochner* era jurisprudence, which rigidly restricted both Congress's power to regulate interstate commerce and state and national power to regulate property; as chief justice, Taft actually rejected both *United States v. E. C. Knight* and *Lochner v. New York* itself.

National Power and Interstate Commerce

As Allen Ragan has pointed out, Chief Justice Taft "lent a ready and willing pen" to the project of centralizing national power over the economy. His opinions defended expansive federal control over interstate commerce and showed an ardent nationalism that belied traditional claims of formalism. Taft argued that the Constitution gave Congress the authority to regulate interstate commerce in order to protect it, foster its growth, and protect the public from tainted goods. Congress possessed, he insisted, "absolute control" over interstate commerce because the national government's power over trade among the states is "exactly what it would be in a government without states."[3] John Marshall, Taft's hero, had gone no further in his seminal opinion in *Gibbons v. Ogden.*

Taft's understanding of the commerce power was heavily influenced by Justice Oliver Wendell Holmes's ruling in *Swift & Co. v. United States* (1905), which marked a turn away from the Supreme Court's older notion of dual sovereignty. According to the dual sovereignty doctrine, the states and the national government held power in "separate and exclusive spheres of sovereignty" and each was "authorized to control autonomous and distinct domains of social life."[4] As the Court famously announced in *United States v. E. C. Knight* (1895), "It is vital that the independence of the [national] commercial power and of the [state] police power, and the delimitation between them . . . should always be recognized and observed." "That which belongs to commerce is within the jurisdiction of the United States," Chief Justice Melville Fuller wrote, "but that which does not belong to commerce is within the jurisdiction of the police power of the state." The state's police power was "essentially exclusive" and national commerce power was "also exclusive"; the Court attempted to draw a bright line between national and federal regulatory power and saw little room for the two to overlap.[5]

When it applied these principles in *Knight*, the Court ruled that although the American Sugar Refining Company held a practical monopoly on sugar refining in the United States, it was not subject to national control. Because refining occurred in a single location, the Court reasoned, it was an intrastate activity and could not be regulated under the interstate commerce clause. Moreover, the Court pointed out that "commerce" was different from mere "manufacturing": because goods are first manufactured then sold in interstate commerce, these activities should be regarded as separate and distinct.[6] It distinguished between commerce itself—understood as the sale and transportation of goods—and manufacturing, which occurred in a single location, and argued that the national government could regulate only the former and never the latter. The sugar industry, the Court believed, could not be viewed holistically. As a result, the national government might be able to regulate the interstate sale of raw sugar to the company and the final sale of refined sugar to out-of-state vendors, but it could not regulate the middle stage during which the raw sugar was refined.

A decade later, Holmes's *Swift* opinion broke from this older view and announced his now-famous metaphor of commerce as a "current." Holmes implicitly rejected the fine distinctions made by the *Knight* Court and insisted "commerce among the States is not a technical legal conception, but a practical one." Thus, when goods are bought in one state and transported to another state for sale, and when by repetition this becomes "a typical, constantly recurring course," the movement and sale of those goods constitutes "a current of commerce among the States." Congress could therefore regulate even intrastate activities if they were "part and incident" of the current of interstate commerce. Taft adopted much of the logic of *Swift* and praised the decision's recognition of "the great changes and development" of modern business and its rearticulation of "the dividing line between interstate and intrastate commerce where the Constitution intended it to be."[7]

The principles laid out in *Swift* allowed Taft to enunciate an extensive and robust understanding of congressional power over the national economy.

Taft advocated a holistic and integrated conceptualization of interstate commerce that encompassed the entire journey of goods in the current of interstate commerce. The national government's powers covered the entire stream of commerce, from the time a commodity was sold and entered interstate commerce to the time it came to rest at its ultimate destination.[8] Congress could regulate the intermediate stages of that journey, which might include temporarily holding goods in some facility, stops to allow inspection or repackaging, and the sale of the goods as a part of the process of transit. Because each of these transitions or pauses was, in its "essential character," a part of interstate commerce and "indispensable to the continuity" of the overall stream of commerce, none of these stages removed an article from interstate commerce. Thus, instead of breaking up interstate commerce into multiple independent, intrastate stages, Taft insisted that intermediate stages were a part of the stream of national commerce.[9]

This argument has critical implications, for it rejected the central logic of the *Knight* decision. Taft acknowledged that in most cases interstate commerce was distinct from manufacture, agriculture, and other purely intrastate activities, because manufacture or production normally occurred before an article's entry into the stream of commerce. However, he also argued that in a complex modern economy, the current of commerce could sometimes encompass even manufacture. Quoting Chief Justice Edward D. White's opinion in *United States v. Ferger*, Taft ruled that the Court must consider not "the intrinsic existence of commerce in the particular subject dealt with" but the "relation of that subject to commerce and its effect upon it." When Congress determined that intrastate activities produced a "direct effect" on interstate commerce, the Court should not "substitute its judgment" for that of the legislature, "unless the relation of the subject to interstate commerce and its effect upon it are clearly nonexistent." Thus, when intrastate activities such as manufacture or mining were inextricably intertwined with interstate commerce, or when they were "likely to obstruct, restrain or burden" it, they could be regulated by the national government.[10]

Taft insisted that commodities were subject to national power from the time they entered the flow of interstate commerce until the time they came to rest in their ultimate destination. Even if those items halted temporarily for repurposing—to be concentrated, repackaged, or even manufactured—before being shipped out of state in a different form, they never truly left the "current" of interstate commerce. Such repurposing activities may not be "interstate commerce in and of themselves" when considered alone, yet even manufacture could be "an essential but subordinate part" of interstate commerce and "subject to national regulation" when it occurred amidst the stream of interstate commerce. Since Congress had power to regulate interstate commerce, the chief justice argued, it must also have the authority incidentally to regulate various intrastate activities that are intermingled with interstate commerce; otherwise its power under the interstate commerce clause would be destroyed. Thus, although Congress could not normally control manufacture, it could control it incidentally when regulating interstate commerce.[11]

Taft's conception of the interstate commerce power both limited state authority and guaranteed the federal government's power over the national economy. He insisted, however, that he was not undermining legitimate state authority. National power to regulate some local activities was simply "incidental . . . and necessary" to congressional power over interstate commerce, but it would not "involve general regulation of intrastate commerce." Nevertheless, he consistently championed the supremacy of the national government within its own proper sphere. As he wrote in 1922, echoing similar language in Justice John Marshall Harlan I's dissent from *Knight*, "Commerce is a unit, and does not regard state lines, and while, under the Constitution, interstate and intrastate commerce are ordinarily subject to regulation by different sovereignties, *yet when they are so mingled together that the supreme authority, the Nation, cannot exercise complete effective control over interstate commerce without incidental regulation of intrastate commerce,* such incidental regulation is not an invasion of state authority."[12] The chief justice's robust defense of congressional power over interstate commerce showed that he was an intellectual heir to John Marshall's ruling in *Gibbons v. Ogden*, but Taft also evidently relied on Marshall's argument for national supremacy in *McCulloch v. Maryland*, since he implicitly argued that the scope of the interstate commerce clause could be understood only in light of the necessary and proper clause.

Within the broadly defined field of interstate commerce, Taft argued, the national government's powers were virtually unlimited. Congress could protect commerce by preventing any obstruction that imposed a "direct and undue burden" on it; this encompassed virtually any acts "which, in the judgment of Congress, are likely to affect interstate commerce prejudicially." The chief justice insisted that the commerce clause granted the government power to regulate to discourage monopolies, prevent speculation on futures when it might manipulate prices of goods in interstate commerce, and prohibit state-level taxes that discriminated against goods imported from other states. In imposing such regulations, Congress was free to "adopt any means" it chose to attain its legitimate end of fostering and protecting interstate commerce.[13]

Two examples may help to illustrate the extent of Taft's understanding of the interstate commerce power. In *Brooks v. United States*, Taft upheld a federal statute penalizing the interstate transit of stolen motor vehicles, even though the theft itself had occurred in a single state. Arguing that the national government could exercise "the police power . . . within the field of interstate commerce" to prevent "harmful results to people of other states," he insisted that federal power could be employed to prevent the transportation of harmful or tainted goods across state lines. The logic of *Brooks* is significant since it legitimates Congress's power to regulate "gross misuse[s] of interstate commerce"; this power permitted Congress to prohibit not only the sale of stolen vehicles but even the interstate sale of lottery tickets, and to regulate morality by banning the white slave trade.[14]

In 1926, Taft argued that goods could become a part of interstate commerce through neglect rather than intent. His opinion in *Thornton v. United States* upheld the Agriculture Department's power to inspect and treat cattle in interstate commerce and to prevent the spread of disease. The government claimed it had the power to treat cattle that had inadvertently strayed across the state line separating Georgia and Florida. Taft sided with the government, ruling that the free roaming constituted "intercourse between states" and placed the cattle under the national government's regulatory scheme since the "failure of [the] owners to restrict their [the cattle's] ranging" across the state line showed "the will of the owners" that their stock should move interstate. The Court ruled the federal government could regulate even the *accidental* movement of commodities across state lines, prior to any sale or formal entry into the stream of commerce.[15]

Notably, despite his strong defense of national regulatory authority, Taft pointed out that some mixed commercial activities fell under the regulatory power of both the national and the state governments.

National sovereignty guaranteed that the federal government's powers would remain preeminent, but Taft acknowledged the legitimacy of state authority over parts of the current of interstate commerce. A state could not tax interstate commerce simply because goods temporarily came to rest out of necessity (e.g., at a port, waiting for the arrival of a cargo ship), nor could it impose special taxes or regulations that discriminate against such commerce. The states could, however, regulate on a narrower basis. For example, unless Congress had previously "occupied the field" with its own regulations, a state could limit the weight of trucks using state highways, regardless of whether those vehicles were engaged in intrastate or interstate commerce. Similarly, state legislatures could enact laws to limit or ban the importation of tainted goods. To the extent that Taft's jurisprudence recognized that state and national power could overlap in at least some cases, he showed his disagreement with the dual sovereignty doctrine by arguing that state and national power to regulate an increasingly integrated economy could not be rigidly separated.[16]

Taft's explication of congressional commerce power evinces his nationalism. He insisted, however, that he was not altering the Constitution's meaning but merely delineating its robust grant of national power and showing the nation's ability to cope with "the natural development of interstate commerce under modern conditions." Rather than expanding national power, the Court recognized that the national government had more opportunities to employ its power because the economy had become increasingly complex and, as a result, intrastate and interstate economic activities were more often blended. The expanded use of national power involved no break from constitutional propriety, Taft argued, since "historically it was one of the chief purposes of the Constitution to bring [such activities] under national protection and control." National power under the Constitution had not expanded; instead, the use of that federal power had increased as the national economy developed: in 1789, interstate traffic constituted only a quarter of all commerce, but by 1910 it made up three-quarters of the nation's trade.[17]

Labor, Regulation, and Due Process

The chief justice's defense of national regulatory power over commerce permitted the government to protect interstate trade against burdensome or discriminatory state regulations. However, Taft also recognized the power of the government to regulate business in order to protect labor. Indeed, despite frequent claims that Taft was essentially a business-friendly Republican unconcerned with the plight of laborers, he frequently displayed "certain sympathies for the working class."[18] On the one hand, Taft opposed secondary boycotts, defended the use of injunctions to prevent irremediable harm to businesses, and argued that "the cornerstone of our civilization is in the proper maintenance of the guarantees of the Fourteenth Amendment and the Fifth Amendment."[19] However, his approach to labor and regulation was more nuanced than these legal principles, taken alone, would suggest. Taft was no ideologue. He believed that labor unions benefited society, he thought that the unregulated market permitted capital to exploit workers, and he rejected the idea that labor regulations could be struck down simply because corporations claimed the legislation limited their right to contract.

Taft condemned various labor organizations for engaging in secondary boycotts and other practices he believed were illegal and unjust, yet it would be unfair to paint him as an opponent of labor or a shill for business. In fact, he adopted a generally favorable approach to unionized labor throughout his career. As civil governor of the Philippines, he encouraged the creation of labor unions in the islands and later insisted on the "absolute necessity" of unions as a means of securing just wages for workers. As president, he supported wide-ranging reforms to benefit laborers, as evidenced by his support for the proposed workmen's compensation bill in 1912, his administration's implementation of an eight-hour day for government contractors, and his creation of the Bureau of Mines and an independent Department of Labor. Finally, he served as joint chairman of the National War Labor Board during World War I and in that capacity "surprised many observers . . . with his moderation and often pro-labor rulings." This is not the record of an antilabor hard-liner.[20]

As a federal judge, Taft cannot be classified as either "pro-business" or "pro-labor." He sided with labor in *Adkins v. Children's Hospital* and in *American Steel Foundries v. Tri-City Trades Council*, but he ruled for management in *Truax v. Corrigan* and *Bailey v. Drexel*. He managed to rule in favor of both labor and management in *Charles Wolff Packing Co. v. Court of Industrial Relations*, as I explain below. Yet since he sought to enunciate constitutional principles in his opinions—and not simply to aid a favored class—any accurate account of his jurisprudence requires us to look beyond a mere count of "conservative" or "liberal" decisions. When we grapple with his legal principles, it becomes clear that Taft honestly tried to ensure justice for both labor and business, to respect the rights of capital while also defending the government's legitimate authority to regulate and protect the weaker party.

Early in his career, Taft played a significant role in explicating the right of workers to combine and strike. In 1894, as a judge on the Sixth Circuit, he ruled that laborers have

> the right to organize into or to join a labor union which should take joint action as to their terms of employment. It is of benefit to them and to the public that laborers should unite in their common interest and for lawful purposes. . . . If they stand together, they are often able . . . to command better prices for their labor than when dealing singly with rich employers, because the necessities of the single employee may compel him to accept any terms offered him. . . . They may unite with other unions. The officers they appoint . . . may advise them as to the proper course to be taken by them in regard to their employment, or . . . may order them . . . peaceably to leave the employ of their employer.[21]

Some of Judge Taft's other rulings angered labor unions, but this passage would come to set the standard for laborers' freedoms and would be repeatedly invoked by workers and their unions.[22]

As chief justice, he would again delineate the rights of labor in *American Steel Foundries v. Tri-City Trades Council*, in which case he reversed an illegitimate injunction issued by the lower court and defended the right of laborers in Granite City, Illinois, to picket. Taft warned that legal picketing may not involve trespass, obstruction of public byways, intimidation, or violence against nonstriking workers, but he also insisted that laborers had a right to assemble, to protest, and to try to convince others to join their cause. Because before his ruling few attempts had been made to determine the legality of picketing, Taft's opinion was actually a significant development intended to "lay down . . . a general rule" for courts.[23]

His decision in *Steel Foundries* has been criticized for not defending the workers more robustly, but Jonathan Lurie recognizes that Taft sought an evenhanded approach that protected the rights of both the strikers and their employers.[24] Certainly, some of the specifics of *Steel Foundries* may appear arbitrary or vague. For example, the chief justice acknowledged a right to strike and picket, but he also seemed to limit this right rigidly when he wrote that the union was entitled only to "one representative for each point of ingress and egress in the plant," and insisted that the picketers must approach those they sought to persuade "singly" as "missionaries."[25] One might reasonably raise questions about these specific guidelines: Why may unions place one picket at each factory entrance, but not two? At what point do the verbal pleas of a missionary become the threatening exhortations of a violent agitator?

However, although Taft obviously sought to lay down general principles, many of the most restrictive aspects of the case had little precedential force. As Taft pointed out, courts of equity should be "flexible" in applying remedies in labor disputes, since "each case must turn on its own circumstances." His admonitions were "not laid down as a rigid rule" but were meant to apply "to this case under the circumstances" because of specific "tendencies to disturbance and conflict" displayed by the strikers in Granite City. The strikers had repeatedly assaulted nonstrikers, offering such serious threats to their safety that at least fifteen workers had been forced to sleep at the plant. These circumstances prompted Taft to insist that the strikers must act as single missionaries. Yet the chief justice insisted that the most restrictive language in his decision applied only to the case at bar. His specific prohibitions could "be varied in other cases." Thus, Taft's opinion did impose significant limitations on the actions of the picketers in Granite City, but it also defended the rights of strikers in every future labor case.[26]

Just as Taft acknowledged the rights of labor but was also willing to recognize certain limitations on those rights, he also defended the property rights of management without precluding the possibility that the government could impose significant regulations on businesses. It is true that Taft's approach to property rights sometimes displayed traditional hallmarks of *Lochner* era jurisprudence. He did believe that the due process clauses of the Fifth and Fifteenth Amendments protected private property and guaranteed the liberty of contract against arbitrary regulation. However, his approach to property rights was far more complex than has often been thought. In fact, Taft argued that *Lochner* was wrongly decided and had been overturned in 1917. As we will see, rather than presenting a "laissez-faire dogma" and an unyielding defense of property as "the bulwark of civilization," as Mason claims, Taft recognized that the individual's right to property was not absolute and could be subject to regulation.[27]

In fact, despite his belief that the due process clauses protected property rights, he also recognized that property could be regulated when appropriate procedural safeguards were guaranteed, as can be seen in *Truax v. Corrigan*. Despite his claim that the institution of private property played a critical role in "the uplifting and the physical and moral improvement of the whole human race," he also insisted that it was legal "to impose limitations upon its uses for lawful purposes."[28] Taft demanded that legal remedies must at least be available when property was harmed or regulated, but he did not defend property as an untouchable and sacrosanct right.[29] As a result, although he did rule in favor of property claims at times,[30] he often rejected such claims.[31]

This insistence on remedies is the key to his most controversial labor decision, *Truax v. Corrigan*. In that case, William Truax claimed that his restaurant had suffered serious economic harm as a result of a prolonged strike and sought an injunction against the strikers. As the Court recounted the events, Truax's former employees had engaged in a lengthy campaign that included attacks on Truax's employees as "scab Mexican labor . . . [and] other opprobrious epithets" and libelous claims that he had chased his employees "down the street with a butcher knife," assaulted his staff to force them to return to work, and even physically attacked his own customers: "Assaults and slugging were a regular part of the bill of fare." However, when Truax appealed to the state courts for an injunction against the picketers, his request was denied because Arizona law forbade the use of injunctions in such labor disputes.[32]

The Supreme Court ruled for Truax 5 to 4. Taft's majority opinion argued that Truax's business was his property, that the state could not permit "a direct injury to [his] fundamental property right," and that the Arizona law violated the Fourteenth Amendment's promise of equal protection by preventing him from seeking legal relief against the picketers. Taft's decision was criticized on two fronts. First, Brandeis argued that Taft undermined the state's legitimate authority to determine when remedies at equity could and could not be employed.[33] Second, Holmes objected to Taft's characterization of a business as property and argued that business is subject to extensive regulation because it is "a course of conduct" rather than "a thing"; moreover, Holmes insisted that Arizona could rightfully forbid the use of injunctions since "there is more danger that the injunction will be abused in labor cases than elsewhere."[34]

Whether or not one finds the dissenters' contentions plausible, it is worth noting that these criticisms largely overlook the central point made by the majority. The majority opinion did not focus on either injunctions alone or on state regulatory power over business interests. Instead, the critical question was whether the state could legally permit damage to Truax's business while also denying him any legal means of seeking relief. Taft struck down the statute because, as interpreted and applied by the state court, it placed the actions of the strikers beyond the power of the law and denied Truax "all remedy for the wrongs . . . suffered." On its face, the statute did no more than forbid the use of injunctions in certain labor disputes, but the Arizona Supreme Court had interpreted the statute in a way that granted the strikers "complete immunity *from any civil or criminal action*," thereby effectively "pronounc[ing] their acts lawful." Thus, the central holding of *Truax* was that the state had violated Truax's due process rights, not specifically by denying him an injunction, but by refusing him *any* procedural means of seeking relief for damage to his property. Arizona owed Truax an opportunity to pursue some legal remedy; it could not simply forbid him access to the courts.[35]

Secondarily, the Court ruled that even if the state permitted Truax to seek redress in a civil suit, nevertheless the anti-injunction statute violated the Fourteenth Amendment's equal protection clause. The law permitted an individual to seek injunctive relief in most cases, but created a special carveout for labor disputes. As a result, Truax could have secured an injunction against anyone who maliciously damaged his business, *except* his former employees. "If competing restaurant keepers had inaugurated the same type of campaign against Truax," Mason writes, "an injunction would necessarily have [been] issued to protect him in the enjoyment of his business." The Court therefore ruled that the state could not deny Truax injunctive relief in this one instance if he would be entitled to it in all other cases.[36]

Although the Court ruled that Arizona must offer Truax a remedy to protect his property rights, Taft's opinion actually stressed the importance of procedural (rather than substantive) protections of property: "The due process clause requires that every man shall have the protection of his day in court." Arizona was required to permit Truax a procedure—through an injunction or, barring that, perhaps through a civil suit for damages—to seek redress for the damage his business had suffered. However, to the extent that Truax "won" the case, his victory simply entitled him to have access to the courts without guaranteeing that he would ultimately prevail. Indeed, although Taft stated his own belief that the picketers had engaged in illegal conduct, the Supreme Court's decision did not impose that judgment on Arizona or its courts. Instead, the chief justice concluded his opinion by writing that the state court should have granted an injunction only after "the defendants [were] required to answer" Truax's complaints and then only "*if* the evidence sustain the averments of the complaint." This language required Arizona to give the restaurateur his day in court, but it did not demand that he be guaranteed any substantive relief.[37]

If Taft and Holmes differed over whether businesses could be considered property in *Truax*, Taft nevertheless agreed with a part of Holmes's dissent. As can be seen in the chief justice's own dissent in *Adkins v. Children's Hospital*, Taft believed that businesses may legitimately be subject to extensive regulation, despite the property interests of their owners. In *Adkins*, the majority opinion of Justice George Sutherland struck down a District of Columbia minimum wage law for women. Sutherland insisted that the Fifth Amendment's due process clause, which included within it a guarantee of freedom of contract, forbade the government from imposing a minimum wage. Because Sutherland believed that employees and employers had an "equal right" to contract to buy or sell labor at any price, he argued that the law took account "of the necessities of only one party" by guaranteeing the worker a set wage without considering the value of that labor to the employer. Sutherland therefore claimed that the statute denied the right of individuals "to freely contract with one another . . . where both are willing, perhaps anxious, to agree" to a lower wage. His decision acknowledged that the Supreme Court had upheld laws limiting working hours, but he insisted that setting maximum hours was substantially different from fixing wages.[38]

In his dissent, Taft delineated serious objections to Sutherland's understanding of equality and freedom in the market. He rejected the claim that employers and employees stood on equal footing and were therefore equally free. Minimum wage legislation, he wrote, is based on the assumption "that employees, in the class receiving least pay, are not upon a full level of equality of choice with their employer, and . . . are prone to accept pretty much anything that is offered." This was not a new theme for Taft. During his time in politics, he had voiced similar concerns, asking, "What could a single laboring man do in the necessary controversies that arise between labor and capital with respect to the adjustment of wages . . . against his wealthy employers, especially when that employer is a great corporation?" In effect, Taft argued that freedom of contract might mean little if practical necessity forced one party to agree to unfair terms.[39]

Taft evidently agreed with Sutherland's argument that the minimum wage law considered the necessity only of the worker, but where Sutherland saw this as a violation of the Constitution, Taft believed such asymmetrical concern was merited and permissible if the relative necessities of labor and capital were themselves unequal. By regulating in defense of the more vulnerable party, the government did not destroy liberty or equality, but helped to protect the liberties of both parties by placing them on a more equal playing field. Taft's dissent suggests that he believed the government may impose economic regulations and protect the weaker party precisely in order to ensure that both parties may contract freely. As a result, Taft's belief in the freedom of contract appears to have convinced him that government intervention in the market was warranted.

In *Adkins*, Taft also rejected Sutherland's distinction between maximum hours laws and minimum wage laws. Because the chief justice believed "in absolute freedom of contract, the one term is as important as the other," he argued that Sutherland's opinion "exaggerate[d] the importance of the wage term of the contract" and held it "inviolate" while permitting regulation of the length of working hours. Since "one [term] is the multiplier, and the other the multiplicand," both affected wages and both limited the freedom of contract to a similar degree. If Congress believed low wages were as great a danger as extended hours, Taft insisted, the Court should not reject its judgment. Even Stanley Kutler, who believes the *Adkins* dissent represented little more than Taft's "rare adherence to judicial restraint," acknowledges that "hardly any opinion prior to the mid-1930s more fully exposed the judicial double standards" used to distinguish wage legislation from hours restrictions.[40]

This disagreement may seem to be of secondary importance, but it is worth remembering that as he challenged the majority's distinction between maximum hours and minimum wage laws, Taft also explicitly attacked *Lochner*. Modern scholarship typically views *Lochner* as representative of an entire era, spanning from the end of the nineteenth century to 1937, but Taft insisted that *Lochner* was an anomaly. The Supreme Court, he wrote, had acknowledged the power of legislatures to limit working hours in *Holden v. Hardy* (1898), and despite retreating from that position in *Lochner*, it had returned to the *Holden* standard with their 1917 ruling in *Bunting v. Oregon*. As a result, he believed "the *Lochner* case was . . . overruled *sub silentio*" by *Bunting*.[41]

Overall, then, Taft's *Adkins* opinion marked his disagreement both with Sutherland and with the *Lochner* legacy. The argument of Taft's dissent "reveals the extent of his economic liberalism better than any of his opinions before or after." It is notable enough that Taft displayed his disagreement with *Lochner* and his recognition that the right to contract might be regulated. However, the very fact that the chief justice produced a dissenting opinion is striking. As we will see in chapter 8, Taft frowned on dissents and believed justices ought to suppress disagreements except in the rarest and most important cases. He dissented in writing only twice during his eight-year tenure on the Court. His public disavowal of Sutherland's decision, as a result, can only be seen as a serious and principled disagreement with the majority's ruling.[42]

Despite the progressive implications of Taft's dissent, his opinion in *Adkins* has often been viewed as the exception rather than the rule. For example, Mason suggests that Taft's dissent was "an aberration." Taft, he intimates, had momentarily slipped into liberalism in *Adkins* but quickly returned to obsessive conservatism, as evidenced by his opinion in *Charles Wolff Packing Co. v. Court of Industrial Relations*. Other scholars have agreed with this general assessment and seen *Wolff* as reactionary.[43] Yet, despite the frequent assertion that *Wolff* was a conservative opinion that displayed Taft's true ideological leanings, the chief justice's support for the minimum wage law in *Adkins* and rejection of an industrial relations statute in *Wolff* can be reconciled.

In *Wolff*, the Court struck down a Kansas law stipulating that the manufacture and preparation of clothing and food were affected with the public interest and therefore proposed to grant an industrial court extensive power to settle labor disputes and fix wages in these industries. The Supreme Court, in an opinion authored by the chief justice, expressed serious reservations about the breadth of Kansas's definition of businesses clothed with the public interest, then turned to the industrial court's power. The law permitted the industrial court to set wages and settle labor disputes, but the Court was most concerned that the statute also limited the right of both the employer and the employee to object to those wages.

Under the law, once wages had been fixed by the industrial court, the "employer is bound by this act to pay the wages fixed" and could not vary them; the employer's only options were to follow the court's orders or go out of business. More troubling, however, was the position of the employee. Laborers were "not required to work at the wages fixed," but workmen were "forbidden, on penalty of fine or imprisonment, to strike against them." Any individual employee could leave his work, but he was banned from organizing and striking in combination with other workers. This, Taft wrote, forced the individual laborer "to give up that means of putting himself on an equality with his employer which action in concert with his fellows gives him." Kansas's law may have been intended to protect labor, but it ultimately denied workers the right to combine and strike, imposing "a more drastic exercise of control . . . upon the employee than upon the employer." Had Taft upheld the Kansas statute, he would have at the same time decimated the very rights to combine and strike that he had defended on the Sixth Circuit and in *Steel Foundries*. Taft has been accused of enunciating a "doctrinaire conservatism" in *Wolff*, but in actuality the Court struck down paternalistic labor legislation in order to protect both the rights of workers and the rights of their employers.[44]

Contrary to the scholarly consensus, Taft's *Wolff* opinion was neither reactionary nor in conflict with his *Adkins* dissent. *Wolff* and *Adkins* actually presented very different constitutional questions. Most importantly, *Adkins* dealt with legislation governing the actual process of negotiating a contract, but the law in *Wolff* went beyond this and restricted what both employers and employees could do after wages had been determined. Moreover, *Wolff* cannot fairly be considered a divisive, ideological decision. Notably, although *Adkins* had divided the Court narrowly 5 to 3 (Brandeis did not participate), *Wolff* was decided unanimously. In *Wolff*, all three dissenters from *Adkins*—Taft, Holmes, and Sanford—in addition to Brandeis, voted to strike down the Kansas law. Indeed, even in conference, not a single justice believed the statute could be sustained.[45]

Overall, this review of Taft's labor decisions indicates that traditional depictions of the chief justice's alleged conservatism have not fully recognized the extent to which he was willing to defend labor even in the face of appeals to due process or the liberty of contract. Although his *Adkins* dissent has often been presented as an aberration, quickly reversed by *Wolff*, a more complete review of Taft's labor cases suggests that *Truax*, as a "conservative" decision, was more of an outlier than his "liberal" dissent in *Adkins*. Taft's labor decisions were far more nuanced and evenhanded than the scholarship has traditionally recognized.[46]

Before concluding, it is necessary to consider Taft's decision in the child labor case *Bailey v. Drexel Furniture Company*. In *Bailey*, Taft spoke for a majority of eight when he struck down a 10 percent federal tax on mines, quarries, mills, canneries, workshops, and factories that employed children. The case did address a labor issue, but Taft's opinion was largely technical and considered congressional tax power rather than a specific dispute between labor and capital. Nowhere in the Court's opinion, for example, does one find a meaningful discussion of property rights, the right to contract, or the rights of laborers or children. As a result, the case does not fit neatly into the foregoing consideration of Taft's labor decisions. Nevertheless, the case has obvious connections with the overall issue of labor regulations. I have argued that Taft recognized broad governmental powers to protect workers. Yet *Bailey*, by striking down a federal attempt to penalize the use of child labor, seems to present glaring evidence that Taft had little sympathy for the most endangered workers in the market.

The truth is somewhat more complex, for in *Bailey*, Taft's constitutional interpretation was in conflict with his policy preferences. He was not a proponent of child labor. As a candidate for the presidency, he praised the District of Columbia's child labor statute as a model law that should "arous[e] the States to similar action"; as president he oversaw the creation of the Bureau of Children, and even as he struck down the tax in *Bailey*, he also noted that the law sought "to promote the highest good."[47] Taft's policy preferences, as a result, cannot be said to have controlled his decision-making. He was acting as a judge, not a politician, and, despite the fact he had previously advocated prohibitions on child labor, he was forced to decide *Bailey* on legal and constitutional grounds.

His majority opinion ruled that the law was unconstitutional and an illegal attempt by Congress to use its tax power to regulate a purely intrastate matter. Taft argued that taxes were imposed "with the primary motive of obtaining revenue," but the "prohibitory and regulatory effect and purpose" of the tax in question were "palpable." Since the power to regulate intrastate commerce belonged to the states, he believed that upholding such a law would effectively sanction Congress's attempt to use its taxing authority to "break down all constitutional limitation" on its powers and "completely wipe out the sovereignty of the states."[48]

Taft's argument was well within the contemporary mainstream. Two points are notable. First, the Court's 1918 child labor decision, *Hammer v. Dagenhart*, had been handed down 5–4, but *Bailey* was decided 8–1.

Holmes and Brandeis, who had dissented in *Hammer*, signed on to Taft's opinion in *Bailey*. Even then Professor Felix Frankfurter responded to the decision by acknowledging that "'humanity' is not the test of constitutionality."[49] Second, the concern that expanding federal power could eventually swallow up state police power was a fear expressed even by justices whose progressive credentials cannot be questioned. A decade after *Bailey*, Brandeis and Benjamin Cardozo voted to strike down wage and hour regulations in *Schechter Poultry Corp. v. United States*. As Cardozo explained, upholding the wage law "would obliterate the distinction between what is national and what is local in the activities of commerce."[50] Regardless of its modern reputation, Taft's decision in *Bailey* must be considered in light of the fact that progressive luminaries embraced similar legal logic and issued similar rulings.

Taft's Judicial Legacy

Taft's jurisprudence left an imprint on American constitutionalism, particularly through his numerous opinions explicating a broad understanding of Congress's power to regulate interstate commerce. His labor cases were fewer in number and addressed a greater variety of topics, making it more difficult to glean an overarching theory, yet they are notable for his explicit defense of the right to strike and picket in *Steel Foundries* and for his dissent in *Adkins*. One may disagree with any of the chief justice's rulings, yet Taft obviously made a good faith effort to judge impartially according to the Constitution. Taft's jurisprudence shows that the Constitution granted the government extensive powers to regulate the national economy and that the fundamental law's protections of rights did not rigidly limit government regulatory power. He did not set out to be a progressive judge, but his case law shows that the Constitution did not forbid or prevent progressive reforms.

This chapter has emphasized Taft's decisions on commerce and labor because they show his approach to two of the most important constitutional issues of his day, issues that would remain at the forefront of political and legal disputes for decades. It was, after all, critical decisions addressing interstate commerce, in *National Labor Relations Board v. Jones & Laughlin Steel* (*NLRB*), and minimum wage legislation, in *West Coast Hotel v. Parrish*, that marked the Court's so-called "switch in time" in 1937. It is notable that despite Taft's reputation for conservatism, in these areas his jurisprudence has been recognized for its broad defense of government power. Numerous scholars, even while voicing significant reservations about Taft's ideology, have recognized that his interstate commerce clause decisions laid the groundwork for Chief Justice Charles Evans Hughes's opinion in *NLRB*, and, less frequently, it has been observed that Taft's *Adkins* dissent helped Hughes defend his decision in *West Coast Hotel*.[51]

The argument for commerce as a "current" that permitted the US government to regulate every stage of a "constant, typically recurring course" cleared the way for *NLRB*. In that case, which addressed national regulations of labor practices in a Pennsylvania manufacturing plant, Hughes placed the plant within the stream of commerce. Relying on the language of the labor board, he argued that it could be seen as a "heart" drawing in raw materials from other states, manufacturing them within a single state, then pumping the finished goods back out into interstate commerce. Hughes argued that even if manufacture is purely intrastate and does not fall directly under Congress's interstate commerce power, it may still be regulated indirectly "by reason of [its] close and intimate relation to interstate commerce" since "effective control" of interstate commerce may at times also "embrace some control" over intrastate manufacture. Hughes defended his reasoning in part by citing Taft's decisions in *Stafford v. Wallace, Board of Trade v. Olsen,* and *Railroad Commission of Wisconsin v. Chicago, Burlington & Quincy Railroad Co.* As Barry Cushman argues, the Taft Court's broad understanding of the interstate commerce power "contained within itself the potential" for broader federal control of the national economy and provided a theoretical basis for the broader application of federal powers. Taft alone did not create the groundwork for *NLRB*, but his case law, alongside the *Shreveport Rate Cases* and Harlan's dissent in *Knight*, helped to set the stage for Hughes's opinion.[52]

Similarly, Taft's dissent in *Adkins* presaged Hughes's decision in *West Coast Hotel*, which overturned *Adkins* by upholding Washington State's minimum wage law for women. Hughes "proceeded on the basic premise advanced by both Taft and Holmes" in their *Adkins* dissents. He contended that the due process clause did protect the freedom of contract, but that this right was subject to regulation, that regulation of wages is permissible because employers and employees do not actually stand on equal footing, and that Sutherland's attempt to distinguish between maximum hours laws and minimum wage laws was unjustifiable.

It may be true, as Stanley Kutler argues, that the "consummate craftsman" Charles Evans Hughes cited Taft's opinions strategically, employing "that impeccable constitutionalist" to buttress his argument. Nevertheless, it is equally true that Hughes could cite Taft's opinions only because their logic and language pointed in the direction of 1937.[53]

It can hardly be suggested that every Taft opinion on record explicitly expresses progressive sympathies or shows how progressive reforms may be implemented under the Constitution. Nor, despite Hughes's reliance on Taft's opinions in *NLRB* and *West Coast Hotel*, would it be reasonable to claim that Taft himself would have endorsed every element of the New Deal or every case decided by the Hughes and Stone Courts. One strongly suspects, to consider just two examples, that he would have flatly rejected both *Home Building & Loan Association v. Blaisdell* and *Wickard v. Filburn*. Taft saw constitutional limits where later Courts would not. Nevertheless, a careful consideration of Taft's decisions shows us that his reputation as an inflexible formalist must be revisited. Ultimately, the logic of his commerce and labor decisions has more in common with *NLRB* and *West Coast Hotel* than the reasoning of *Knight* or *Lochner*.

8 | Chief Justice as Chief Executive
Judicial Reforms on the Taft Court

William Howard Taft is the only American to have served as the head of two branches of the national government. Less well known is the fact that Taft is responsible for making the chief justice the genuine head of the judiciary. Whatever his shortcomings as president, Taft was a remarkable success as chief justice and strengthened and reshaped the Supreme Court and the federal court system. As a result of his lobbying, Congress created the Conference of Senior Circuit Judges in 1922 (now the Judicial Conference) and gave the chief justice power to transfer federal judges between circuits in order better to keep abreast of casework. Three years later, Congress passed the 1925 Judges' Bill, which expanded the Supreme Court's certiorari jurisdiction and freed it to focus on critical cases of constitutional and statutory interpretation. These reforms, taken together, made the chief justice the formal head and chief executive of the federal judiciary and greatly increased the power of the Supreme Court as a whole. Felix Frankfurter wrote that for his reform work, "Chief Justice Taft had a place in history . . . next to Oliver Ellsworth, who originally devised the judicial system."[1]

This chapter will first detail Taft's efforts to transform the role of the chief justice into an explicitly political and executive office. Most scholars acknowledge that Taft was a capable administrator on the bench; only a few, however, observe that he sought to expand the chief justice's political power by making him the chief executive of the entire federal judiciary.[2] Because Chief Justice Taft interjected himself into the realm of policy, his work cannot be seen as mere administration. He did not act as a bureaucratic functionary or consider merely how best to carry out his duties. He also operated as a chief executive for the Court by advising Congress on how the Court should be modernized to meet the changing needs of the country and what the Court's duties ought to be. Through his efforts, Taft provided the federal courts with an executive head capable of leading judicial reform efforts and maintaining clear lines of responsibility within the judicial system.

Second, I consider the Judges' Bill, which helped to restructure the federal judiciary, streamlined the judicial process, and made the Supreme Court the final court of appeal for important national legal issues. By expanding the Court's certiorari jurisdiction, the Judges' Bill freed it from the laborious duty of hearing appeals on trivial legal questions and gave the Court broader discretion in choosing which cases it would hear. Further, the bill elevated the Supreme Court and transformed it into the true apex of the federal judiciary while also ensuring its power to review even state court decisions that bore on critical national controversies. This in turn increased the authority of the chief justice; as the Court focused more exclusively on major legal disputes, the chief justice gained proportionately greater power through his ability to assign cases and his leadership in creating and maintaining majorities to support the Court's rulings.

Notably, Taft's efforts were in line with progressive reform goals. Not only did he improve the efficiency of the administration of justice, he pursued many of his reforms explicitly in order to aid poor litigants. Many scholars now agree that Chief Justice Taft shared some of the progressives' concerns—particularly in his interest in efficiency and broad conception of national powers—but his efforts to ensure equal justice to the poor have generally gone unnoticed. Indeed, some even believe his administrative reforms were reactionary. Peter Fish, for instance, argues that Taft was a "conservative" reformer who accepted efficiency-based reforms "to ward off specific threats to an independent federal judiciary and to preserve a social and political equilibrium." He concludes that Taft's interest in judicial reform was "but rhetoric" to hide his true desire to strengthen the Court as a defender of property against democratic reformers.[3]

On the contrary, I argue that Taft's reforms were actually progressive and advanced progressive ideals. Taft recognized that structural reforms would promote social reform, since increasing the efficiency of the courts decreased the costs of litigation and made the administration of justice more affordable and available to the poor. Many progressives disparaged the federal courts and sought to curb judicial power, but Taft saw that fostering greater efficiency would redound to the benefit of needy litigants and help to address progressive concerns without undermining the authority of the courts. In this way, he presented a reform agenda for the judiciary and simultaneously strengthened the Court, defended individual rights, and affirmed the integrity of constitutional government.

The Chief Justice

In the early twentieth century, the country was developing and modernizing, but the structure of the judiciary lagged far behind; the federal courts were decentralized and bogged down by unwieldy procedures. Because most chief justices had been stringently apolitical—most even refused to advise Congress as it attempted to reform the judiciary, leaving that role to the attorney general—the courts lacked a judicial spokesman who could express the judiciary's needs to the political branches. As chief justice, Taft embraced distinctly political and executive duties. He became the Court's official representative to the political branches and believed it was his duty "to suggest needed reforms and to become rather active in pressing them" upon the legislature. Taft assumed an explicitly political role. Robert Post observes, "In Taft's eyes, the chief justiceship was much closer in spirit and responsibility to the English position of Lord Chancellor." This officer, Taft pointed out, was "the highest judicial officer of the realm" and also played a political role as "a member of the Cabinet, of the House of Lords and of the Government controlling legislation."[4]

To this end, Taft entered office with a reform agenda for the Court. In a 1922 article for the *American Bar Association Journal*, which can easily be seen as the new chief justice's "state of the judiciary" missive, Taft proposed three specific reform measures. First, to address the increase in the number of federal cases, Taft called on Congress to create additional judgeships and establish a judicial conference that could provide "executive direction" to the judicial force. Second, to simplify and streamline the federal rules of procedure, he requested that Congress permit the Supreme Court to reformulate the rules of procedure for suits at common law (just as it had already been authorized to formulate rules for equity and admiralty). Finally, he argued that the mandatory jurisdiction of the high court should be reduced and its certiorari jurisdiction concomitantly increased; by giving the Court broad discretion over its docket, he hoped to free it from hearing trivial disputes and allow it to focus exclusively "on all important questions of general law with respect to which there is a lack of uniformity in the intermediate Federal courts of appeal." The Court should decide key constitutional questions and settle disagreements between circuit courts while leaving less important cases to the lower courts. Although Taft's hopes for simplifying judicial procedure would not be achieved during his tenure, he inaugurated a period of reform, convinced Congress to create the Judicial Conference, and expanded the Court's certiorari jurisdiction.[5]

The chief justice used his considerable political influence to vigorously support the 1922 and 1925 bills. In addition to personally testifying before Congress and repeatedly seeking the backing of Solicitor General James M. Beck, Taft encouraged various bar associations to endorse his proposals and lobbied for assistance from his extensive network of allies in Congress, the judiciary, the bar, and even among newspapermen. Consequently, he was able not only to encourage Congress to consider what reforms might be necessary for the judiciary, but also to direct the legislative debate and advance the specific policies he believed were most critical. His success relied on informal power and personal influence, but by his efforts Taft transformed the office of chief justice, setting a precedent for future chief justices to act as "chief judicial reformer[s]."[6]

In 1921 when Taft assumed the chief justiceship, the federal courts faced two connected problems: the judiciary needed a greater number of district judges to keep up with its rapidly growing workload, and it lacked "a head charged with the responsibility of the use of the judicial force." There was "a hierarchical system of courts, [but] not of judges"; the high court was technically supreme and could review the decisions of lower courts, yet the judiciary lacked any formal structure that permitted either the chief justice or senior circuit judges to preside over their colleagues in executive or administrative matters. The 1922 reform bill helped to ameliorate these two problems by increasing the size of the federal judiciary and by creating an institutional executive force headed by the chief justice, in the form of the Conference of Senior Circuit Judges.[7]

Only a few days after he was sworn in, Taft emphasized the need for executive direction in the judiciary: "We must have machinery of quasi-executive character to mass our Judicial force where the congestion is, or is likely to be." He lobbied Congress for a "flying squadron" of eighteen new federal judges, assigned not to specific circuits or districts but to the nation at large. Under his plan, the chief justice would have the power to move these judges to the districts most in need of additional personnel, either to clear backlogs or keep up with the districts' workloads.[8] Taft's suggestion went far beyond mere administrative efficiency. According to his proposed plan, the president would appoint eighteen new judges with the advice and consent of the Senate, but the chief justice would have the power to determine, with the advice and consent of a committee of judges, in which districts these judges would hold court. Shifting low-level civil servants between offices for the sake of efficiency would undoubtedly be an administrative duty, but Taft asked for a power that was essentially executive.

The political implications of the transfer power raised substantial objections in Congress, especially in regard to prohibition and the enforcement of federal criminal law. Some feared, for instance, that judges from "dry" districts would be moved indiscriminately to "wet" areas, or vice versa. Taft insisted that the chief justice would not play prohibition politics, since he would be unable to assign a judge to hear any specific type of case. Yet even aside from the enforcement of the Volstead Act, the power to transfer judges would have enormous political repercussions. Since Taft was deeply concerned with rising disrespect for law and the apparent inability of some state courts to punish criminals and maintain order, it is possible that he would have been tempted to move rigid law-and-order judges to areas known for lax enforcement of the law. The power to transfer judges would give the chief justice a politically significant role in taking care that the laws were faithfully implemented.[9]

Congress rebuffed Taft's proposal for a group of at-large judges, but did agree to create a total of twenty-four new district judgeships. Moreover, Congress created a mechanism by which judges could be transferred between courts. It allowed senior circuit judges to move district judges between districts within their respective circuits and permitted the chief justice to move district judges between circuits, with the agreement of the senior circuit judge in both circuits. Essentially, Congress created two levels of executive chiefs by increasing the formal powers of both the chief justice and the senior circuit judges.[10]

Taft's endeavors to create an executive head of the judiciary were further realized with the creation of the Conference of Senior Circuit Judges, which served a key bureaucratic function by providing detailed reports on the work of each circuit and district, including the amount of business completed and remaining in each court. This information allowed the conference to understand "the condition of the calendar district by district . . . the localities that are over-burdened, those that keep abreast of their work, and those that have a surplus of judicial time." Critically, Taft believed that reports on the productivity of individual judges would "stimulate effective work of each judge in the reduction of arrears." If a district or circuit remained continuously behind, the statistics and reports helped the chief justice and the local senior circuit judge understand the needs of that court and strive to remedy delays, thereby ensuring, in Frankfurter and Landis's words, "a systematic examination of business and personnel." Further, Taft interposed the chief justice into the process of judicial legislation, for he employed the annual reports of the Judicial Conference to inform Congress and the country about the state of the judiciary and recommend measures necessary for the health of the court system.[11]

As a result of the new formal powers granted him by the 1922 act, Taft saw the potential to expand further the chief justice's informal influence. Taft is famous for advising presidents on judicial appointments and lobbying for the creation of an independent Supreme Court building. However, his extensive work to unify the federal courts by soliciting needed information from lower court judges and his willingness to serve as a general manager and unofficial disciplinarian also demonstrate his executive management of the judiciary.

As chief justice, Taft advised (sometimes uninvited) Warren Harding, Calvin Coolidge, and Herbert Hoover on judicial selection and at times wielded significant influence over judicial appointments. It is evident that Taft had the greatest influence during the Harding administration, when he played at least some role in advising the president on the selection of Justices George Sutherland, Pierce Butler, and Edward Sanford. Harding's attorney general, Harry M. Daugherty, apparently promised that he would only put forward judicial nominees of whom Taft approved. Taft's influence was seen most clearly in the appointment of Butler. Not only did he personally advise Butler during the nomination and confirmation process, he testified before the Senate Judiciary Committee to defend Butler's reputation after La Follette attempted to paint the nominee as a corporate lawyer with inappropriate ties to railroads. His influence with Coolidge and Hoover was less pronounced, but even during his later years Taft seems to have had some pull with the White House. During Hoover's presidency, Taft enjoyed a collegial relationship with Attorney General William Mitchell, who at times sought the chief justice's advice on judicial appointments to the lower courts. According to Donald Anderson's account, Taft sought "to dictate his successor even on his deathbed" and "would not resign from his office until he learned that [Charles Evans] Hughes had been nominated." Even if Anderson's story verges on the apocryphal, Hoover did actually believe that "Taft would more readily resign if he knew that Hughes would succeed him."[12]

Ultimately, it is impossible to pinpoint the extent to which Taft's recommendations influenced any president in nominating a candidate for the high bench. Taft had a large role in promoting Butler's appointment and played at least some part in supporting Sutherland, Sanford and Harlan F. Stone, but in many cases his preferred candidate was passed over. Nevertheless, he seems to have wielded a veto over Supreme Court nominations. Walter Murphy writes, "If Taft was only partially successful in getting his own candidates on the Court, he was completely successful in keeping out men who he thought would misinterpret the Constitution or increase dissension within the Court."[13]

Of course, Taft's actions have raised significant questions of propriety, but Taft dismissed any scruples he may have had. He believed that as chief justice he had a duty to guarantee that the Supreme Court did its work efficiently and well, to protect the reputation of his Court, and to ensure that the judiciary would be both a bastion of constitutionalism and open to reform.

Upon taking the center seat, Taft was faced with a Court behind in its work, in part because of the infirmity of its older members. Between 1921 and 1924, Mahlon Pitney suffered a nervous breakdown, William Day and Oliver Wendell Holmes underwent serious illnesses, and Joseph McKenna's mind, Taft believed, was deteriorating. The chief justice sought to ensure that new justices would be capable of fulfilling their duties on the Court and supported the appointment of jurists who were "hard hitting, industrious . . . and very able lawyer[s]" marked by "eminent ability and judicial experience" and who possessed the respect of "the Bar and the community."[14]

Furthermore, Taft recognized that the Court's legitimacy could be called into question because of the decades-long dominance of Republicans at the presidential level. Between William McKinley's 1897 inauguration and 1921, when Harding named Taft chief justice, four Republican presidents had appointed eleven supreme court justices and Woodrow Wilson, the sole Democratic president during those years, had appointed only three. As chief justice, Taft argued that a bipartisan bench was necessary in order to protect the Court's reputation. For instance, he informed Harding that Butler was "a Democrat of the Cleveland type." He insisted that it would "aid the Court to increase the number of Democrats on the bench, there now being only two" and wrote Justice Willis Van Devanter that appointing a Democrat to the Supreme Court "would be a good thing for the Court and politically."[15]

Finally, Taft insisted that the Court needed jurists who were progressive but also deeply attached to the Constitution. Contrary to traditional claims that Taft became a reactionary in his old age and sought to use the Court as a bulwark against progressive reforms, he actually believed that it was the Court's duty to uphold and defend progressive policies that met constitutional muster. In a 1922 letter to Elihu Root, he explained that he sought a delicate balance: "We ought not to have too many men on the Court who are . . . reactionary on the subject of the Constitution"; instead, he hoped for "men who are liberal but who still believe that the cornerstone of our civilization is in the proper maintenance of the guarantees of the Fourteenth Amendment and the Fifth Amendment." This was not a new theme for Taft; in 1919 he insisted that lawyers should play a role in protecting progress and maintaining "the nice balance between private right and public necessity . . . in order that individual initiative and the spur of the advance of all by the advance of each shall not be lost." Taft hoped for the appointment of jurists who combined his own mixture of progressivism and constitutionalism.[16]

Moreover, Taft's influence went beyond judicial appointments and extended to a general managerial role in overseeing the personnel of the courts. He used his personal influence to improve the administration of justice throughout the federal judiciary, often writing to his fellow judges in order to ascertain the conditions in their district or circuit and to request their suggestions for reform. The lower court judges seemed to appreciate the gesture, understanding that the chief justice was making a real effort to show that they were all "parts of an articulated system of courts."[17]

At times, Taft's efforts were disciplinary. He wrote personal letters asking slow judges to quicken their efforts. To one judge who had put off deciding a case for four years, Taft wrote, "I write in the interest of the administration of justice, and for the reputation of the Federal Judiciary. . . . I urge that you drop everything else and decide this case." To another, he stressed the importance of dispensing speedy justice: "I think it is a source of considerable irritation among litigants that their cases are not decided. . . . One can acquiesce in an adverse conclusion by taking an appeal, but when two people have no means of taking an appeal, it leaves both in a situation of which they may properly complain." Taft even reminded one judge that "my pride in you as one of my appointments is so great, that I thought it [appropriate] . . . to call this [delay] to your attention."[18] The chief justice employed his influence both to increase the efficiency of the courts and to protect the judiciary's reputation against legitimate complaints.

These letters went beyond mere verbal prodding, for the chief justice and the conference had before them actual data from each court. The conference helped to institutionalize an informal sense of responsibility in the federal judges; Taft explained that by making the judges "feel as if they are under real observation by the other judges and the country" the conference "solidifies the Federal judiciary" and brought "all the district judges within a mild disciplinary circle." Of course, Taft had no formal authority over the decisions made by any federal judge. The purpose of creating executive power in his office was not to dominate lower court judges. As Taft himself acknowledged, "Judges should be independent in their judgments," but the chief justice had a legitimate role to play in prompting efficient work, since judges "should be subject to some executive direction as to the use of their services."[19]

Taft also engaged in political affairs when he successfully lobbied Congress for funds to construct the modern Supreme Court Building. Taft did not live to see the erection of the Court's current home, but his efforts ensured the project's eventual success. At the laying of the cornerstone for the new building in 1932, Chief Justice Hughes observed, "We are indebted to the late Chief Justice William Howard Taft more than to anyone else. . . . This building is the result of his intelligent persistence." It is thanks to Taft that the Supreme Court no longer meets beneath the Capitol. And this physical independence from the legislature—now as then—plays a role in guaranteeing the political independence of the third branch.[20]

Taft had become chief justice when the judiciary was disjointed and lacking in structure and accountability. Through the creation of the Judicial Conference he secured a tremendous reform that united the judiciary under the leadership of the chief justice. By expanding his influence beyond mere administrative duties to explicitly political matters, Taft promoted strong appointments to the bench, sought to ensure judicial accountability, and worked to advance the judiciary's unity and independence.

The Supreme Court

If the 1922 act that created the Judicial Conference made the chief justice the formal head of the judiciary, the Judges' Bill of 1925 solidified the Supreme Court's authority over the lower federal courts and over state courts. By 1925, the growth of the federal government, modernization of industry, claims by military contractors in the wake of World War I, and litigation under the Volstead Act had overburdened the Supreme Court's docket. This problem was exacerbated by the antiquated structure of the federal courts. Although the 1891 Evarts Act had constituted circuit courts made up of two circuit court judges and one Supreme Court justice, these had relatively limited jurisdiction and did not function as true intermediate courts of appeal. The obligatory jurisdiction of the high court typically made up at least 75 percent of its docket. As a result, litigants often waited up to two years for a hearing, and the Court sometimes took another three years to hand down a decision in an important case. The Judges' Bill alleviated these difficulties by substantially restricting the Court's mandatory jurisdiction and increasing its discretionary certiorari jurisdiction.[21] By expanding the Supreme Court's certiorari jurisdiction, it gave the Court the power to control its own docket. As a result, Taft's work to promote the 1925 law reinforced the already burgeoning power of the chief justice and further unified the judiciary by transforming the Supreme Court into the nation's highest court of appeals.

The 1922 law had strengthened the chief justice's ability to ask Congress for legislation to aid the Court, and by 1925 Taft was using that power enthusiastically. Because the American Bar Association had convinced Congress that a jurisdiction bill would be too complicated for the legislature to formulate on its own, Taft created a drafting committee made up of Justices Day, Van Devanter, and James McReynolds, which was later aided by both Sutherland and the chief justice himself. The entire Court—with the exception of Brandeis, who disagreed privately— endorsed the bill, and Taft, Van Devanter, and McReynolds spent two or three days each lobbying for it on Capitol Hill. The bill was approved by a voice vote in the House and after only brief debate in the Senate.[22]

The Judges' Bill limited direct appeals to the Supreme Court to a small class of cases, thereby requiring most cases to be filtered through the circuit courts and reducing the high court's burden. Freed from the burden of hearing trivial cases and direct appeals, the Court could limit its docket to cases of true national importance. It retained mandatory jurisdiction over cases in which a state supreme court had struck down a federal statute or a state statute was held to be valid against a claim of unconstitutionality or conflict with a federal law. At the same time, the Court's newly expanded certiorari jurisdiction permitted it to review important circuit court decisions, review a state court's decision that determined the constitutionality of a federal statute or treaty, affected the validity of a state statute said to be repugnant to the US Constitution, laws, or treaties, or any decision in a case affecting "any title, right, privilege, or immunity" claimed under the Constitution.[23]

Essentially, the Judges' Bill turned the Supreme Court into the final appellate court for important national issues involving individual rights or the power of the federal government. It could oversee federal jurisprudence and also intervene at the state level when local courts hindered national power or denied national rights. The Supreme Court could now focus solely on its higher duties: "First to secure uniformity of decision between those courts in the nine circuits, and second to bring up cases involving questions of importance which it is in the public interest to have decided by this Court."[24] As a result of its new discretionary power, the Court gained a tremendous amount of political authority and was guaranteed a major role in buttressing the power of the federal government. In this way, the bill not only expanded the influence of the Supreme Court over lower courts, but also granted it the power to hear and decide critical issues relating to federalism, individual rights, and public policy.

As the Supreme Court began to focus on a different class of cases, the chief justice's influence over the Court rose, particularly in the realm of cultivating strong majorities in support of key decisions. Taft employed personal persuasion and his power to assign cases to dissuade dissents, mass the Court around majority opinions, and strengthen the Court's institutional reputation. It is some mark of his success that he is credited with suppressing more than 200 dissenting votes during his tenure.[25]

As chief justice, Taft had the authority to assign opinions in any case in which he voted with the majority. Since Taft voted against the majority in only nineteen cases during his tenure, he could almost always assign an opinion to a justice who would produce a clear, well-written decision that would unite the Court and deter dissents. From his brother justices, he demanded "carefully craft[ed] opinions to meet the concerns of all of the Justices," and he was willing to reassign a case simply because a justice's draft majority opinion failed to win sufficiently strong support.[26]

For example, the opinion in *Sonneborn Brothers v. Cureton* had origin-ally been assigned to McReynolds, but Taft took over the case himself when McReynolds's draft opinion incited serious objections and prompted the Court to hear a second round of arguments. Taft gave careful consideration to the potential dissenters' views and authored a more conciliatory opinion. McReynolds authored a two-paragraph concurrence expressing his own ideas, but the Court backed Taft's opinion unanimously. Similarly, when McReynolds's opinion in *Railroad Commission v. Southern Pacific Co.* failed to convince the more liberal members of the Court, Taft finally reassigned the majority opinion to himself. Holmes and Brandeis approved of his new opinion and joined the majority; even McReynolds submitted, after initially protesting and threatening to dissent. Taft held himself to a similarly high standard and graciously altered his opinions in order to conciliate his fellow justices. For instance, he deterred dissenting opinions by eliminating a protracted explanation of the interstate commerce clause from his opinion in *Wisconsin v. Illinois*. As he wrote to Justice Butler, although it was "a real sacrifice of my personal preference," he believed "it is the duty of us all to control our personal preferences to the main object of the Court."[27]

Moreover, Taft recognized that due concern for the constitutional and legal objections of potential dissenters would help to unite the Court. He frequently accepted criticisms or concerns from draft dissents and blended these ideas into his own opinions to appease the dissenting justices. In *United Mine Workers v. Coronado Coal Co.* (*Coronado I*), for example, Taft "made important concessions to the would-be dissenters" and held that, although a union and its local branches could be sued for lawless acts during a strike, the national board of the United Mine Workers could not be held liable for the actions of local strikers unless it had actually encouraged the illegal activities. Brandeis was satisfied with the compromise and the decision was handed down unanimously. Similarly, in the *Steel Foundries* case, Taft unified a fractured Court; he modified an injunction against violent picketing and also clearly defended the workers' right to picket, thereby integrating arguments supported by the liberal wing of the Court. As a result, Holmes joined the majority and Brandeis concurred separately, noting that he concurred "in substance in the opinion and the judgment of the Court," rather than dissenting.

Having won over the liberals, Taft also convinced the more conservative Pitney to suppress his objections because "it is so unusual to get as many of the Court together . . . that we better let it go as the opinion has been approved." Justice Clark opposed the majority opinion, but he did not write a dissent.[28]

Thus, Taft demonstrated that carefully refined legal arguments could hold appeal for virtually the entire high court. Even Brandeis, more than any other justice the ideological opposite of Taft, admitted that the chief justice showed great skill in addressing his constitutional concerns. With respect to *Southern Pacific*, Brandeis wrote, "I had written a really stinging dissent. . . . I suppressed my dissent because . . . the worst things [in the majority opinion] were removed by the Chief." Similarly, he accepted Taft's opinion in *Chicago & Northwestern Railway Co. v. Nye Schneider Fowler Co.* because "the opinion handles the matter so deftly that I think there will be no such lasting harm done as to require dissent. So as our Junior [justice] says: 'I'll shut up.'"[29]

Taft's successes in suppressing dissents arose in large part from his personality and generosity. Holmes praised the genial chief justice: "Never before . . . have we gotten along with so little jangling and dissension." Taft used personal persuasion to convince his fellow justices to modify their views or compromise for the sake of unity. When the Court was deciding *American Railway Express Co. v Kentucky*, he recognized that Brandeis had valid complaints against McReynolds's majority opinion. Taft evidently managed to make Brandeis's more liberal views palatable to McReynolds's more conservative ear; the result was that McReynolds adopted Brandeis's arguments as his own. This compromise evidently caused Brandeis, Holmes, and Stone to suppress dissents and the Court decided the case 7 to 2, with Sutherland and Butler dissenting without opinion.[30]

These efforts to maintain unanimity were part of Taft's strategy for countering the more radical political forces of the day, since he believed dissents damaged the Court's legitimacy. As Taft wrote to Justice Stone, the whole Court should recognize that "the continuity and weight of our opinions on important questions of law should not be broken any more than we can help by dissents." The entire Court, including even Brandeis and Holmes, who are now remembered for their dissents, understood that frequent and public airing of disagreements would simply provide fodder for attacks on the judiciary. Holmes was known to be reticent "to express his dissent, once he's 'had his say' on a given subject." For his part, Brandeis determined that since "I have differed from the court recently" in three different dissents, he had "concluded that, in this case, I had better 'shut up.'" Following an effort by Senator William Borah of Idaho to require a seven-vote majority on the Supreme Court in order to strike down a federal statute, Brandeis recounted that the Court had "deemed [it] inadvisable to express dissent and add another 5 to 4 [decision]. . . . The whole policy is to suppress dissents, that is the one positive result of Borah['s] 7 to 2 business."[31]

Throughout his tenure, Taft worked tirelessly to protect and strengthen the reputation of the judiciary by "massing the court" to hand down unanimous, or nearly unanimous, decisions. The percentage of unanimous Supreme Court opinions had declined sharply just before Taft's ascent to the center seat. In 1912, almost 90 percent of the Court's opinions were unanimous, but that number had fallen, dropping to a low of just over 60 percent in 1919. In Taft's first term as chief justice, the Court's unanimity rate for published opinions spiked back up above 90 percent; throughout his tenure, the Court maintained unanimity in an average of 84 percent of its published opinions and 91.4 percent of its total decisions. In addition, the Taft Court almost wholly eliminated one-vote decisions, with only 0.95 percent of cases being decided by a single vote.[32]

Through his efforts to ensure the passage of the Judges' Bill, Taft helped to buttress the Court as a whole, but he also saw the potential to expand the prerogatives and influence of the chief justice. Further, by using his personal influence alongside the chief justice's assigning power, Taft unified and strengthened the Court as an institution, protected its reputation, and guarded its influence. Taft has often been criticized for his judicial temperament, which supposedly rendered him incapable of seizing political opportunities or forcefully wielding executive power. But his actions as chief justice suggest a more complex picture; as Jeffrey Rosen points out, "If Taft had chafed in the White House as a judicial president, he thrived in the Supreme Court as a presidential chief justice."[33] Taft may have been a judge at heart, but his leadership on the Court shows that he also had the mind of an executive.

Progressive Reforms in Service of the Constitution

As the federal government's role expanded, the courts had been called upon to address the vast new fields of litigation that arose from the government's broadening role in American life. Taft saw that the courts needed to be strengthened to meet the new demands placed on all three branches of the government. In this sense, his work to rejuvenate and strengthen the courts clearly aligned with the Progressive Era's expansion of the role of government. Taft's reform efforts on the Court were in line with progressive goals insofar as they centralized national power and institutionalized a more efficient and scientific means of evaluating and responding to the judiciary's needs; as Justin Crowe points out, Taft participated in "Progressive era state-building." Moreover, we should not forget that Taft believed his judicial reforms would actually advance social reforms, most notably by making access to the courts of justice more affordable for poor litigants. Thus, even as he advanced efficiency-based reforms, he also recognized that these efforts promoted social progress.[34]

In contrast to more radical progressives who distrusted the courts, Taft pointed to the critical role played by the Court in protecting the inalienable rights of individuals, rich and poor alike. However, he also recognized the legitimacy of many progressive complaints against the courts, and sought to provide remedies for these concerns without damaging the federal judiciary. He believed that much of the anger against the federal judiciary arose not because the courts had struck down unconstitutional laws, but because they were inefficient and failed to treat poor litigants fairly. Thus, where many progressives argued that the judges were unelected, life-tenured defenders of wealth and property, Taft sought to reform the courts so as to protect the poor against moneyed interests. He hoped that by "promoting dispatch in the disposition of litigation and reducing the cost thereof to the poor litigant" he could help to remedy "the only real arguments that they [radical progressives] have against our judicial system," and to legitimize and strengthen the federal judiciary. He worked by traditional constitutional means to achieve the ends sought by progressives.[35]

Even before he became chief justice, Taft had argued that the greatest defect of the national government was its "failure to secure expedition and thoroughness in the enforcement of public and private rights in our courts." Because the judicial machinery was "slow and expensive," it often failed to secure speedy justice and undermined the public's faith in the courts, the justice of the laws, and ultimately the Constitution itself. Additionally, the slowness of the judicial system did not harm all litigants

CHIEF JUSTICE AS CHIEF EXECUTIVE | 173

equally. Instead, inefficient courts often helped the rich at the expense of the poor, as delays provided "a great advantage for that litigant who has the longest purse. . . . The wealthy defendant can almost always secure a compromise . . . because of the necessities of the poor plaintiff." In his efforts to ensure justice for all, Taft showed his agreement with concerns Woodrow Wilson had espoused in *Constitutional Government* when Wilson acknowledged that "the average integrity of the American bench is extraordinarily high." But Wilson worried, "Are not poor men in fact excluded from our courts by the cost and length of their processes?" Taft believed that it was his duty to alleviate this "unequal burden" by reducing the "delays and expense of litigation."[36]

By creating true intermediate courts of appeal and limiting the Supreme Court's mandatory jurisdiction, the Judges' Bill had reduced the costs of litigation by ensuring that most cases were appealed no more than once: from a district to a circuit court. Theoretically, guaranteeing poor litigants as many appeals as possible would seem to be both just and prudent. But Taft argued that in practice, a right of appeal through numerous courts typically allowed a rich litigant, whether an individual or a corporation, "to hold these [poorer] litigants off from what is their just due by a lawsuit for . . . a period [of several years], with all the legal expenses incident" to a lengthy legal battle. By limiting the number of possible appeals in most cases, the 1925 bill promoted a less expensive process and protected the poorer party.[37]

Similarly, Taft's plans for reforming and simplifying the federal judiciary's antiquated system of procedure would have reduced the expense of litigation. Under the Conformity Act of 1872, Congress required federal district and circuit courts to adopt state rules of procedure for all civil cases at common law, effectively requiring the judiciary to use four dozen systems of procedure. Taft believed that, just as the Supreme Court was authorized to make rules for equity and admiralty, Congress ought to delegate rulemaking for procedures at common law to the judiciary. His efforts were stymied by legislative inaction, but the reforms he championed would be achieved a decade later when Congress delegated rulemaking power to the Court and approved the Federal Rules of Civil Procedure.

Additionally, Taft worked to decrease the direct costs of litigation in a number of small ways. As he wrote to Brandeis, "I am itching to reduce expenses to the litigants in our Court." During his tenure, he cut the Court's printing costs almost in half. Having long believed that employing court officials on a fee-based income unduly raised costs for litigants, he shifted the Supreme Court's clerk to a fixed salary. And, in response to a plea from a defense lawyer, Taft convinced the administration and Congress to guarantee a criminal defendant a free copy of his indictment, ensuring the accused would not have to pay to access his own court records.[38]

The Taft Court also began to expand federal protections of individual rights. Modern commentators have criticized Taft as a reactionary for his votes in free speech cases such as *Gitlow v. New York* and for his majority opinion in the search and seizure case *Olmstead v. United States.* Regardless of one's view of the correctness of those decisions, it is worth recalling that Taft knew his judicial reforms would strengthen the Court's ability to protect individual rights. The Judges' Bill freed the Court to give appropriate attention to "genuine issues of constitutional right of individuals" and thereby expanded the national government's role in protecting rights against state action. For Taft, this was a critical part of the judiciary's duty. He fiercely opposed efforts to restrict the federal judiciary's jurisdiction over claims of federal rights because he believed that such limitations would unduly weaken the Court; however, he also recognized that for southern Blacks, such restrictions would mean "a practical deprivation" of their "Federal rights and protection"; the Court's jurisdiction, he insisted, helped avoid such "injustice due to sectional prejudice."[39]

Moreover, the Judges' Bill allowed the Supreme Court to begin the process of incorporating the Bill of Rights through the Fourteenth Amendment's due process clause. In his *Popular Government* (1913), Taft wrote that the Fourteenth Amendment "vests in the National Government the power and duty to protect, against the aggression of a State, every person within the jurisdiction of the United States in most of the personal rights, violation of which by Congress is forbidden in the first eight amendments to the Constitution."[40] A dozen years later, the passage of the Judges' Bill coincided with the beginning of the process of incorporation; it was enacted in 1925, the same year the Court handed down its first incorporation case, *Gitlow v. New York.* As chief justice, Taft was a part of the *Gitlow* majority, and also supported the Court's decisions in *Meyer v. Nebraska* and *Pierce v. Society of Sisters.*[41] By convincing Congress to free the Court from the burden of hearing trivial appeals, he ensured the high court could turn its attention to the protection of national rights through the process of incorporation.[42]

Clearly, Taft's efforts as chief justice reveal his desire to promote efficiency and speed in the federal courts. Further, his own testimony suggests that he was interested in encouraging social reform as well as efficiency-based reform. By reducing expenses and simplifying procedures, he showed that the Constitution and the federal courts created under it could continue to function justly and fairly even as the country developed. His work aligned with progressive goals, but he pursued those goals by conservative means and worked within the existing constitutional system while avoiding more radical measures that might have destroyed the judiciary's authority.

The Legacy of the Taft Court

In an era of change and reform, the Court's function would inevitably have been altered. Had Taft appointed Hughes chief justice in 1910, rather than elevating Edward D. White to the center seat, reform might have come sooner. On the other hand, it is impossible to say how the Court's role would have developed. Reforms may have been inevitable, but the specific reforms Taft achieved were hardly certain. Taft entered office with a distinct political program he convinced Congress to enact within four years of his ascent to the center seat; the reform bills of 1922 and 1925 owed their passage largely to his efforts. Indeed, Alpheus Mason argues that "as a judicial architect, Taft is without peer," since even Hughes built upon the foundation laid by Taft.[43]

Kenneth Starr has argued that Taft's efforts helped to maintain the constitutional system of separation of powers by making the Court sufficiently "strong and independent . . . [to] fulfill its constitutional purpose." Taft faced no easy task, for at the time he assumed the bench "the federal courts were perilously close to abdicating their role." By expanding the role of the chief justice and making the Supreme Court a true court of final appeal, Taft helped to strengthen the judiciary and made it a fully coequal branch of the national government. As Allen Ragan observed, if Taft was conservative in his desire for slow, steady reform in many areas, he was a "decided liberal" in the realm of judicial reform, "if not a confirmed radical." By working to respond to reasonable complaints about excessive costs and inefficiency, Taft demonstrated that the courts and the constitutional system of separation of powers could be maintained alongside progressive change. In effect, by making the administration of justice more just, Taft hoped to prove to the nation that the Constitution, and the Courts created by Article III, were worthy of being maintained.[44]

Conclusion

This book complicates a traditional narrative that has emphasized Taft's devotion to law and the Constitution at the expense of his progressivism. For decades, scholars have largely followed the model of Henry Pringle's *Life and Times of William Howard Taft* (1939) and argued that Taft's "judicial temperament" and adherence to the Constitution made him a weak president and an intransigent chief justice who actively worked to retard the pace of progressive reform. Political scientists Peri Arnold and Donald Anderson, for their part, have claimed Taft had no firm commitment to constitutional orthodoxy, and instead emphasized the temperamental critique, explaining that Taft's political education as an administrator and judge rendered him an inept political actor whose legalistic tendencies and political errors undermined and weakened the reform movement. Although a few revisionist studies have modified these assessments, the general understanding of Taft's political project remains largely consistent. It is claimed that because of his judicial attachment to law and his constitutional conservatism, Taft impeded progressive reform. The Constitution, impliedly, plays a negative role in the political life of the nation; it prevents change because its primary function is to hinder the use of government power.

I argue instead that we may understand Taft and his political project more fully by recognizing that Taft was seriously committed to both constitutionalism and progressivism. Not only did he believe the Constitution was not opposed to progressive policy initiatives, but he also showed how conservative constitutionalism could actually buttress and strengthen progressive reforms. Taft recognized that the Constitution does impose limits on government, but he demonstrated that it could play a positive and constructive role in American political life by empowering the government to act and by undergirding and protecting the reform legislation the government implemented. Moreover, he recognized that if the Constitution could come to the aid of progressivism, political reform might also redound to the benefit of the Constitution by showing its continued relevance and workability in modern America. Rather than being diametrically opposed, Taft's progressive policies and constitutional principles formed a coherent political project.

Taft's career helps to display the complexity and breadth of the Progressive movement. Numerous factions of the larger movement can easily be identified: progressives who emphasized the need for reform to eliminate poverty, protect labor, preserve and manage natural resources, improve education, root out corruption in government, encourage efficiency and administrative expertise, or promote morality. These reformers were variously motivated by religion, hope in the progressive improvement of the species, or empathy for those who had been harmed or left behind by rapidly changing circumstances. They were united by their belief that the Industrial Revolution had resulted in tremendous social and economic problems and that these new challenges should be addressed and ameliorated through government action.

These complexities help us to recognize Taft's progressive credentials. Taft was a genuine progressive, but he melded his progressivism with his constitutionalism. He was therefore both a progressive and an opponent of radicals, such as Herbert Croly, who believed that social reform demanded institutional transformation and a radical break from traditional constitutionalism. Taft is the prime example of constitutional progressivism; he and his allies supported significant policy changes, but balked at the idea of constitutional transformation. Charles Evans Hughes and Elihu Root are other notable proponents of a brand of progressivism that is liberal in its policy priorities but conservative in its constitutionalism. During the Progressive Era, both called for expanded government action to improve public morals and public health, reduce the power of trusts, protect labor, and encourage public service. At the same time, they defended the traditional Constitution.[1]

Although Taft's efforts to promote significant policy-level reforms demonstrate his progressivism, his major contribution to American political thought is his understanding of the Constitution as a fundamental law, not a policy-oriented document. Taft's constitutionalism is remarkable because his principles seem foreign to modern legal discourse. In many ways, Taft can be thought of as an originalist, yet his originalism was marked by a belief in robust national powers. Describing executive power in words he could easily have used to characterize the powers of the entire national government, he insisted that the Constitution grants "wide powers, not rigidly limited."[2] Taft recognized that the Constitution did limit government powers, yet he argued that the fundamental law's primary function was to create and empower the national government, not to restrict its actions.

In this way, Taft differs from many modern originalists insofar as he argued that the Constitution is primarily permissive, not restrictive. Today's originalists often appeal to the ideals of the founding era to argue that the Constitution created unyielding restrictions on the national government's powers in order to preserve individual rights and state power. In contrast, Taft pointed out that the Constitution was constructed as a replacement for the disastrously weak system created by the Articles of Confederation. Taft argued that the Constitution was not implemented in order to protect the states from the central government, but to empower a strong, workable national government and to replace the confederated system with a truly united nation.[3]

Taft's constitutionalism allowed him to argue that the Constitution may be the instrument by which progressive reform is furthered. Yet it is notable that Taft respected the Constitution's limits and disdained those who attempted to tear down or disregard the restrictive elements of the Constitution. He recognized that the Constitution may sometimes slow the pace of progress or even inhibit government action, but he also believed that its limits and restrictions must be respected if reform is to be permanent and stable. Initiatives accomplished through constitutional means will be undergirded and maintained by the fundamental law. He reminds us that without the protection of the Constitution, even beneficial and humane policy reforms may be fleeting.

Of course, Taft's understanding of the Constitution did not permit any and all progressive reform efforts. He did recognize the basic restraints contained in the Constitution: the system of checks and balances, limits on national authority, and restrictions on government action in order to protect individual rights. Despite this, he believed that in the constitutional scheme, powers were essential and primary while restrictions on their use were secondary. In Taft's understanding of constitutional history, John Marshall and Alexander Hamilton were the heroes for their articulation of expansive national powers, and Thomas Jefferson and John C. Calhoun—whom he happily lumped together—were cast as the villains for their stringent interpretation of the Constitution.[4]

For all this, it is necessary to acknowledge the limitations of Taft's constitutionalism before concluding this study. Taft was not always true to his own method of interpreting the Constitution. For example, he believed in the nondelegation doctrine, which bars Congress from delegating legislative power to administrative agencies, but he also suggested that he was willing to abandon it—or at least significantly weaken it—in some narrow instances when its constraints became too inconvenient.[5] Similarly, his 1912 decision to send military supplies to the Mississippi valley in response to flooding, in the absence of congressional appropriations, stood in clear violation of his understanding of the constitutional system of separation of powers. Taft usually adhered to his own constitutional standards, but in a few cases, he was willing to bend the rules for the sake of political expediency.

Regardless, neither his belief in constitutional constraints on governmental action nor his occasional inconsistencies undermine Taft's belief in a strong national government that is both empowered and limited by the Constitution. In fact, Taft's vision of constitutional power was more expansive than that propounded by his opponents on both ends of the political spectrum. It is not surprising that the strict constructionists on the right disagreed with his arguments since they believed the Constitution imposed exacting limitations on the national government. But ironically, many radical progressives actually seem to have agreed with a version of this conservative viewpoint, for the strict constructionists had so successfully used their stringent constitutional interpretation to block progressive reforms that some radical progressives had given up on the Constitution. Having been so often frustrated by restrictive court opinions of the stripe of *E. C. Knight* and *Lochner*, some progressives had evidently come to believe that the strictures of the Constitution were as rigid as their conservative opponents claimed. When Herbert Croly called for the creation of a "new order" and Roosevelt insisted that constitutional structures must be weakened to make way for "pure democracy," both seemed to tacitly accept the strict constructionist viewpoint, seeing in it evidence that the Constitution was outdated, unsuited to the twentieth century, and in need of fundamental transformation.

As a result of this surprising agreement, both strict constructionists and radical progressives propounded an understanding of the Constitution that was, to Taft's mind, deeply flawed. They ultimately saw the fundamental law as brittle and time-bound, neither open to change nor capable of developing in the face of changing circumstances. Some conservatives, because of their desire to hinder change, along with many radical progressives, out of their frustration with the Constitution's restraints, essentially agreed that the Constitution was a restrictive document written to enact only policies appropriate to the eighteenth and nineteenth centuries. The major distinction between the groups, as a result, was that conservatives typically appreciated these older policies and held on to the Constitution as a permanent bulwark against change, while the radicals called for constitutional transformation in order to facilitate reform.

In this way, both sides risked subverting the fundamental law by treating the Constitution as little more than a servant of their favored policies. At least some conservatives adhered to their view of the Constitution because it mandated their policies and no others, while many radical progressives attacked the strictures of the Constitution precisely because they feared it would prevent their policies from being enacted. Their attachment to or rejection of the Constitution, as a result, appeared to depend largely on the fundamental law's ability to demand or permit their policy priorities. Both sides debased the Constitution to the extent that they failed to recognize its character as a fundamental law.

In contrast, Taft recognized that the Constitution transcended contemporary policy conflicts and played a foundational role in political life. To his mind, the Constitution was not an instrument by which factions or parties could mandate or forbid certain policies. Instead, it was a fundamental law that conceived a nation, created the government's essential institutional structures, and constructed a means by which individual rights could be protected. It devised and empowered a government capable of serving the people of the United States, a government that could develop and adapt as conditions changed. Taft's constitutionalism, as a result, was nonpartisan, for it was not implicated in or subservient to any set of policies. By showing that the Constitution transcended mere policy disputes, Taft offered a vision that allows us to appreciate the Constitution's potential to survive across time and be open to change without itself changing or losing its integrity as a fundamental law.

Taft's constitutional progressivism may speak to modern debates over constitutional interpretation and constitutional change. A century later, little has changed in the realm of constitutional interpretation. Today, as at the beginning of the twentieth century, both conservatives and liberals too often focus narrowly on the limitations of the written

Constitution and too frequently succumb to the temptation to use it as a weapon by which their policies may be mandated and their opponents' policies forbidden. These views not only misunderstand the Constitution's empowering function, but undermine its foundational place in the American regime, since they degrade it from its status as a fundamental law and instead treat it as a tool to be used to win victories at the level of public policy.

Contemporary liberals tend to adhere to a modern version of Croly's call for constitutional transformation, adopting either a notion of a "living Constitution" or a more radical constructivism. Living constitutionalism, as David Strauss has defined it, is "the view that what the Constitution requires changes over time, even if the document is not formally amended." Strauss admits that the Constitution "is a fixed point of our constitutional system" whose "text cannot be ignored," but he also argues that the text of the Constitution is primarily helpful "in noncontroversial areas." Thus, the Constitution is useful because it creates structures of government, but its text can only partially resolve our most important and controversial political disputes. Essentially, living constitutionalists recognize that the Constitution imposes a certain framework and a structure within which political decisions must be made, but they also seek to move beyond the text of the document in order to allow American experience and culture to alter the meaning of the Constitution. The actual text of the Constitution becomes less useful over time, since the document's meaning must be updated by political and judicial precedents—court opinions, statutes, customs, "trends in society"—and more general "judgments of fairness and good policy." In *America's Unwritten Constitution* (2012), Akhil Amar makes a similar argument, looking beyond the formal amendment process to more subtle ways of altering the Constitution's meaning. Amar argues that vague words in the Constitution—such as "equal," "unreasonable," and "unusual"—should be "read idealistically," for they are "brilliantly designed to keep the American Constitution in touch with the American people even in the absence of formal Article V amendments." As Strauss's reference to "good policy" concedes and Amar implies, the Constitution must be made useful by transforming it to fit modern policy priorities.[6]

But the more extreme form, toward which "living constitutionalism" often trends, is a call for outright transformation of the Constitution's meaning. Constructivism, which James Fleming has appropriately titled a "Constitution-perfecting theory," would allow each generation to reinterpret the Constitution to align with contemporary values. Ronald Dworkin, constructivism's foremost proponent, argues that judges should take the old "concepts" of liberty, equality, or freedom contained in the Constitution and update them to fit modern "conceptions" of fairness and justice. Because future generations should be faithful to the concepts—but not the conceptions—underlying the Constitution, political actors are charged with making the Constitution the best it can be, according to their own ideas of equality and justice. They are to fuse constitutional law with moral philosophy and improve the nation to the extent of their ability. Ultimately, Dworkin's theory is so broad that it destroys any real limits on government action, for it sees the Constitution as embodying little more than vague moral principles that should lead us to support whatever justice-, equality-, and freedom-promoting policies are (for the moment) fashionable.[7]

Opposing these liberal constitutional theorists are originalists who insist that the Constitution must be interpreted as it was understood at the time of its drafting. As Justice Antonin Scalia wrote—commenting on Taft's approach in *Myers*—originalists interpret the Constitution in light of its text, its structure, and "the contemporaneous understanding of the [Constitution] . . . (particularly the understanding of the First Congress and of the leading participants in the Constitutional Convention), the background understanding . . . [from] the English constitution, and . . . [practices from] the various state constitutions in existence when the federal Constitution was adopted." Originalists, Randy Barnett has argued in *Restoring the Lost Constitution*, look to the original public meaning of the Constitution and consider "the public meaning of the words of the Constitution, as understood by the ratifying conventions and the general public." The Constitution's words, both the original Constitution of 1787 and its various amendments, must be read as they were understood at the time of the drafting. This may be achieved through reliance on period dictionaries and consideration of the historical context in which the text was written.[8]

Broadly speaking, Taft concurred with much of this interpretive approach, as his *Myers* opinion makes clear. However, Taft departed from some modern originalists when he demanded that the Constitution's grants of power should receive a "liberal construction." This insistence rests on his belief that the Constitution, as a fundamental law, contains provisions that are "necessarily incomplete or lacking in detail." One suspects he would have agreed with Marshall's famous dicta in *McCulloch*,

"We must never forget that it is a *Constitution* we are expounding." Taft believed the Constitution's sometimes spare text needed to be construed and interpreted in light of the necessities of government. He called on the federal courts to recognize that the Constitution's strictures were sufficiently "elastic" to "permit a construction" that would allow the fundamental law to remain relevant and "conform to the growth and necessities of the country." Again, one is reminded of Marshall's argument, construing legislative powers through the necessary and proper clause, that we have "a Constitution intended to endure for ages to come, and consequently to be adapted to the various crises of human affairs." Taft insisted that the nation needed no new interpretation of the Constitution of 1787; when interpreting the fundamental law, the Supreme Court never "varies or amends the Constitution," but it may legitimately recognize "new applications" of government power to modern circumstances. It was not the Constitution that developed, but the country. Similarly, although the fundamental law did not change, save through the formal amendment process, the government it created might adapt and grow over time. The Constitution did not change, but it was open to changing circumstances. Taft's strong nationalism and his belief in the elasticity of the Constitution's text distinguishes him from many modern originalists.[9]

The attraction of Taft's version of originalism is that it recognized the fundamental law as timeless and permissive, rather than time-bound and restrictive, and thereby rejected the temptation to break down distinctions between constitutional interpretation and policy preferences. Taft offered a vision of a fundamental law that has legitimacy in part because it is not tied to the policy priorities of any faction or party. Instead, he offered a principled understanding of our fundamental law, which permits the Constitution to maintain its integrity even as the government created by the Constitution may develop and change to respond to new challenges. Taft's approach not only rejected the living constitutionalism or constructivism that ultimately subverts the Constitution, but may also offer a corrective to those originalists who succumb to the temptation to see the Constitution as a policy document, not a fundamental law.

In this context, Barnett's *Restoring the Lost Constitution* is singularly useful, for it shows the extent to which Barnett's method of constitutional interpretation is tied up with his libertarian sympathies. He proposes a set of constitutional amendments that would, he hopes, restore the "lost" Constitution. He suggests placing more explicit restrictions on Congress's power to regulate interstate commerce, limiting the treaty power to matters clearly within the realm of national authority, and prohibiting the Supreme Court from altering the Constitution's meaning by appealing to the law of nations or the laws of foreign countries. One may disagree with any of these proposals, but they are all consistent with his general argument: that the national government has expanded its own powers far beyond the intent of the framers. Yet some of his proposals focus less on constitutional principles than on libertarian policy preferences. He would require a three-fifths vote in both houses of Congress to pass a tax increase, impose term limits on members of Congress, and create a formal process by which the states may repeal federal laws. Most notably, he would repeal the Sixteenth Amendment and prohibit income taxes, permitting instead an uniform sales tax and essentially forcing Congress to fund the government through the "fair tax." Barnett correctly argues out that the Sixteenth Amendment eliminated key "structural obstacles to the growth of national power" and "altered the federal system," before pointing out that it permits a form of taxation that "many advocates of liberty think . . . is theft." If Amar would permit unofficial amendments outside the formal process of Article V in order to achieve liberal results, Barnett indicates that the Sixteenth Amendment—which he concedes is "constitutionally authorized"— is somehow illegitimate and must be repealed in order to restore the orthodoxy enshrined in the "lost Constitution." The Constitution, were it interpreted and amended as Barnett wishes, would be demoted to the level of a policy document, mandating many libertarian policies and banning most progressive policies.[10]

Despite varied methods and goals, the proponents of these diverse modes of interpretation too often succumb to the same failures as the reactionaries and radicals of Taft's day. They do not seem to believe, as Taft did, that the Constitution may remain stable and maintain its integrity while at the same time being able to cope with modern circumstances and emerging challenges. For some conservative originalists, the Constitution's grants of power are so limited that it has become stagnant and tied down to the policies in vogue in the early republic. For many liberals, the Constitution's restrictions are so rigid and problematic that they must be circumvented in order to advance modern "conceptions" of justice and equality. In an odd way, a form of rigid originalism may have won, for even many liberal constitutional theorists seem to implicitly concede that the Constitution of 1787 is utterly inflexible.

Taft offers a viable and principled alternative to these schools of political thought, for he shows that the Constitution is neither organic and "living" nor left in the grip of the eighteenth century. Taft, were he alive today, would almost certainly have sympathized with Scalia's definition of originalism, yet his understanding of the Constitution's meaning was vastly different from that proposed by many modern originalists. Taft recognized the Constitution for what it was: a replacement for the stilted Articles of Confederation that created a strong and energetic national government. He consistently adopted a "liberal construction" of national powers, praising Marshall's extensive efforts to protect the nascent powers of United States against those who would have undermined the Constitution and the government it created. Contrary to his reputation as a formalist, Taft argued that the Marshall Court had done good service in "exalting and broadening the national sovereignty and minimizing the power of the states." Taft may fairly be considered an originalist, but his originalism was colored by his nationalism and his belief that the Constitution's grants of power were far more important than the limitations it imposed on the use of that power.[11]

Taft's understanding of the Constitution asks us to recognize its fundamental character and invites us to transcend partisan policy disputes as we seek to understand its implications. By granting the national government expansive powers, the Constitution created a government capable of enacting policies suited to 1787, to 1912, and even to today. It permits a vast array of policies without demanding we accept either Barnett's libertarianism or Dworkin's understanding of fairness. Neither, however, does the Constitution forbid most policies. With exceptions to protect individual rights and federalism, it would permit the government to adopt either libertarian policies or to promote modern liberal conceptions of fairness and justice through liberal public policies. We might say that Taft believed that the Constitution is not "living" in an organic sense, for it does not grow and change, but he also recognized that it is capable of surviving over the centuries. It remains stable without crippling the government or preventing it from responding to sometimes radically unstable circumstances. Taft recognized the need to both maintain the integrity of the Constitution as a fundamental law and show its openness to change.

Through his pointed critique, Taft offered political wisdom that may be attractive to liberals and conservatives alike. By showing the Constitution's openness to change and its ability to survive in the modern world, Taft articulated a nationalist understanding of the fundamental law and showed its ability to permit and strengthen progressive reform. At the same time, he did recognize the limitations imposed by the Constitution. As his efforts to legalize Roosevelt's reforms demonstrate, the Constitution demands method and regularity; it requires the government to work through set channels and eschews informal and unilateral action. Taft managed to show that the Constitution could permit reform while also maintaining principles of constitutional restraint that guide and direct reform through regular processes. If Taft's progressive policies showed the Constitution's continued relevance and viability, his conservative restraint helped to protect the integrity of the fundamental law.

Notes

Preface

1. Mark Carnes, "William Howard Taft," in *To the Best of My Ability: The American Presidents,* ed. James McPherson (New York: Dorling Kindersley Limited, 2004), 194.
2. Irwin Hood Hoover, *Forty-Two Years in the White House* (Boston: Houghton Mifflin Co., 1934), 111.
3. "Taft Causes Hotel Deluge," *New York Times,* June 19, 1915.

Introduction

1. Enclosure (draft letter to Charles Hammond), Taft to Rudolph Forster (May 12, 1912), William Howard Taft Papers, Manuscript Division, Library of Congress; William Howard Taft, "Speech of William Howard Taft: Accepting the Republican Nomination for President of the United States," S. Doc. 902, 62nd Congress, 2nd Session (1912), 5–6; Theodore Roosevelt, "Who Is a Progressive?" *Outlook* 100 (April 1912): 809; Theodore Roosevelt, "A Short Political Creed," *Outlook* 100 (March 1912): 721.
2. Lewis Gould, *Four Hats in the Ring: The 1912 Election and the Birth of Modern American Politics* (Lawrence: University Press of Kansas, 2008), 7.
3. Taft, "Speech Accepting the Nomination," 6; George Kibbe Turner, "How Taft Views His Own Administration: An Interview with the President," *McClure's Magazine* 35 (January 1910): 221; Taft, "Address of Hon. William H. Taft, President of the United States. Delivered in Boston, Mass. Thursday, April 25, 1912," S. Doc. No. 615, 62nd Congress, 2nd Session (1912), 4–5.
4. Statement of President Taft to Harry Dunlap of the *New York World* (November 14, 1912); Taft to J. Warren Keifer (June 28, 1912), Taft Papers (emphasis added).
5. Antonin Scalia, "Originalism: The Lesser Evil," *Cincinnati Law Review* 57 (1989): 851–852; Taft to Elihu Root (December 21, 1922), Taft Papers. For Taft's interpretive approach, see Myers v. United States, 272 U.S. 52 (1926), 110–115, 120–122, 136, 174–175; Taft to Pierce Butler (January 7, 1929), Taft Papers.

6. William Howard Taft, *The Collected Works of William Howard Taft*, ed. David Burton (Athens: Ohio University Press, 2001–2004), 3:282–283.

7. Peri Arnold, *Remaking the Presidency: Roosevelt, Taft, and Wilson, 1901–1916* (Lawrence: University Press of Kansas, 2009), 71.

8. Henry Pringle, *The Life and Times of William Howard Taft* (New York: Farrar & Rinehart, 1939), 1:129, 416, 483.

9. Alpheus Thomas Mason, *William Howard Taft: Chief Justice* (New York: Simon & Schuster, 1964), 303.

10. Paolo Coletta, *The Presidency of William Howard Taft* (Lawrence: University Press of Kansas, 1973), 12, 27, 48.

11. Lewis Gould, *The William Howard Taft Presidency* (Lawrence: University Press of Kansas, 2009), xi, 45, 66, 199. See also Gould, *Four Hats in the Ring*; Lewis Gould, *Chief Executive to Chief Justice: Taft betwixt the White House and Supreme Court* (Lawrence: University Press of Kansas, 2013).

12. Jeffrey Rosen, *William Howard Taft* (New York: Times Books, 2018), 2, 68, 133.

13. Jonathan Lurie, *William Howard Taft: The Travails of a Progressive Conservative* (Cambridge: Cambridge University Press, 2012), 16, 143.

14. Jonathan Lurie, *The Chief Justiceship of William Howard Taft, 1921–1930* (Columbia: University of South Carolina Press, 2019), 185, 206, 225.

15. Donald Anderson, *William Howard Taft: A Conservative's Conception of the Presidency* (Ithaca, NY: Cornell University Press, 1973), 4, 296, 305 (emphasis added).

16. Arnold, *Remaking the Presidency*, 94, 96, 128.

17. Jonathan O'Neill, "William Howard Taft and the Constitutional Presidency in the Progressive Era," in *Progressive Challenges to the American Constitution: A New Republic*, ed. Bradley C. S. Watson (New York: Cambridge University Press, 2017), 197.

18. Sidney Milkis, "William Howard Taft and the Struggle for the Soul of the Constitution," in *Toward an American Conservatism: Constitutional Conservatism during the Progressive Era*, ed. Joseph Postell and Jonathan O'Neill (New York: Palgrave Macmillan, 2013), 64–65, 70; see also Sidney Milkis, *Theodore Roosevelt, the Progressive Party, and the Transformation of American Democracy* (Lawrence: University Press of Kansas, 2009), 86–91, 107–122.

19. Taft to William Allen White (February 26, 1908), Taft Papers; Lurie, *Progressive Conservative*, 11; Pringle, *Life and Times*, 1:62–63.

20. Joseph Foraker to Taft (April 3, 1888), Taft Papers; Pringle, *Life and Times*, 1:95.

21. Herbert Duffy, *William Howard Taft* (New York: Minton, Balch, & Co., 1930), 24; Lurie, *Progressive Conservative*, 24–25.

22. Oscar King Davis, *William Howard Taft: The Man of the Hour* (Philadelphia: P. W. Ziegler Co., 1908), 98 (quote), 78; Lurie, *Progressive Conservative*, 29–30, 37.

23. Helen Herron Taft, *Recollections of Full Years* (New York: Dodd, Mead & Co., 1914), 35; Ralph Eldin Minger, *William Howard Taft and United States Foreign Policy: The Apprenticeship Years, 1900–1908* (Urbana: University of Illinois Press, 1975), 4–6, 21; Lurie, *Progressive Conservative*, 41; Gould, *Taft Presidency*, 4.

24. Davis, *Man of the Hour*, 128–130, 137–142; Lurie, *Progressive Conservative*, 42–52; Helen Taft, *Recollections*, 267–269.

25. Gould, *Taft Presidency*, 4; Pringle, *Life and Times*, 1:268; "President off to Hunt," *New York Times*, April 4, 1905.

26. Taft, *Collected Works*, 1:200, 289; 3:163; 5:34; 8:9, 14; Taft, "Statement of President Taft in Cincinnati" (November 5, 1912); Taft to Charles Nagel (October 11, 1910), Taft Papers.

27. Milkis, *Transformation of American Democracy*, 47.

28. Herbert Croly, *The Promise of American Life* (Princeton, NJ: Princeton University Press, 2014), 169; Herbert Croly, *Progressive Democracy* (New Brunswick, NJ: Transaction Publishers, 2009), 2, 14, 19, 332 (emphasis added).

29. Arthur M. Schlesinger Jr., ed., *History of American Presidential Elections: 1789–1968* (New York: Chelsea House Publishers, 1971), 3:2186–2187; Milkis, *Transformation of American Democracy*, 156–157.

30. Theodore Roosevelt, *The Works of Theodore Roosevelt: National Edition* (New York: Charles Scribner's Sons, 1926), 17:119–120, 123; "Roosevelt Favors Recall of President," *New York Times*, September 20, 1912.

31. Milkis, "Struggle for the Soul of the Constitution," 76–77.

32. Taft, *Collected Works*, 5:17, 21–22, 36–38 (emphasis added).

33. William Howard Taft, *Our Chief Magistrate and His Powers* (Durham, NC: Carolina Academic Press, 2002), 12–13; Turner, "Taft Views," 211; Taft, "The Administration of Justice—Its Speeding and Cheapening," *Central Law Journal* 72, no. 11 (1911): 193; Taft, *Collected Works*, 1:297; 5:116; 8:4.

34. Taft, *Collected Works*, 5:87, 89, 136.

35. Taft, *Collected Works*, 5:92–93 (emphasis added). For the observation on the Constitution's potential, I am indebted to David Nichols, *The Myth of the Modern Presidency* (University Park: Pennsylvania State University Press, 1994), 31.

36. Taft, "Speech Accepting the Nomination," 11; Taft, *Collected Works*, 3:31–32; Woodrow Wilson, *Constitutional Government* (New York: Columbia University Press, 1964), 192.

37. Taft, *Collected Works*, 4:151–152 (emphasis added); 3:265.

38. Taft, *Collected Works*, 1:10, 2:9; Taft, "The Attacks on the Courts and Legal Procedure," *Kentucky Law Journal* 5, no. 2 (1916): 24.

Chapter 1. "Maintenance and Enforcement"

1. Arthur M. Schlesinger Jr., ed., *History of American Presidential Elections: 1789–1968* (New York: Chelsea House Publishers, 1971), 3:2102 (quote), 2053, 2055, 2058; William Howard Taft, *The Collected Works of William Howard Taft*, ed. David Burton (Athens: Ohio University Press, 2001–2004), 3:44; "Bryan Concludes Platform Attack," *New York Times*, June 24, 1908.

2. Taft, *Collected Works*, 3:6–7.

3. Taft to William Nelson (February 23, 1909), William Howard Taft Papers, Manuscript Division, Library of Congress (emphasis added); "Taft Is Sworn in Senate Hall," *New York Times*, March 5, 1909; Archibald Butt, *The Letters of Archie Butt: Personal Aide to President Roosevelt* (Garden City, NY: Doubleday, Page, & Co., 1924), 283.

4. Archibald Butt, *Taft and Roosevelt: The Intimate Letters of Archie Butt, Military Aide* (Garden City, NY: Doubleday, Doran & Company, Inc., 1930), 2:593; Taft to Horace Taft (June 6, 1909), Taft Papers.

5. Stephen Skowronek, *The Politics Presidents Make* (Cambridge, MA: Belknap Press of Harvard University Press, 1997), 41, 228–229.

6. "President Taft," *New York Times*, March 5, 1909; see also "Taft a 'Safer' President," *New York Times*, March 5, 1909.

7. Donald Anderson, *William Howard Taft: A Conservative's Conception of the Presidency* (Ithaca, NY: Cornell University Press, 1973), 230–231; Paolo Coletta, *The Presidency of William Howard Taft* (Lawrence: University Press of Kansas, 1973), 98–100.

8. Sidney Milkis, "William Howard Taft and the Struggle for the Soul of the Constitution," in *Toward an American Conservatism: Constitutional Conservatism during the Progressive Era*, ed. Joseph Postell and Jonathan O'Neill (New York: Palgrave Macmillan, 2013), 70; Jonathan O'Neill, "William Howard Taft and the Constitutional Presidency in the Progressive Era," in *Progressive Challenges to the American Constitution: A New Republic*, ed. Bradley C. S. Watson (New York: Cambridge University Press, 2017), 205–208; Jonathan Lurie, *William Howard Taft: The Travails of Progressive Conservative* (Cambridge: Cambridge University Press, 2012), 108–109.

9. Peri Arnold, *Remaking the Presidency: Roosevelt, Taft, and Wilson, 1901–1916* (Lawrence: University Press of Kansas, 2009), 117–118; James Penick, "The Age of the Bureaucrat: Another View of the Ballinger–Pinchot Controversy," *Forest History Newsletter* 7, no. 1/2 (1963): 16.

10. James Penick, *Progressive Politics and Conservation* (Chicago: University of Chicago Press, 1968), 10 (quote), 42–46; Penick, "Age of the Bureaucrat," 19; Taft to Philander Knox (October 9, 1909), Taft Papers; Lewis Gould, ed., *My Dearest Nellie: The Letters of William Howard Taft to Helen Herron Taft, 1909–1912* (Lawrence: University Press of Kansas, 2011), 73.

11. An Act for the Relief of Settlers on Public Lands, 21 Stat. 140 (1880), 141.

12. Richard Ellis, *The Development of the American Presidency* (New York: Routledge, 2018), 276; Skowronek, *Politics Presidents Make*, 250.

13. Theodore Roosevelt, *An Autobiography* (New York: Charles Scribner's Sons, 1946), 363, 405–406; Garfield quoted in *Investigation of the Department of the Interior and of the Bureau of Forestry* (Washington, DC: Government Printing Office, 1911), 9:5322; Gifford Pinchot, *Breaking New Ground* (Washington, DC: Island Press, 1998), 389; Arnold, *Remaking the Presidency*, 120.

14. Ellis, *Development of the American Presidency*, 276.

15. Skowronek, *Politics Presidents Make*, 250; Milkis, "Struggle for the Soul of the Constitution," 70.

16. Taft to Gifford Pinchot (September 13, 1909), quoted in Coletta, *Presidency of Taft*, 89.

17. Max Ball, *Department of the Interior Bulletin 623: Petroleum Withdrawals and Restorations Affecting the Public Domain* (Washington, DC: Government Printing Office, 1916), 133–135.

18. Oscar Lawler, "Memorandum and Brief upon the Subject of the Power of the Executive to Make Withdrawals of Public Lands" (April 6, 1910); Richard Ballinger, "Speech at Providence, Rhode Island" (January 29, 1910), Taft Papers.

19. Ball, *Department of the Interior Bulletin 623*, 24, 135; for the text and extent of these orders, see 150–181.

20. Ball, *Department of the Interior Bulletin 623*, 135; Taft, *Collected Works*, 3:218–219.

21. Taft, *Collected Works*, 3:220.

22. Pickett Act, 36 Stat. 847 (1910), 847.

23. Pinchot, *Breaking New Ground*, 296; Henry Pringle, *The Life and Times of William Howard Taft* (New York: Farrar and Rinehart, Inc., 1939), 1:479; Coletta, *Presidency of Taft*, 88; "Taft Backs Up Pinchot," *New York Times*, March 17, 1909.

24. Lurie, *Progressive Conservative*, 109–111; Steven Skowronek, *Building a New American State: The Expansion of National Administrative Capacities, 1877–1920* (Cambridge: Cambridge University Press, 1982), 180, 190; Taft to George Wickersham (October 7, 1909), Taft Papers.

25. Anderson, *Conservative's Conception*, 76–77; Lewis Gould, *The William Howard Taft Presidency* (Lawrence: University Press of Kansas, 2009), 70, 73, 77–78.

26. Pinchot, *Breaking New Ground*, 450; Taft to Gifford Pinchot (January 7, 1910), Taft Papers.

27. Coletta, *Presidency of Taft*, 98; Taft, *Collected Works*, 4:85; "President Taft's Own View: An Authorized Interview by Francis E. Leupp," *Outlook* 99 (December 1911): 814; George Kibbe Turner, "How Taft Views His Own Administration: An Interview with the President," *McClure's Magazine* 35, no. 2 (1910): 218.

28. Lewis Gould, *The Presidency of Theodore Roosevelt* (Lawrence: University Press of Kansas, 2011), 210.

29. Anderson, *Conservative's Conception*, 78–81; Coletta, *Presidency of Taft*, 154, 160–165; Gould, *Taft Presidency*, 98, 164–165; Lurie, *Progressive Conservative*, 143–145.

30. Sherman Act, 26 Stat. 209 (1890), 209; James Richardson, ed., *A Compilation of the Messages and Papers of the Presidents, 1789–1908* (Washington, DC: Bureau of National Literature and Art, 1908), 11:1289; Theodore Roosevelt, "The Trusts, the People, and the Square Deal," *Outlook* 99 (December 1911): 656.

31. Gould, *Presidency of Roosevelt*, 208 (quote), 205–206, 208.

32. Gould, *Presidency of Roosevelt*, 208–209.

33. Taft, *Collected Works*, 4:168–171, 333–334; George Wickersham, "The Policies and the Record of the Taft Administration" (August 14, 1912), Taft Papers.

34. Anderson, *Conservative's Conception*, 63; Taft to Elbert F. Baldwin (December 24, 1908), quoted in Gould, *Taft Presidency*, 25; Coletta, *Presidency of Taft*, 255.

35. Taft, *Collected Works*, 3:45 (quote), 422–425; 4:170–171.

36. Roosevelt, *Autobiography*, 439, 442; Doris Kearns Goodwin, *The Bully Pulpit: Theodore Roosevelt, William Howard Taft, and the Golden Age of Journalism* (New York: Simon & Schuster, 2013), 529–530.

37. Roosevelt, *Autobiography*, 440; Gould, *Presidency of Roosevelt*, 240; Goodwin, *Bully Pulpit*, 529.

38. "The Progress of the World," *The American Review of Reviews* 44, no. 6 (December 1911): 658; Coletta, *Presidency of Taft*, 159.

39. Quoted in Goodwin, *Bully Pulpit*, 669; Donald Anderson, "Commentary," in Taft, *Collected Works*, 5:166.

40. Taft, *Collected Works*, 3:37–38; 4:168, 334; 5:217–231; Enclosure, Taft to J. C. Hemphill (May 19, 1911), Taft Papers.

41. Taft to Henry L. Higginson (September 8, 1911), quoted in Pringle, *Life and Times*, 2:655.

42. Taft, *Collected Works*, 3:135.

43. Roosevelt, "The Trusts, the People, and the Square Deal," 652.

44. Taft, *Collected Works*, 3:7.

Chapter 2. Party Leadership and Legislation

1. Taft to Herbert Hadley (February 23, 1909), quoted in Michael Bromley, *William Howard Taft and the First Motoring Presidency, 1909–1913* (Jefferson, NC: McFarland & Company, 2007), 29–30.

2. Sidney Milkis, *Theodore Roosevelt, the Progressive Party, and the Transformation of American Democracy* (Lawrence: University Press of Kansas, 2009), 3; William Howard Taft, *The Collected Works of William Howard Taft*, ed. David Burton (Athens: Ohio University Press, 2001–2004), 1:18, 281; 8:12.

3. Milkis, *Transformation of American Democracy*, 3–4; Taft, *Collected Works*, 1:282; 3:193.

4. Henry Pringle, *The Life and Times of William Howard Taft* (New York: Farrar and Rinehart, Inc., 1939), 1:428; Jeffrey Rosen, *William Howard Taft* (New York: Times Books, 2018), 3, 62.

5. William Howard Taft, *Our Chief Magistrate and His Powers* (Durham, NC: Carolina Academic Press, 2002), 14, 53; Taft, *Collected Works*, 1:55–56, 59.

6. Arthur M. Schlesinger Jr., ed., *History of American Presidential Elections: 1789–1968* (New York: Chelsea House Publishers, 1971), 3:2103–2104; "To Make Mistakes Is Human," *American Economist* 49, no. 1 (1912): 8.

7. Archibald Butt, *Taft and Roosevelt: The Intimate Letters of Archie Butt, Military Aide* (Garden City, NY: Doubleday, Doran & Company, Inc., 1930), 1:334.

8. Lewis Gould, *The William Howard Taft Presidency* (Lawrence: University Press of Kansas, 2009), 57–59, 92.

9. "Fight to Go on Monday," *New York Times*, March 14, 1909; Theodore Roosevelt to Taft (November 10, 1908), William Howard Taft Papers, Manuscript Division, Library of Congress; Taft to Sen. Joseph L. Bristow (December 5, 1908), quoted in Donald Anderson, *William Howard Taft: A Conservative's Conception of the Presidency* (Ithaca, NY: Cornell University Press, 1973), 101.

10. Taft to Elihu Root (November 25, 1908), Taft Papers; "Overtures to Taft Made by Speaker," *New York Times*, November 28, 1908; "Taft Would Avert Fight on Speaker," *New York Times*, March 10, 1909; Gould, *Taft Presidency*, 51–52.

11. James Tawney to Taft (November 25, 1908), Taft Papers; Gould, *Taft Presidency*, 52–53; Bromley, *Motoring Presidency*, 143; Paolo Coletta, *The Presidency of William Howard Taft* (Lawrence: University Press of Kansas, 1973), 62.

12. Coletta, *Presidency of Taft*, 62, 64, 66–67; Bromley, *Motoring Presidency*, 148, 151, 166.

13. Taft, *Collected Works*, 3:134; see also 1:215.

14. Butt, *Intimate Letters*, 1:124; Coletta, *Presidency of Taft*, 67.

15. Taft to Horace Taft (June 27, 1909), Taft Papers.

16. See George Wickersham to Taft (June 16, 1909); Frank Cole to Fred Carpenter (June 17, 1909); J. A. Fowler to Taft (June 17, 1909); George Wickersham to Taft (June 21, 1909); George Wickersham to Taft (June 23, 1909); Frank Cole to Fred Carpenter (June 24, 1909), Taft Papers.

17. Coletta, *Presidency of Taft*, 69; George Kibbe Turner, "How Taft Views His Own Administration: An Interview with the President," *McClure's Magazine* 35 (January 1910): 212; Taft, *Collected Works*, 3:242–243.

18. Taft to Nelson Aldrich (July 29, 1909), Taft Papers; Butt, *Intimate Letters*, 1:163; Gould, *Taft Presidency*, 58–60.

19. Taft to Horace Taft (June 27, 1909), Taft Papers; Turner, "Taft Views," 212–213; Taft, *Collected Works*, 3:169, 177; Lewis Gould, ed., *My Dearest Nellie: The Letters of William Howard Taft to Helen Herron Taft, 1909–1912* (Lawrence: University Press of Kansas, 2011), 61.

20. James Tawney to Taft (August 18, 1909), Taft Papers; Gould, *Taft Presidency*, 60–62.

21. Taft, *Collected Works*, 3:180, 182.

22. Gould, *Taft Presidency*, 63; Lewis Gould, *Four Hats in the Ring: The 1912 Election and the Birth of Modern American Politics* (Lawrence: University Press of Kansas, 2008), 12–13.

23. Taft, *Collected Works*, 4:106–109, 117–120; Coletta, *Presidency of Taft*, 144–151.

24. Gould, *Taft Presidency*, 51; Jonathan Lurie, *William Howard Taft: The Travails of a Progressive Conservative* (Cambridge: Cambridge University Press, 2012), 107–108.

25. Gwendolyn Mink, *Old Labor and New Immigrants in American Political Development* (Ithaca, NY: Cornell University Press, 1986), 210; Taft, *Collected Works*, 3:18, 54.

26. Hepburn Act, 34 Stat. 584 (1906), 584, 590; Taft, *Collected Works*, 2:45.

27. Taft, *Collected Works*, 3:408–409; George Wickersham to Taft (September 2, 1909), quoted in Pringle, *Life and Times*, 1:523.

28. Coletta, *Presidency of Taft*, 128–129; Gould, *Taft Presidency*, 98, 101.

29. George Wickersham, "The Policies and the Record of the Taft Administration" (August 14, 1912), Taft Papers; Bromley, *Motoring Presidency*, 248–249; Anderson, *Conservative's Conception*, 130; Chauncey Depew to Elihu Root (June 23, 1910), quoted in Anderson, *Conservative's Conception*, 131.

30. Mann–Elkins Act, 36 Stat. 539 (1910), 539–540; George Wickersham, "The Policies and the Record of the Taft Administration" (August 14, 1912), Taft Papers; Taft, *Collected Works*, 3:409.

31. Hepburn Act, 34 Stat. 584 (1906), 592; Mann–Elkins Act, 36 Stat. 539 (1910), 543.

32. Mann–Elkins Act, 36 Stat. 539 (1910), 544, 549–550; Taft, *Collected Works*, 3:409.

33. Steven Skowronek, *Building a New American State: The Expansion of National Administrative Capacities, 1877–1920* (Cambridge: Cambridge University Press, 1982), 252, 262 (quotes), 254–255.

34. George Wickersham, "The Policies and the Record of the Taft Administration" (August 14, 1912), Taft Papers; Taft, *Collected Works*, 1:205, 3:9–11; 4:75–76.

35. Safety Appliance Act, 36 Stat. 298 (1910), 298.

36. Taft, *Collected Works*, 3:54; 4:63, 217, 335; J. M. Mathews, "Employers' Liability and Workmen's Compensation," *American Political Science Review* 5, no. 4 (1911): 585–590.

37. Taft, *Collected Works*, 4:216, 250–251.

38. Taft, *Collected Works*, 4:252; Taft, "Message of the President of the United States: Transmitting The Report of the Employers' Liability and Workmen's Compensation Commission," S. Doc. 338, 62nd Congress, 2nd Session (1912), 120–123. The bill will hereafter be cited as "Sutherland Commission."

39. Taft, *Collected Works*, 4:252–253.

40. Sutherland Commission, 115–117.

41. Taft, "Speech of William Howard Taft: Accepting the Republican Nomination for President of the United States," S. Doc. 902, 62nd Congress, 2nd Session (1912), 6; Taft, "Message Transmitting Report of the Employers' Liability Commission," 6; Sutherland Commission, 107; see Employers' Liability Cases, 207 U.S. 463 (1908), 494–498; Second Employers' Liability Cases, 223 U.S. 1 (1912), 48–49.

42. Coletta, *Presidency of Taft*, 48.

43. "To Pass Liability Bill," *New York Times*, May 5, 1912; "Phillips Asks Clark's Aid," *New York Times*, August 20, 1912; Lurie, *Progressive Conservative*, 169; Schlesinger, ed., *Presidential Elections*, 3:2189.

44. Coletta, *Presidency of Taft*, 65 (quote), 71.

45. Coletta, *Presidency of Taft*, 133, 255; George Wickersham, "The Policies and the Record of the Taft Administration" (August 14, 1912), Taft Papers.

46. Anderson, *Conservative's Conception*, 134; Coletta, *Presidency of Taft*, 114–115; "Reluctant Congress Bent to Taft's Will," *New York Times*, June 21, 1910.

47. Taft believed *Pollock* could be circumvented via an excise tax on corporate dividends; see Turner, "Taft Views," 213.

48. Stephen Skowronek, *The Politics Presidents Make* (Cambridge, MA: Belknap Press of Harvard University Press, 1997), xvi, 13–15, 41.

49. Skowronek, *Politics Presidents Make*, 254–255.

50. Anderson, *Conservative's Conception*, 60; Butt, *Intimate Letters*, 1:260.

Chapter 3. To "Perfect the Machinery"

1. Peter Fish, "William Howard Taft and Charles Evans Hughes: Conservative Politicians as Chief Judicial Reformers," *The Supreme Court Review* 1975, no. 1 (1975): 125; Paolo Coletta, *The Presidency of William Howard Taft* (Lawrence: University Press of Kansas, 1973), 132.

2. William Howard Taft, *The Collected Works of William Howard Taft*, ed. David Burton (Athens: Ohio University Press, 2001–2004), 3:7.

3. Lewis Gould, *The William Howard Taft Presidency* (Lawrence: University Press of Kansas, 2009), 121.

4. Taft, *Collected Works*, 4:226–242; Coletta, *Presidency of Taft*, 130.

5. Taft, *Collected Works*, 4:227, 230; Coletta, *Presidency of Taft*, 130; Peri Arnold, *Making the Managerial Presidency: Comprehensive Reorganization Planning, 1905–1996* (Lawrence: University Press of Kansas, 1998), 34, 37.

6. Taft, *Collected Works*, 4:226; William Howard Taft, *Our Chief Magistrate and His Powers* (Durham, NC: Carolina Academic Press, 2002), 65.

7. Walter Scholes and Marie Scholes, *The Foreign Policies of the Taft Administration* (Columbia: University of Missouri Press, 1970), 24–26; Coletta, *Presidency of Taft*, 208, 212–213; Steven Skowronek, *Building a New American State: The Expansion of National Administrative Capacities, 1877–1920* (Cambridge: Cambridge University Press, 1982), 224–227.

8. "Federal Budget Proposed," *New York Times*, June 2, 1912; Donald Anderson, *William Howard Taft: A Conservative's Conception of the Presidency* (Ithaca, NY: Cornell University Press, 1973), 86.

9. William Howard Taft, "The Need for a National Budget: Message from the President of the United States Transmitting Report of the Commission on Economy and Efficiency on the Subject of the Need for a National Budget," H. Doc. 851, 62nd Congress, 2nd Session (1912), 4; Charles Stewart, *Budget Reform Politics: The Design of the Appropriations Process in the House of Representatives, 1865–1921* (Cambridge: Cambridge University Press, 2006), 179–188; Skowronek, *Building a New American State*, 188.

10. Sundry Civil Appropriations Act, 37 Stat. 360 (1912), 415.

11. Steven Calabresi and Christopher Yoo, *The Unitary Executive: Presidential Power from Washington to Bush* (New Haven, CT: Yale University Press, 2008), 251; Arnold, *Managerial Presidency*, 45; "Taft Insistent, Orders a Budget," *New York Times*, September 20, 1912.

12. Taft to Franklin MacVeagh (September 19, 1912), William Howard Taft Papers, Manuscript Division, Library of Congress.

13. Taft to Franklin MacVeagh (September 19, 1912), Taft Papers.

14. Taft to Franklin MacVeagh (September 19, 1912), Taft Papers (emphasis added); Taft, *Chief Magistrate*, 47, 125.

15. Rene Ballard, "The Administrative Theory of William Howard Taft," *The Western Political Quarterly* 7, no. 1 (1954): 73; Taft, *Chief Magistrate*, 8–9; Calabresi and Yoo, *Unitary Executive*, 251.

16. Jonathan O'Neill, "William Howard Taft and the Constitutional Presidency in the Progressive Era," in *Progressive Challenges to the American Constitution: A New Republic*, ed. Bradley C. S. Watson (New York: Cambridge University Press, 2017), 199.

17. Taft, *Chief Magistrate*, 5; Taft, *Collected Works*, 4:71, 244; Woodrow Wilson, *Constitutional Government* (New York: Columbia University Press, 1964), 68.

18. Taft, *Collected Works*, 4:71, 244; Commission on Economy and Efficiency, "The Need for a National Budget" in Taft, "Message Transmitting Report of the Commission," 145.

19. Taft, *Collected Works*, 3:73, 163; 4:245 (emphasis added).

20. Taft, *Chief Magistrate*, 59–60; Taft, *Collected Works*, 1:55; 4:233.

21. Taft, *Collected Works*, 3:71; 4:232–234; Coletta, *Presidency of Taft*, 138.

22. Anderson, *Conservative's Conception*, 91; Appropriations Act, 16 Stat. 495 (1871), 514–515.

23. Taft, *Chief Magistrate*, 58, 60; Anderson, *Conservative's Conception*, 91; Coletta, *Presidency of Taft*, 137–138.

24. "Salary Bill Veto Sustained by House," *New York Times*, August 16, 1912; Taft to William O. Bradley (March 7, 1911), Taft Papers.

25. Taft to Frank Hitchcock (March 27, 1912); Taft to Frank Hitchcock (July 3, 1912), Taft Papers.

26. Taft to Frank Hitchcock (February 26, 1910); Taft to William O. Bradley (August 9, 1912), Taft Papers.

27. Taft to John Lord O'Brian (August 10, 1912), Taft Papers; Felix Frankfurter and Harlan Phillips, *Felix Frankfurter Reminisces: An Intimate Portrait as Recorded in Talks with Dr. Harlan B. Phillips* (New York: Reynal & Company, 1960), 54; Sidney Milkis, *Theodore Roosevelt, the Progressive Party, and the Transformation of American Democracy* (Lawrence: University Press of Kansas, 2009), 81–82.

28. Taft to George Norris (January 11, 1910); Taft to Franklin MacVeagh (June 28, 1911), Taft Papers.

29. Taft, *Collected Works*, 3:368; "Improving the Foreign Service," *New York Times*, January 23, 1911.

30. Taft, *Collected Works*, 4:232; Taft, *Chief Magistrate*, 70–71.

31. Taft, *Chief Magistrate*, 67, 70–72.

32. Taft, *Collected Works*, 4:336–338; Taft, *Chief Magistrate*, 31.

33. Taft, *Collected Works*, 4:338–339; Joseph Story, *Commentaries on the Constitution of the United States* (Boston: Billiard, Gray, and Company, 1833), 2:333–337.

34. Taft, *Chief Magistrate*, 31; Taft, *Collected Works*, 4:337; "Taft Comes Out for Single Term," *New York Times*, November 17, 1912.

35. Taft, *Chief Magistrate*, 18, 52; "Taft Comes Out for Single Term," *New York Times*, November 17, 1912.

36. Taft, *Collected Works*, 4:336–337; "Taft Comes Out for Single Term," *New York Times*, November 17, 1912.

37. "Taft Comes Out for Single Term," *New York Times*, November 17, 1912; Taft, *Chief Magistrate*, 31.

38. Taft, *Collected Works*, 4:336–337.

39. Woodrow Wilson, *Cabinet Government in the United States* (Stamford, CT:

The Overbrook Press, 1947), 2–13, 16–18; "Taft Comes Out for Single Term," *New York Times*, November 17, 1912.

40. Wilson, *Cabinet Government*, 9–13.

41. Woodrow Wilson, *Congressional Government: A Study in American Politics* (Cleveland: World Publishing Co., 1973), 170; Walter Lippmann, "Introduction," in Wilson, *Congressional Government*, 15; see also Wilson, *Cabinet Government*, 26–29.

42. Jeffrey Tulis, *The Rhetorical Presidency* (Princeton, NJ: Princeton University Press, 1987), 120–123.

43. Wilson, *Constitutional Government*, 56; Wilson, *Cabinet Government*, 31.

44. Milkis, *Transformation of American Democracy*, 21.

Chapter 4. Partisanship and the Presidency

1. Taft to M. A. McRae (November 12, 1904), William Howard Taft Papers, Manuscript Division, Library of Congress.

2. Donald Anderson, *William Howard Taft: A Conservative's Conception of the Presidency* (Ithaca, NY: Cornell University Press, 1968), 43, 58; Doris Kearns Goodwin, *The Bully Pulpit: Theodore Roosevelt, William Howard Taft, and the Golden Age of Journalism* (New York: Simon & Schuster Paperbacks, 2013), 521.

3. Lewis Gould, *The William Howard Taft Presidency* (Lawrence: University Press of Kansas, 2009), 21 (quote); Michael Korzi, "William Howard Taft, the 1908 Election, and the Future of the American Presidency," *Congress & the Presidency* 43, no. 2 (2016): 227–254.

4. Sidney Milkis, *Theodore Roosevelt, the Progressive Party, and the Transformation of American Democracy* (Lawrence: University Press of Kansas, 2009), 86; Gould, *Taft Presidency*, 21; Herbert Duffy, *William Howard Taft* (New York: Minton, Balch, & Co., 1930), 220–221.

5. Peri Arnold, *Remaking the Presidency: Roosevelt, Taft, and Wilson, 1901–1916* (Lawrence: University Press of Kansas, 2009), 116 (quote), 73, 103; Anderson, *Conservative's Conception*, 12–13, 41–43.

6. Paolo Coletta, "Election of 1908," in Arthur M. Schlesinger Jr., ed., *History of American Presidential Elections: 1789–1968* (New York: Chelsea House Publishers, 1971), 3:2065–2066.

7. Coletta, "Election of 1908," 3:2050, 2058, 2073; William Howard Taft, *The Collected Works of William Howard Taft*, ed. David Burton (Athens: Ohio University Press, 2001–2004), 3:9–11, 21–22, 31–32.

8. Milkis, *Transformation of American Democracy*, 102.

9. Enclosure, F. E. Warren to Taft (January 18, 1911); Charles Norton to Charles Hilles (March 26, 1911), Taft Papers.

10. Archibald Butt, *Taft and Roosevelt: The Intimate Letters of Archie Butt,*

Military Aide (Garden City, NY: Doubleday, Doran & Company, Inc., 1930), 1:372; Taft to Charles Norton (December 5, 1910); Charles Norton to Charles Hilles (March 26, 1911); Taft to Eugene Hale (January 23, 1911), Taft Papers.

11. Paolo Coletta, *The Presidency of William Howard Taft* (Lawrence: University Press of Kansas, 1973), 54–55; Gould, *Taft Presidency*, 146–148.

12. Gould, *Taft Presidency*, 162–164, 174; Coletta, *Presidency of Taft*, 231.

13. Gil Troy, *See How They Ran* (New York: The Free Press, 1991), 113.

14. Taft to Clarence Kelsey (May 22, 1912), Taft Papers; Gould, *Taft Presidency*, 178–182.

15. Gould, *Taft Presidency*, 181; Coletta, *Presidency of Taft*, 236–237; Nicholas Murray Butler to Taft (November 12, 1915), Taft Papers.

16. Coletta, *Presidency of Taft*, 236; Gould, *Taft Presidency*, 180–181; Lewis Gould, *Four Hats in the Ring: The 1912 Election and the Birth of Modern American Politics* (Lawrence: University Press of Kansas, 2008), 67; Goodwin, *Bully Pulpit*, 699–700; Gilbert Roe, "The Truth about the Contests," *La Follette's Weekly Magazine* 4, no. 31 (1912): 15.

17. Taft to C. A. Ricks (June 26, 1912), Taft Papers; George Mowry, "Election of 1912," in Arthur M. Schlesinger Jr., ed., *History of American Presidential Elections: 1789–1968* (New York: Chelsea House Publishers, 1971), 3:2145 (quote), 2159.

18. Lewis Gould, ed., *My Dearest Nellie: The Letters of William Howard Taft to Helen Herron Taft, 1909–1912* (Lawrence: University Press of Kansas, 2011), 265; "Not a 'Third Ticket,'" *New York Times*, July 6, 1912; "Roosevelt Electors to Stay," *New York Times*, September 24, 1912; "Taft on California Reverse," *New York Times*, October 11, 1912.

19. Gould, *Taft Presidency*, 158.

20. "Taft Is Notified: Cincinnati Joyful," *New York Times*, July 29, 1908.

21. Taft to William Worthington (May 29, 1912); Taft to Mrs. Buckner Wallingford (July 14, 1912); Taft to Charles Wilby (May 3, 1912), Taft Papers (emphasis added); Taft, "Speech of William Howard Taft Accepting the Republican Nomination for President of the United States," S. Doc. 902, 62nd Congress, 2nd Session (1912), 11.

22. Taft, "Address of Hon. William H. Taft, President of the United States. Delivered in Boston, Mass. Thursday, April 25, 1912," S. Doc. No. 615, 62nd Congress, 2nd Session (1912), 5; Taft to Adolphus Busch (December 4, 1912); Taft to Howard Hollister (ca. April 1912); Taft to Joseph Gaffney (August 16, 1912), Taft Papers; Stephen Knott, *The Lost Soul of the American Presidency: The Decline into Demagoguery and the Prospects for Renewal* (Lawrence: University Press of Kansas, 2019), 110.

23. Taft to Howard Hollister (ca. April 1912); Taft to Theodore Roosevelt (March 21, 1909); Taft Papers; Butt, *Intimate Letters*, 1:298.

24. Taft, "Boston Address," 7, 17; Henry Pringle, *The Life and Times of William*

202 | NOTES TO PAGES 89–95

Howard Taft (New York: Farrar and Rinehart, Inc., 1939), 2:784; Gould, *Taft Presidency*, 177–178; Gould, *Four Hats*, 64–65.

25. Taft to Charles Wilby (May 3, 1912), Taft Papers; Taft, "Boston Address," 4–5.

26. Milkis, *Transformation of American Democracy*, 190–191; Gould, ed., *My Dearest Nellie*, 211, 230.

27. Taft to Clarence Kelsey (November 8, 1912); Statement of President Taft in Cincinnati (November 5, 1912); Taft to Mrs. William Edwards (August 2, 1912), Taft Papers; Taft to Clarence Kelsey (November 8, 1912), quoted in Pringle, *Life and Times*, 2:841; Gould, ed., *My Dearest Nellie*, 227.

28. Statement of President Taft to Harry Dunlop of the *New York World* (November 14, 1912); Taft to Mrs. Buckner Wallingford (July 14, 1912); Taft to Whitelaw Reid (April 7, 1910), Taft Papers; Gould, ed., *My Dearest Nellie*, 211.

29. Anderson, *Conservative's Conception*, 194–195; Coletta, *Presidency of Taft*, 242–243; Jonathan Lurie, *William Howard Taft: The Travails of a Progressive Conservative* (Cambridge: Cambridge University Press, 2012), 170; Pringle, *Life and Times*, 2:760–761.

30. Gould, ed., *My Dearest Nellie*, 203, 279; Butt, *Intimate Letters*, 1:236, 298; Taft to John W. Hill (November 10, 1912), Taft Papers.

31. Taft to Clarence Kelsey (November 8, 1912), quoted in Pringle, *Life and Times*, 2:841; Taft, "Statement of President Taft in Cincinnati" (November 5, 1912), Taft Papers.

32. Butt, *Intimate Letters*, 1:272.

33. Mowry, "Election of 1912," 3:2164. Mowry's numbers are estimates, but they are quite reasonable in light of the popular vote split in the general election: Roosevelt led Taft 27 percent to 23 percent.

34. Jeffrey Tulis, *The Rhetorical Presidency* (Princeton, NJ: Princeton University Press, 1987), 46–47, 95–116, 133–135.

35. Taft, *Collected Works*, 3:147–148; Gould, *Taft Presidency*, 149–151; Tulis, *Rhetorical Presidency*, 118 (quote), 106–107.

36. Taft, *Collected Works*, 3:156–159, 162–165.

37. "Taft in the East Talks to Big Crowds," *New York Times*, October 20, 1908; Korzi, "Taft and the 1908 Election," 234; Butt, *Intimate Letters*, 1:316; Coletta, *Presidency of Taft*, 262.

38. "Taft Prophesies 100,000 in New York," *New York Times*, November 1, 1908; "Taft Tells League Bryan Is a Menace," *New York Times*, September 23, 1908; "Host Greets Taft, Hughes," *New York Times*, October 29, 1908; Korzi, "Taft and the 1908 Election," 242–248.

39. Sidney Milkis, "William Howard Taft and the Struggle for the Soul of the Constitution," in *Toward an American Conservatism: Constitutional Conservatism during the Progressive Era*, ed. Joseph Postell and Jonathan O'Neill (New York: Palgrave Macmillan, 2013), 64; Tulis, *Rhetorical Presidency*, 78, 108.

40. "What Taft Plans at Yale," *New York Times*, February 26, 1913 (quote); "Taft Plans Work on National Lines," *New York Times*, November 10, 1912; "Taft, Professor, Works for Ideals of Taft, President," *New York Times*, May 25, 1913.

41. "William H. Taft," *New York Times*, March 4, 1913; Stephen Skowronek, *The Politics Presidents Make* (Cambridge, MA: The Belknap Press, 1997), 254–255.

42. Theodore Roosevelt, *The Works of Theodore Roosevelt: National Edition* (New York: Charles Scribner's Sons, 1926), 17:297–298.

Chapter 5. The Professor on the Presidency

1. Theodore Roosevelt, *An Autobiography* (New York: Charles Scribner's Sons, 1946), 363.

2. Roosevelt, *Autobiography*, 357, 365.

3. For noteworthy scholarly disagreement with TR's argument, see L. Peter Schultz, "William Howard Taft: A Constitutionalist's View of the Presidency," *Presidential Studies Quarterly* 9, no. 4 (1979): 402–414; Lance Robinson, "Theodore Roosevelt and William Howard Taft: The Constitutional Foundations of the Modern Presidency," in *The Constitutional Presidency*, ed. Joseph Bessette and Jeffrey Tulis (Baltimore: Johns Hopkins University Press, 2009), 76–95; Jonathan O'Neill, "William Howard Taft and the Constitutional Presidency in the Progressive Era," in *Progressive Challenges to the American Constitution: A New Republic*, ed. Bradley C. S. Watson (New York: Cambridge University Press, 2017), 196–225.

4. Taft, *Our Chief Magistrate and His Powers* (Durham, NC: Carolina Academic Press, 2002), 4, 139–140; Roosevelt, *Autobiography*, 357.

5. Roosevelt, *Autobiography*, 386.

6. Robinson, "Roosevelt and Taft," 78.

7. John Locke, *Two Treatises of Government*, ed. Ian Shapiro (New Haven, CT: Yale University Press, 2003), 173 (chap. 14, sec. 164); Thomas Jefferson to John B. Colvin (September 20, 1810), in *Thomas Jefferson: Writings*, ed. Merrill D. Peterson (New York: Literary Classics of the United States, Inc., 1984), 1231; Jeremy Bailey, *Thomas Jefferson and Executive Power* (Cambridge: Cambridge University Press, 2010), 179. For modern Jeffersonians, see Arthur Schlesinger Jr., *The Imperial Presidency* (Boston: Houghton Mifflin Co., 1973), 7–10; David Adler, "The Framers and Executive Prerogative: A Constitutional and Historical Rebuke," *Presidential Studies Quarterly* 42, no. 2 (2012): 376–389.

8. Larry Arnhart, "'The God-Like Prince': John Locke, Executive Prerogative, and the American Presidency," *Presidential Studies Quarterly* 9, no. 2 (1979): 124; George Thomas, "As Far as Republican Principles Will Admit: Presidential Prerogative and Constitutional Government," *Presidential Studies Quarterly* 30, no. 3 (2000): 548.

9. Benjamin Kleinerman, whose essentially Lockean approach critiques both camps, believes a president's extralegal actions may "*become* constitutional," but also suggests the Constitution (initially) forbids some actions necessary for the nation's survival; Kleinerman, *The Discretionary President: The Promise and Peril of Executive Power* (Lawrence: University Press of Kansas, 2009), x–xi, 170–179 (emphasis original).

10. Taft, *Chief Magistrate*, 4, 78, 88–89, 139–140. Taft's approach is similar to that of Herbert Storing, "The Presidency and the Constitution," in *Toward a More Perfect Union*, ed. Joseph Bessette (Washington, DC: AEI Press, 1995), 377–385.

11. Taft, *Chief Magistrate*, 140; Louis Fisher, *Constitutional Conflicts between Congress and the President*, 6th ed. (Lawrence: University Press of Kansas, 2014), 17.

12. Taft, *Chief Magistrate*, 47, 125. Note, however, that though the president may not control the officer's execution of ministerial functions, he may remove him from office (ibid., 81); see Myers v. United States, 272 U.S. 52 (1926), 135.

13. Taft, *Chief Magistrate*, 2, 78; Schultz, "Constitutionalist's View," 404, 408.

14. Taft, *Chief Magistrate*, 94, 126.

15. Taft, *Chief Magistrate*, 97 (quotes), 89–91, 96–97 (examples); In Re Debs, 158 U.S. 564 (1885), 578–583.

16. Taft, *Chief Magistrate*, 93 (quotes), 94, 98–99.

17. Taft, *Chief Magistrate*, 94, 100 (quotes), 94–96, 114–115.

18. Robinson, "Roosevelt and Taft," 78.

19. Taft, *Chief Magistrate*, 96.

20. "Guard Engineers in Georgia Strike," *Chicago Tribune*, May 29, 1909; "Federal Officials End Georgia Strike," *New York Times*, May 30, 1909; Archibald Butt, *Taft and Roosevelt: The Intimate Letters of Archie Butt, Military Aide* (Garden City, NY: Doubleday, Doran & Company, Inc., 1930), 1:110; Department of Commerce and Labor, "Memorandum to the Secretary" (August 10, 1909), William Howard Taft Papers, Manuscript Division, Library of Congress.

21. Roosevelt, *Autobiography*, 357.

22. Roosevelt, *Autobiography*, 473–474, 476.

23. Roosevelt, *Autobiography*, 475–476; see also Roosevelt to Winthrop Murray Crane (October 22, 1922), in *The Letters of Theodore Roosevelt*, ed. Elting Morison (Cambridge, MA: Harvard University Press, 1951), 3:359–366.

24. Taft, *The Collected Works of William Howard Taft*, ed. David Burton (Athens: Ohio University Press, 2001–2004), 4:176; Henry Pringle, *The Life and Times of William Howard Taft* (New York: Farrar and Rinehart, Inc., 1939), 2:700–701, 706–708.

25. Taft, *Collected Works*, 4:180; Taft to A. B. Farquhar (September 11, 1912), Taft Papers.

26. Taft to Leonard Wood (March 12, 1911); for a representative letter to

a journalist, see Taft to J. C. Hemphill (March 25, 1911), Taft Papers; Donald Anderson, *William Howard Taft: A Conservative's Conception of the Presidency* (Ithaca, NY: Cornell University Press, 1968), 267–268; Paolo Coletta, *The Presidency of William Howard Taft* (Lawrence: University Press of Kansas, 1973), 190.

27. Taft to Richard E. Sloan (April 18, 1911), Taft Papers.

28. "50,000 Need Food in Flood District," *New York Times*, April 7, 1912; Taft to Henry Stimson (April 4, 1912), Taft Papers. Six years before, as Roosevelt's secretary of war, he had issued a similar order to send military supplies to California in response to an earthquake; see Taft to James Phelan (May 1, 1906), Taft Papers.

29. Roosevelt, *Autobiography*, 363; Taft, *Chief Magistrate*, 147.

30. See Kleinerman, *Discretionary President*, 115–116.

31. Abraham Lincoln, *The Collected Works of Abraham Lincoln*, ed. Roy Basler (New Brunswick, NJ: Rutgers University Press, 1953), 4:429–430 (emphasis added); Louis Fisher, *Presidential War Power*, 3rd ed. (Lawrence: University Press of Kansas, 2013), 48.

32. 12 Stat. 319 (1861); 12 Stat. 589 (1862); Lincoln, *Collected Works*, 5:336, 434–435; 6:23–24; 28–30.

33. Lincoln, *Collected Works*, 5:421, 423; 6:29; 7:281–282.

34. Taft, *Chief Magistrate*, 53.

35. Taft, *Chief Magistrate*, 2, 57–58, 138.

36. Taft, *Chief Magistrate*, 156.

Chapter 6. The Chief Justice on the Presidency

1. William Howard Taft, *Our Chief Magistrate and His Powers* (Durham, NC: Carolina Academic Press, 2002), 56–57. *Myers* was Taft's second removal power opinion; in Wallace v. United States, 257 U.S. 541 (1922), the Court sustained the president's removal of a US Army officer but avoided the major constitutional issue.

2. Steven Calabresi and Christopher Yoo, *The Unitary Executive: Presidential Power from Washington to Bush* (New Haven, CT: Yale University Press, 2008), 248–250, 268; Edward Corwin, *The President's Removal Power under the Constitution* (New York: National Municipal League, 1927), v–vi, 7; Louis Fisher, *Constitutional Conflicts between Congress and the President* (Lawrence: University Press of Kansas, 2014), 70–72; Jonathan Lurie, *The Chief Justiceship of William Howard Taft, 1921–1930* (Columbia: University of South Carolina Press, 2019), 121–125; Alpheus Thomas Mason, *William Howard Taft: Chief Justice* (New York: Simon & Schuster, 1964), 253–254; Allen Ragan, *Chief Justice Taft* (Columbus: Ohio State Archaeological and Historical Society, 1938), 63–68.

3. Only a single scholar seems to have noted Taft's nuances. See Robert Post,

"Tension in the Unitary Executive: How Taft Constructed the Epochal Opinion of *Myers v. United States*," *Journal of Supreme Court History* 45, no. 2 (2020): 183–185.

4. The most comprehensive modern analysis of *Myers* is J. David Alvis, Jeremy Bailey, and F. Flagg Taylor, *The Contested Removal Power, 1789–2010* (Lawrence: University Press of Kansas, 2013), 106–140. My work differs in emphasis, particularly on civil service reform.

5. 19 Stat. 78 (1876), 80.

6. Taft to Pierce Butler (September 16, 1925), William Howard Taft Papers, Manuscript Division, Library of Congress.

7. Myers v. United States, 272 U.S. 52 (1926), 116–118.

8. *Myers*, 119–120, 122 (quoting Oliver Ellsworth at the First Congress).

9. US Const. art. II, §2.

10. *Myers*, 161.

11. *Myers*, 132–135.

12. *Myers*, 131 (quoting Madison at the First Congress).

13. *Myers*, 173 (quote), 275–283 (Brandeis dissent); Corwin, *Removal Power*, 3–7.

14. *Myers*, 128 (quoting Madison at the First Congress).

15. *Myers*, 161–162. Taft's argument was made in a rather obtuse manner: "Whether the action of Congress in removing the necessity for the advice and consent of the Senate, and putting the power of appointment in the President alone, would make his power of removal in such case any more subject to Congressional legislation than before is a question this Court did not decide in [*United States v. Perkins*]. . . . Under the reasoning upon which the legislative decision of 1789 was put, it might be difficult to avoid a negative answer, but it is not before us and we do not decide it" (see Alvis, Bailey, and Taylor, *Contested Removal Power*, 133).

16. *Myers*, 135.

17. *Myers*, 161.

18. *Myers*, 161; Beck quoted in Alvis, Bailey, and Taylor, *Contested Removal Power*, 130.

19. See Corwin, *Removal Power*, 7, 63; Alvis, Bailey, and Taylor, *Contested Removal Power*, 132; Post, "Tension in the Unitary Executive," 183–185.

20. *Myers*, 161–163, 173–174; Pendleton Act, 22 Stat. 403 (1883), 406.

21. Post, "Tension in the Unitary Executive," 183–185.

22. Taft also insisted cabinet officers could never be classified, since they cannot legitimately be considered "inferior officers" (Taft, *Our Chief Magistrate*, 55–56).

23. Aditya Bamzai, "Taft, Frankfurter, and the First Presidential For-Cause Removal," *University of Richmond Law Review* 52 (2018): 691, 736–737, 748.

24. *Myers*, 135. Taft evidently spoke of superior officers in this passage, yet

the logic of his argument—particularly when considered in light of Bamzai's article and Taft's additionally commentary in *Our Chief Magistrate* (81)—provides useful evidence for his broad understanding of presidential power over classified inferior officers.

25. *Myers*, 161–163, 173–174.

26. Woodrow Wilson, "The Study of Administration," *Political Science Quarterly* 2, no. 2 (1887): 207–209, 221.

27. Wilson, "Study of Administration," 208, 212–213, 215.

28. Wilson, "Study of Administration," 216 (quote), 221.

29. Corwin, *Removal Power*, xii.

30. Herbert Croly, *The Promise of American Life* (Princeton, NJ: Princeton University Press, 2014), 387–388; David Nichols, "The Promise of Progressivism: Herbert Croly and the Progressive Rejection of Individual Rights," *Publius* 17, no. 2 (1987): 33.

31. Croly, *Promise of American Life*, 396–397, 406.

32. Croly, *Promise of American Life*, 412, 415–416 (emphasis added); Herbert Croly, *Progressive Democracy* (New Brunswick, NJ: Transaction Publishers, 2009), 251.

33. Croly, *Promise of American Life*, 398, 404–405, 415–416.

34. Humphrey's Executor v. United States, 295 U.S. 602 (1935), 618–619.

35. *Humphrey's Executor*, 628 (original emphasis).

36. *Humphrey's Executor*, 625.

37. Alvis, Bailey, and Taylor, *Contested Removal Power*, 141 (quote), 145–159.

38. *Humphrey's Executor*, 625.

Chapter 7. Jurisprudence

1. Alpheus Thomas Mason, *William Howard Taft: Chief Justice* (New York: Simon & Schuster, 1964), 15, 291; Robert McCloskey, *The American Supreme Court*, 5th ed., rev. Sanford Levinson (Chicago: University of Chicago Press, 2010), 106; Jonathan Lurie, *The Chief Justiceship of William Howard Taft, 1921–1930* (Columbia: University of South Carolina Press, 2019), 148, 229.

2. Robert Post, "Chief Justice William Howard Taft and the Concept of Federalism," *Constitutional Commentary* 9 (1992): 200–203, 213, 215–216, 220–221; Robert Post, "Federalism in the Taft Court Era: Can It Be 'Revived'?," *Duke Law Journal* 51 (2002): 1517; Allan Ragan, *Chief Justice Taft* (Columbus: Ohio State Archaeological and Historical Society, 1938), 18, 43; Jeffrey Rosen, *William Howard Taft* (New York: Times Books, 2018), 120–122.

3. Ragan, *Chief Justice*, 44; Taft to Pierce Butler (January 7, 1929); Taft to Harlan F. Stone (August 31, 1928), William Howard Taft Papers, Manuscript Division, Library of Congress.

4. Post, "Federalism in the Taft Court," 1518.

5. United States v. E. C. Knight Co., 156 U.S. 1 (1895), 11–13.

6. *Knight*, 12–13. Taft rejected *Knight* as a useful precedent; see William Howard Taft, *The Collected Works of William Howard Taft*, ed. David Burton (Athens: Ohio University Press, 2001–2004), 5:199–203.

7. Swift & Co. v. United States, 196 U.S. 375 (1905), 398–399; Board of Trade v. Olsen, 262 U.S. 1 (1923), 35.

8. Stafford v. Wallace, 258 U.S. 495 (1922), 515–519; Sonneborn Brothers v. Cureton, 262 U.S. 506 (1923), 514.

9. Carson Petroleum Co. v. Vial, 279 U.S. 95 (1929), 107 (quoting Texas & New Orleans R. Co. v. Sabine Tram Co., 227 U.S. 111 [1913], 126); *Stafford*, 515–516; *Olsen*, 33, 36.

10. See United Mine Workers v. Coronado Coal Co., 259 U.S. 344 (1922), 407–408; United Leather Workers v. Herkert, 265 U.S. 457 (1924), 465, 470–471; *Stafford*, 521 (quoting United States v. Ferger, 250 U.S. 199 [1919], 203), 525; Dayton-Goose Creek Railway Co. v. ICC, 263 U.S. 456 (1924), 485.

11. *Stafford*, 516, 519, 521–522 (quoting Ferger, 203); *Carson Petroleum*, 106–108.

12. Railroad Commission of Wisconsin v. Chicago, Burlington & Quincy Railroad Company, 257 U.S. 563 (1922), 588 (emphasis added), 590 (hereafter cited as Wisconsin v. Chicago); cf. *Knight*, 32–33.

13. *Stafford*, 521, 528; *Wisconsin v. Illinois*, 278 U.S. 367 (1929), 415 (quotes). See also *Stafford*, 514–515; *Olsen*, 39; *Sonneborn Brothers*, 516–520.

14. Brooks v. United States, 267 U.S. 432 (1925), 436–439.

15. Thornton v. United States, 271 U.S. 414 (1926), 425.

16. *Carson Petroleum*, 106–108; Morris v. Duby, 274 U.S. 135 (1927), 143; Oregon-Washington R. & Nav. Co. v. Washington, 270 U.S. 87 (1926), 101. Taft evidently built on the logic of Cooley v. Board of Wardens, 53 U.S. 299 (1851), 318–319, but he did not cite the case.

17. *Stafford*, 518–519; Taft, *Collected Works*, 5:92–93.

18. Ragan, *Chief Justice*, 18.

19. Taft to Elihu Root (December 21, 1922), Taft Papers.

20. Taft, *Collected Works*, 1:181; 2:163; Lewis Gould, *Chief Executive to Chief Justice: Taft betwixt the White House and Supreme Court* (Lawrence: University Press of Kansas, 2013), 105.

21. Thomas v. Cincinnati, N. O. & T. P. R. Ry. Co., 62 Fed. 803 (C.C.S.D. Ohio 1894), 817.

22. Alpheus Thomas Mason, "The Labor Decisions of Chief Justice Taft," *University of Pennsylvania Law Review* 78, no. 5 (1930): 599–600.

23. American Steel Foundries v. Tri-City Trades Council, 257 U.S. 184 (1921), 203–205; Mason, "Labor Decisions of Taft," 609 (quote), 588.

24. Lurie, *Chief Justiceship*, 25–27; Stanley Kutler, "Chief Justice Taft and the

Delusion of Judicial Exactness: A Study in Jurisprudence," *Virginia Law Review* 48, no. 8 (1962): 1408–1410.

25. *Steel Foundries*, 206–207.

26. *Steel Foundries*, 206–207.

27. Mason, *Chief Justice*, 15, 292.

28. Taft, *Collected Works*, 2:9.

29. Truax v. Corrigan, 257 U.S. 312 (1921), 332.

30. See, e.g., *Truax*; Charles Wolff Packing Co. v. Court of Industrial Relations, 262 U.S. 522 (1923); Appleby v. City of New York, 271 U.S. 364 (1926); Appleby v. Delaney, 271 U.S. 403 (1926).

31. E.g., *Adkins*; *Olsen*; Hetrick v. Village of Lindsey, 265 U.S. 384 (1924); Dayton-Goose Creek Railway; Sutter Butte Canal Co. v. Railroad Commission, 279 U.S. 125 (1929).

32. *Truax*, 325–326.

33. *Truax*, 374–376; Pitney and Clarke dissented along similar lines (*Truax*, 347–349).

34. *Truax*, 342–343. For scholarly criticism of the majority opinion, see Lurie, *Chief Justiceship*, 28–29; Mason, *Chief Justice*, 237–242; Kutler, "Judicial Exactness," 1414–1417.

35. *Truax*, 328, 330 (emphasis added).

36. *Truax*, 331; Mason, "Labor Decisions of Taft," 611.

37. *Truax*, 327, 332, 341 (emphasis added).

38. *Adkins*, 545, 554–555, 557.

39. *Adkins*, 562; Taft, *Collected Works*, 1:181.

40. *Adkins*, 564; Kutler, "Judicial Exactness," 1424.

41. *Adkins*, 564.

42. Ragan, *Chief Justice*, 40. Taft's two written dissents came in *Adkins* and Sloan Shipyards v. United States Shipping Board Emergency Fleet Corp., 258 U.S. 549 (1922). See also his quasi-dissenting opinion in FTC v. Curtis Publishing Co. (*FTC*), which begins "Mr. Chief Justice Taft, doubting"; *FTC*, 260 U.S. 568 (1923), 582.

43. Mason, *Chief Justice*, 251; McCloskey, *American Supreme Court*, 107; Kutler, "Judicial Exactness," 1417. Even Lurie sees the *Adkins* dissent as little more than adherence to *stare decisis* (Lurie, *Chief Justiceship*, 59–60).

44. Charles Wolff Packing Co. v. Court of Industrial Relations, 262 U.S. 522 (1923), 540–541; Kutler, "Judicial Exactness," 1417.

45. Barry Cushman, "Inside the Taft Court: Lessons from the Docket Books," *The Supreme Court Review* 2015, no. 1 (2016): 360–361.

46. Following *Adkins*, Taft voted twice to strike down minimum wage laws, evidently on *stare decisis* grounds; see Cushman, "Inside the Taft Court," 381–383.

47. Taft, *Collected Works*, 2:71; *Bailey*, 37. Taft opposed a constitutional

amendment that would bring child labor under federal control, but he did so at least in part because he recognized that the states themselves were already beginning to regulate child labor more carefully; see Post, "Federalism in the Taft Court," 1561n166.

48. *Bailey*, 37–38.

49. Felix Frankfurter, "Child Labor and the Court," *New Republic* 31 (July 1922): 248.

50. Schechter Poultry Corp. v. United States, 295 U.S. 495 (1935), 554.

51. Barry Cushman, "A Stream of Legal Consciousness: The Current of Commerce Doctrine from *Swift* to *Jones & Laughlin*," *Fordham Law Review* 61, no. 1 (1992): 115–122, 124–127; Stanley Kutler, "Chief Justice Taft, National Regulation, and the Commerce Power," *Journal of American History* 51, no. 4 (1965): 651, 666–668; Kutler, "Judicial Exactness," 1424; Mason, *Chief Justice*, 302–303; Post, "Concept of Federalism," 216–217.

52. National Labor Relations Board v. Jones & Laughlin Steel Corp., 301 U.S. 1 (1937), 27, 37–38; Cushman, "Stream of Legal Consciousness," 125; Kutler, "National Regulation," 668.

53. Kutler, "Judicial Exactness," 1424; Kutler, "National Regulation," 668; West Coast Hotel Co. v. Parrish, 300 U.S. 379 (1937), 391–396.

Chapter 8. Chief Justice as Chief Executive

1. Felix Frankfurter, *Felix Frankfurter on the Supreme Court*, ed. Philip Kurland (Cambridge, MA: The Belknap Press of Harvard University Press, 1970), 488.

2. Robert Post, "Judicial Management and Judicial Disinterest: The Achievements and Perils of Chief Justice William Howard Taft," *Journal of Supreme Court History* 23, no. 1 (1998): 56–57, 67; Kenneth Starr, "William Howard Taft: The Chief Justice as Judicial Architect," *University of Cincinnati Law Review* 60, no. 4 (1992): 963, 965–966.

3. Peter Fish, "William Howard Taft and Charles Evans Hughes: Conservative Politicians as Chief Judicial Reformers," *Supreme Court Review* 1975 (1975): 124, 145 (quotes), 124–125, 144–145.

4. Justin Crowe, "The Forging of Judicial Autonomy: Political Entrepreneurship and the Reforms of William Howard Taft," *The Journal of Politics* 69, no. 1 (2007): 75; Taft to Frank Hiscock (April 12, 1922), William Howard Taft Papers, Manuscript Division, Library of Congress; Post, "Judicial Management," 59; William Howard Taft, "Attacks on the Courts and Legal Procedure," *Kentucky Law Journal* 5, no. 2 (1916): 14; Matthew Brogdon, "Constitutional Foundations of the Modern Judiciary: Recovering the Institutional Logic and Structural Integrity of Article III" (forthcoming; manuscript on file with the author), 190.

5. William Howard Taft, "Three Needed Steps of Progress," *American Bar Association Journal* 8, no. 1 (1922): 35 (quotes), 34–36.

6. Fish, "Judicial Reformers," 124; Crowe, "Judicial Autonomy," 78–80; Alpheus Thomas Mason, *William Howard Taft: Chief Justice* (New York: Simon & Schuster, 1964), 140.

7. Taft, "Attacks on the Courts," 16; Felix Frankfurter and James Landis, *The Business of the Supreme Court: A Study in the Federal Judicial System* (New Brunswick, NJ: Transaction Publishers, 2007), 218.

8. Taft to Louis Brandeis (July 27, 1921), quoted in Mason, *Chief Justice*, 199 (quote), 100.

9. Taft to Frank H. Hiscock (April 12, 1922), Taft Papers; William Howard Taft, "Possible and Needed Reforms in Administration of Justice in Federal Courts," *American Bar Association Journal* 8, no. 10 (1922): 602; Fish, "Judicial Reformers," 135–136.

10. An Act To amend the Judicial Code, in reference to appeals and writs of error, 42 Stat. 837 (1922), 837, 839.

11. Taft, "Attacks on the Courts," 16; Frankfurter and Landis, *Business of the Supreme Court*, 243–245.

12. Henry Taft to Taft (October 26, 1922); Taft to Pierce Butler (October 25, 1922); Taft to Pierce Butler (November 2, 1922); Taft to Pierce Butler (November 17, 1922), Taft Papers; Allen Ragan, *Chief Justice Taft* (Columbus: Ohio State Archaeological and Historical Society, 1938), 96–97; Mason, *Chief Justice*, 189–190; Donald Anderson, "Building National Consensus: The Career of William Howard Taft," *University of Cincinnati Law Review* 68 (1999–2000): 349; Merlo Pusey, *Charles Evans Hughes* (New York: Macmillan Company, 1951): 2:652.

13. Walter Murphy, "In His Own Image: Mr. Chief Justice Taft and Supreme Court Appointments," *Supreme Court Review* 1961 (1961): 188; Walter Murphy, "Chief Justice Taft and the Lower Court Bureaucracy: A Study in Judicial Administration," *Journal of Politics* 24, no. 3 (1962): 460–461, 468–473.

14. Taft to Warren Harding (December 4, 1922), Taft Papers; Murphy, "In His Own Image," 165, 184–185.

15. Taft to Warren Harding (October 30, 1922); Taft to Pierce Butler (October 25, 1922); Taft to Willis Van Devanter (September 16, 1922), Taft Papers.

16. Taft to Elihu Root (December 21, 1922), Taft Papers. Taft's reference to the Fifth and Fourteenth Amendments must be understood in light of his permissive attitude toward regulations of property (chapter 7). Taft quoted in Ross Davies, "Debate and Switch: William Howard Taft on Law as a Vocation," *Journal of Law* 6, no. 1 (2016): 4.

17. Frankfurter and Landis, *Business of the Supreme Court*, 242; Post, "Judicial Management," 56. See Taft to Each Senior Circuit Judge (December 19, 1921);

Taft to All Circuit and District Judges (November 29, 1924); Taft to All Circuit and District Judges (June 16, 1925), Taft Papers.

18. Taft to John A. Peters (October 11, 1927); Taft to William Runyon (March 12, 1928); Taft to Ferdinand Geiger (November 17, 1927), Taft Papers.

19. Taft to Robert Taft (October 2, 1927), Taft Papers; Taft, "Needed Steps," 35.

20. Charles Evans Hughes, "Address of Chief Justice Hughes," *American Bar Association Journal* 18, no. 11 (1932): 728.

21. Robert Post, "The Supreme Court Opinion as Institutional Practice: Dissent, Legal Scholarship, and Decisionmaking in the Taft Court," *Minnesota Law Review* 85 (2001): 1329–1330; Starr, "Judicial Architect," 964, 967; Ragan, *Chief Justice*, 107.

22. Crowe, "Judicial Autonomy," 80; Frankfurter and Landis, *Business of the Supreme Court*, 274n62, 278–80; Mason, *Chief Justice*, 109, 218.

23. The Court would hear cases on direct appeal from a district court in only a few areas: certain cases arising under the antitrust law or the interstate commerce law, a limited class of criminal appeals, and attempts to enjoin the enforcement of a state statute because it violated the federal Constitution; see Judges' Bill, 43 Stat. 936 (1925), 937–939; Post, "Supreme Court Opinion," 1272n23.

24. Taft, writing in Magnum Import Co., Inc. v. Coty, 262 U.S. 159 (1923), 163.

25. David Danelski, "The Influence of the Chief Justice in the Decisional Process of the Supreme Court," in *The Chief Justice: Appointment and Influence*, ed. David Danelski and Artemus Ward (Ann Arbor: University of Michigan Press, 2016), 45n120.

26. Sandra Day O'Connor, "William Howard Taft and the Importance of Unanimity," *Journal of Supreme Court History* 28, no. 2 (2003): 161; Mason, *Chief Justice*, 211.

27. Alexander Bickel, *The Unpublished Opinions of Mr. Justice Brandeis: The Supreme Court at Work* (Cambridge, MA: The Belknap Press of Harvard University Press, 1957), 111–114; Mason, *Chief Justice*, 211–212; Taft to Pierce Butler (January 7, 1929), Taft Papers.

28. American Steel Foundries v. Tri-City Trades Council, 257 U.S. 184 (1921), 213; Bickel, *Unpublished Opinions*, 97–98; David Danelski, "The Chief Justice and the Supreme Court" (PhD diss., University of Chicago, 1961), 180–181, 189–191; Danelski, "Influence of the Chief Justice," 45n120; Taft to Mahlon Pitney (December 3, 1921), Taft Papers.

29. Melvin Urofsky, "The Brandeis–Frankfurter Conversations," *The Supreme Court Review* 1985 (1985): 329; Louis Brandeis to Taft (undated note, Reel #614, Taft Papers), quoted in Post, "Supreme Court Opinion as Institutional Practice," 1341n220.

30. Holmes quoted in O'Connor, "Unanimity," 160; Bickel, *Unpublished Opinions*, 212.

31. Taft to Harlan F. Stone (January 26, 1927); Louis Brandeis to Taft (December 23, 1922), Taft Papers; Urofsky, "Brandeis–Frankfurter Conversations," 330.

32. Taft to Charles P. Taft, II (May 12, 1929), Taft Papers; Post, "Supreme Court Opinion as Institutional Practice," 1310, 1313; Peter Renstrom, *The Taft Court: Justices, Rulings, and Legacy* (Santa Barbara, CA: ABC-CLIO, 2003), 99; Lee Epstein et al., *The Supreme Court Compendium: Data, Decisions, and Developments* (Washington, DC: Congressional Quarterly, Inc., 1994), 161.

33. Jeffrey Rosen, *William Howard Taft* (New York: Times Books, 2018), 3.

34. Crowe, "Judicial Autonomy," 76; Fish, "Judicial Reformers," 134–135.

35. Taft, "Attacks on the Courts," 24.

36. Taft, "Delays and Defects in the Enforcement of Law in this Country," *North American Review* 187 (January–June 1908): 851; William Howard Taft, "The Administration of Justice—Its Speeding and Cheapening," *Central Law Journal* 72, no. 11 (1911): 193–194; Woodrow Wilson, *Constitutional Government* (New York: Columbia University Press, 1964), 153.

37. Taft, "Administration of Justice," 195.

38. Taft to Louis Brandeis (December 18, 1926); Taft Papers; Crowe, "Judicial Autonomy," 78; David O'Brien, *Storm Center: The Supreme Court in American Politics*, 10th ed. (New York: W. W. Norton, 2014), 147; Post, "Judicial Management," 58–59; Mason, *Chief Justice*, 196–197.

39. William Howard Taft, "The Jurisdiction of the Supreme Court under the Act of February 13, 1925," *Yale Law Journal* 35, no. 1 (1925): 2–3; Taft to Henry Taft (April 5, 1928); Taft to Casper Yost (April 5, 1928), Taft Papers.

40. William Howard Taft, *The Collected Works of William Howard Taft*, ed. David Burton (Athens: Ohio University Press, 2001–2004), 5:87.

41. Thanks to Barry Cushman's recent study of the justices' docket books, we now know that Taft supported *Pierce* even in conference, and did not simply acquiesce to the decision publicly; see Cushman, "Inside the Taft Court: Lessons from the Docket Books," *The Supreme Court Review* 2015, no. 1 (2016): 363–364; see also Taft's opinion in the "Chinese bookkeeping case," which endorsed the general principles of *Meyer* and *Pierce* in a Fifth Amendment context; Yu Cong Eng v. Trinidad, 271 U.S. 500 (1926), 526–527.

42. Brogdon, "Constitutional Foundations," 306–308.

43. Crowe, "Judicial Autonomy," 83; Mason, *Chief Justice*, 301.

44. Starr, "Judicial Architect," 964; Ragan, *Chief Justice*, 110.

Conclusion

1. Charles Evans Hughes, *Conditions of Progress in Democratic Government* (New Haven, CT: Yale University Press, 1910); Elihu Root, *The Citizen's Part in Government* (New York: Charles Scribner's Sons, 1907); Root, *Experiments in Government and the Essentials of the Constitution* (Princeton, NJ: Princeton University Press, 1913). See also James Stoner, "Rational Compromise: Charles Evans Hughes as a Progressive Originalist," in *Toward an American Conservatism: Constitutional Conservatism during the Progressive Era,* ed. Joseph Postell and Jonathan O'Neill (New York: Palgrave Macmillan, 2013), 209–234; William Schambra, "The Election of 1912 and the Origins of Constitutional Conservatism," in Postell and O'Neill, eds., *Toward an American Conservatism,* 95–119.

2. William Howard Taft, *Our Chief Magistrate and His Powers* (Durham, NC: Carolina Academic Press, 2002), 4.

3. William Howard Taft, *The Collected Works of William Howard Taft,* ed. David Burton (Athens: Ohio University Press, 2001–2004), 5:19–21, 86–91.

4. Taft, *Collected Works,* 1:282, 298; 3:436, 5:87–90.

5. J. W. Hampton, Jr. & Co. v. United States, 276 U.S. 394 (1928), 406–409; Taft, *Collected Works,* 1:194–195. To justify a departure from the nondelegation doctrine, Taft apparently relied on dicta from Buttfield v. Stranahan, 192 U.S. 470 (1904), 496.

6. David Strauss, "Can Originalism Be Saved?," *Boston University Law Review* 92, no. 4 (2012): 1161; David Strauss, "We the People, They the People, and the Puzzle of Democratic Constitutionalism," *Texas Law Review* 91 (2013): 1970–1971; Akhil Reed Amar, *America's Unwritten Constitution: The Precedents and Principles We Live By* (New York: Basic Books, 2012), 144, 303–304.

7. James Fleming, "Constructing the Substantive Constitution," *Texas Law Review* 72, no. 2 (1993): 214; Ronald Dworkin, *Taking Right Seriously* (Cambridge, MA: Harvard University Press, 1977), 134–137.

8. Antonin Scalia, "Originalism: The Lesser Evil," *Cincinnati Law Review* 57 (1989): 852; Randy Barnett, *Restoring the Lost Constitution: The Presumption of Liberty* (Princeton, NJ: Princeton University Press, 2004), 101 (quote), 107.

9. McCulloch v. Maryland, 17 U.S. 316 (1819), 407 (emphasis added), 415; Taft, *Collected Works,* 5:20, 116, 136, 195.

10. Barnett, *Lost Constitution,* 208, 358, 413–416.

11. Taft, *Collected Works,* 5:19–21, 88–89.

Bibliography

Adler, David. "The Framers and Executive Prerogative: A Constitutional and Historical Rebuke." *Presidential Studies Quarterly* 42, no. 2 (2012): 376–389.

Alvis, J. David, Jeremy Bailey, and F. Flagg Taylor. *The Contested Removal Power, 1789–2010.* Lawrence: University Press of Kansas, 2013.

Amar, Akhil Reed. *America's Unwritten Constitution: The Precedents and Principles We Live By.* New York: Basic Books, 2012.

Anderson, Donald. "Building National Consensus: The Career of William Howard Taft." *University of Cincinnati Law Review* 68 (2000): 323–356.

———. *William Howard Taft: A Conservative's Conception of the Presidency.* Ithaca, NY: Cornell University Press, 1973.

Arnhart, Larry. "'The God-Like Prince': John Locke, Executive Prerogative, and the American Presidency." *Presidential Studies Quarterly* 9, no. 2 (1979): 121–130.

Arnold, Peri. *Making the Managerial Presidency: Comprehensive Reorganization Planning, 1905–1996.* Lawrence: University Press of Kansas, 1998.

———. *Remaking the Presidency: Roosevelt, Taft, and Wilson, 1901–1916.* Lawrence: University Press of Kansas, 2009.

Bailey, Jeremy. *Thomas Jefferson and Executive Power.* Cambridge: Cambridge University Press, 2010.

Ball, Max. *Department of the Interior Bulletin 623: Petroleum Withdrawals and Restorations Affecting the Public Domain.* Washington, DC: Government Printing Office, 1916.

Ballard, Rene. "The Administrative Theory of William Howard Taft." *Western Political Quarterly* 7, no. 1 (1954): 65–74.

Bamzai, Aditya. "Taft, Frankfurter, and the First Presidential For-Cause Removal." *University of Richmond Law Review* 52 (2018): 691–748.

Barnett, Randy. *Restoring the Lost Constitution: The Presumption of Liberty.* Updated ed. Princeton, NJ: Princeton University Press, 2004.

Bickel, Alexander. *The Unpublished Opinions of Mr. Justice Brandeis: The Supreme Court at Work.* Cambridge, MA: The Belknap Press of Harvard University Press, 1957.

Brogdon, Matthew. "Constitutional Foundations of the Modern Judiciary: Recovering the Institutional Logic and Structural Integrity of Article III." Forthcoming.

Bromley, Michael. *William Howard Taft and the First Motoring Presidency, 1909–1913.* Jefferson, NC: McFarland & Company, 2007.

Butt, Archibald. *The Letters of Archie Butt: Personal Aide to President Roosevelt.* New York: Doubleday, Page, & Co., 1924.

———. *Taft and Roosevelt: The Intimate Letters of Archie Butt, Military Aide.* 2 vols. Garden City, NY: Doubleday, Doran & Company, Inc., 1930.

Calabresi, Steven, and Christopher Yoo. *The Unitary Executive: Presidential Power from Washington to Bush.* New Haven, CT: Yale University Press, 2008.

Carnes, Mark. "William Howard Taft." In *To the Best of My Ability: The American Presidents,* edited by James McPherson, 188–195. New York: Dorling Kindersley Limited, 2004.

Coletta, Paolo. "Election of 1908." In *History of American Presidential Elections: 1789–1968,* edited by Arthur Schlesinger Jr., 3:2049–2090. New York: Chelsea House Publishers, 1971.

———. *The Presidency of William Howard Taft.* Lawrence: University Press of Kansas, 1973.

Corwin, Edward. *The President's Removal Power under the Constitution.* New York: National Municipal League, 1927.

Croly, Herbert. *Progressive Democracy.* New Brunswick, NJ: Transaction Publishers, 2009.

———. *The Promise of American Life.* Princeton, NJ: Princeton University Press, 2014.

Crowe, Justin. "The Forging of Judicial Autonomy: Political Entrepreneurship and the Reforms of William Howard Taft." *The Journal of Politics* 69, no. 1 (2007): 73–87.

Cushman, Barry. "Inside the Taft Court: Lessons from the Docket Books." *The Supreme Court Review* 9 (2016): 345–410.

———. "A Stream of Legal Consciousness: The Current of Commerce Doctrine from *Swift* to *Jones & Laughlin.*" *Fordham Law Review* 61 (1992): 105–160.

Danelski, David. "The Chief Justice and the Supreme Court." PhD diss., University of Chicago, 1961.

———. "The Influence of the Chief Justice in the Decisional Process of the Supreme Court." In *The Chief Justice: Appointment and Influence,* edited by David Danelski and Artemus Ward, 19–46. Ann Arbor: University of Michigan Press, 2016.

Davies, Ross. "Debate and Switch: William Howard Taft on Law as a Vocation." *Journal of Law* 6 (2016): 1–6.

Davis, Oscar King. *William Howard Taft: The Man of the Hour.* Philadelphia: P. W. Ziegler Co., 1908.

Duffy, Herbert. *William Howard Taft.* New York: Minton, Balch, & Co., 1930.

Dworkin, Ronald. *Taking Right Seriously.* Cambridge, MA: Harvard University Press, 1977.

Ellis, Richard. *The Development of the American Presidency.* 3rd ed. New York: Routledge, 2018.

Epstein, Lee, Jeffrey Segal, Harold Spaeth, and Thomas Walker. *The Supreme Court Compendium: Data, Decisions, and Development.* Washington, DC: Congressional Quarterly, Inc., 1994.

Fish, Peter. "William Howard Taft and Charles Evans Hughes: Conservative Politicians as Chief Judicial Reformers." *The Supreme Court Review* 1975 (1975): 123–145.

Fisher, Louis. *Constitutional Conflicts between Congress and the President.* 6th ed. Lawrence: University Press of Kansas, 2014.

———. *Presidential War Power.* 3rd ed. Lawrence: University Press of Kansas, 2013.

Fleming, James. "Constructing the Substantive Constitution." *Texas Law Review* 72, no. 2 (1994): 211–304.

Frankfurter, Felix. "Child Labor and the Court." *The New Republic* 31 (July 1922): 248–250.

———. *Felix Frankfurter on the Supreme Court.* Edited by Philip Kurland. Cambridge, MA: The Belknap Press of Harvard University Press, 1970.

Frankfurter, Felix, and James Landis. *The Business of the Supreme Court: A Study in the Federal Judicial System.* New Brunswick, NJ: Transaction Publishers, 2007.

Frankfurter, Felix, and Harlan Phillips. *Felix Frankfurter Reminisces: An Intimate Portrait as Recorded in Talks with Dr. Harlan B. Phillips.* New York: Reynal & Company, 1960.

Goodwin, Doris Kearns. *The Bully Pulpit: Theodore Roosevelt, William Howard Taft, and the Golden Age of Journalism.* New York: Simon & Schuster Paperbacks, 2013.

Gould, Lewis. *Chief Executive to Chief Justice: Taft betwixt the White House and Supreme Court.* Lawrence: University Press of Kansas, 2013.

———. *Four Hats in the Ring: The 1912 Election and the Birth of Modern American Politics.* Lawrence: University Press of Kansas, 2008.

———. *The Presidency of Theodore Roosevelt.* 2nd ed. Lawrence: University Press of Kansas, 2011.

———. *The William Howard Taft Presidency.* Lawrence: University Press of Kansas, 2009.

———, ed. *My Dearest Nellie: The Letters of William Howard Taft to Helen Herron Taft, 1909–1912.* Lawrence: University Press of Kansas, 2011.

Hoover, Irwin Hood. *Forty-Two Years in the White House.* Boston: Houghton Mifflin Co., 1934.

Hughes, Charles Evans. "Address of Chief Justice Hughes." *American Bar Association Journal* 18, no. 11 (1932): 728–729.

———. *Conditions of Progress in Democratic Government.* New Haven, CT: Yale University Press, 1910.

Investigation of the Department of the Interior and of the Bureau of Forestry. Washington, DC: Government Printing Office, 1911.

Kleinerman, Benjamin. *The Discretionary President: The Promise and Peril of Executive Power.* Lawrence: University Press of Kansas, 2009.

Knott, Stephen. *The Lost Soul of the American Presidency: The Decline into Demagoguery and the Prospects for Renewal.* Lawrence: University Press of Kansas, 2019.

Korzi, Michael. "William Howard Taft, the 1908 Election, and the Future of the American Presidency." *Congress & the Presidency* 43, no. 2 (2016): 227–254.

Kutler, Stanley. "Chief Justice Taft and the Delusion of Judicial Exactness: A Study in Jurisprudence." *Virginia Law Review* 48, no. 8 (1962): 1407–1426.

———. "Chief Justice Taft, National Regulation, and the Commerce Power." *Journal of American History* 51, no. 4 (1965): 651–668.

Leupp, Francis. "President Taft's Own View: An Authorized Interview." *Outlook* 99 (December 1911): 811–818.

Lincoln, Abraham. *The Collected Works of Abraham Lincoln.* 8 vols. Edited by Roy Basler. New Brunswick, NJ: Rutgers University Press, 1953.

Locke, John. *"Two Treatises of Government" and "A Letter Concerning Toleration."* Edited by Ian Shapiro. New Haven, CT: Yale University Press, 2003.

Lurie, Jonathan. *The Chief Justiceship of William Howard Taft, 1921–1930.* Columbia: University of South Carolina Press, 2019.

———. "Chief Justice Taft and Dissents: Down with the Brandeis Briefs!" *Journal of Supreme Court History* 32, no. 2 (2007): 178–189.

———. *William Howard Taft: The Travails of a Progressive Conservative.* Cambridge: Cambridge University Press, 2012.

Mason, Alpheus Thomas. "The Labor Decisions of Chief Justice Taft." *University of Pennsylvania Law Review* 78, no. 5 (1930): 585–625.

———. *William Howard Taft: Chief Justice.* New York: Simon & Schuster, 1964.

Mathews, J. M. "Employers' Liability and Workmen's Compensation." *American Political Science Review* 5, no. 4 (1911): 585–590.

McCloskey, Robert. *The American Supreme Court.* 5th ed. Revised by Sanford Levinson. Chicago: University of Chicago Press, 2010.

Milkis, Sidney. *Theodore Roosevelt, the Progressive Party, and the Transformation of American Democracy.* Lawrence: University Press of Kansas, 2009.

———. "William Howard Taft and the Struggle for the Soul of the Constitution." In *Toward an American Conservatism: Constitutional Conservatism during the Progressive Era,* edited by Joseph Postell and Jonathan O'Neill, 63–94. New York: Palgrave Macmillan, 2013.

Minger, Ralph Eldin. *William Howard Taft and United States Foreign Policy: The Apprenticeship Years, 1900–1908.* Urbana: University of Illinois Press, 1975.

Mink, Gwendolyn. *Old Labor and New Immigrants in American Political Development.* Ithaca, NY: Cornell University Press, 1986.

Morison, Elting, ed. *The Letters of Theodore Roosevelt,* Vol. 3. Cambridge, MA: Harvard University Press, 1951.

Mowry, George. "Election of 1912." In *History of American Presidential Elections:*

1789–1968, edited by Arthur Schlesinger Jr., 3:2135–2166. New York: Chelsea House Publishers, 1971.

Murphy, Walter. "Chief Justice Taft and the Lower Court Bureaucracy: A Study in Judicial Administration." *The Journal of Politics* 24 no. 3 (1962): 453–476.

———. "In His Own Image: Mr. Chief Justice Taft and Supreme Court Appointments." *The Supreme Court Review* 1961 (1961): 159–193.

Nichols, David. *The Myth of the Modern Presidency*. University Park: Pennsylvania State University Press, 1994.

———. "The Promise of Progressivism: Herbert Croly and the Progressive Rejection of Individual Rights." *Publius* 17, no. 2 (1987): 27–39.

O'Brien, David. *Storm Center: The Supreme Court in American Politics*. 10th ed. New York: W. W. Norton, 2014.

O'Connor, Sandra Day. "William Howard Taft and the Importance of Unanimity." *Journal of Supreme Court History* 28, no. 2 (2003): 157–164.

O'Neill, Jonathan. "William Howard Taft and the Constitutional Presidency in the Progressive Era." In *Progressive Challenges to the American Constitution: A New Republic*, edited by Bradley C. S. Watson, 196–225. New York: Cambridge University Press, 2017.

Penick, James. "The Age of the Bureaucrat: Another View of the Ballinger–Pinchot Controversy." *Forest History Newsletter* 7, no. 1/2 (1963): 15–21.

———. *Progressive Politics and Conservation: The Ballinger–Pinchot Affair*. Chicago: University of Chicago Press, 1968.

Peterson, Merrill, ed. *Thomas Jefferson: Writings*. New York: Literary Classics of the United States, Inc, 1984.

Pinchot, Gifford. *Breaking New Ground*. Washington, DC: Island Press, 1998.

Post, Robert. "Chief Justice William Howard Taft and the Concept of Federalism." *Constitutional Commentary* 9 (1992): 199–222.

———. "Federalism in the Taft Court Era: Can It Be 'Revived'?" *Duke Law Journal* 51, no. 5 (2002): 1513–1639.

———. "Judicial Management and Judicial Disinterest: The Achievements and Perils of Chief Justice William Howard Taft." *Journal of Supreme Court History* 23, no. 1 (1998): 50–78.

———. "The Supreme Court Opinion as Institutional Practice: Dissent, Legal Scholarship, and Decisionmaking in the Taft Court." *Minnesota Law Review* 85 (2001): 1267–1390.

———. "Tension in the Unitary Executive: How Taft Constructed the Epochal Opinion of *Myers v. United States*." *Journal of Supreme Court History* 45, no. 2 (2020): 167–193.

Pringle, Henry. *The Life and Times of William Howard Taft*. 2 vols. New York: Farrar and Rinehart, Inc., 1939.

"The Progress of the World." *The American Review of Reviews* 44, no. 6 (1911): 643–677.

Pusey, Merlo. *Charles Evans Hughes.* Vol. 2. New York: Macmillan Company, 1951.

Ragan, Allan. *Chief Justice Taft.* Columbus: Ohio State Archaeological and Historical Society, 1938.

Renstrom, Peter. *The Taft Court: Justices, Rulings, and Legacy.* Santa Barbara, CA: ABC-CLIO, 2003.

Richardson, James, ed. *A Compilation of the Messages and Papers of the Presidents, 1789–1908.* Vol. 11. Washington, DC: Bureau of National Literature and Art, 1908.

Robinson, Lance. "Theodore Roosevelt and William Howard Taft: The Constitutional Foundations of the Modern Presidency." In *The Constitutional Presidency,* edited by Joseph Bessette and Jeffrey Tulis, 76–95. Baltimore: Johns Hopkins University Press, 2009.

Roe, Gilbert. "The Truth about the Contests." *La Follette's Weekly Magazine* 4, no. 31 (1912): 7–9, 15.

Roosevelt, Theodore. *An Autobiography.* New York: Charles Scribner's Sons, 1946.

———. "A Short Political Creed." *Outlook* 100 (March 1912): 720–722.

———. "The Trusts, the People, and the Square Deal." *Outlook* 99 (December 1911): 649–656.

———. "Who Is a Progressive?" *Outlook* 100 (April 1912): 809–814.

———. *The Works of Theodore Roosevelt: National Edition.* Vol. 17. Edited by Hermann Hagedorn. New York: Charles Scribner's Sons, 1926.

Root, Elihu. *The Citizen's Part in Government.* New York: Charles Scribner's Sons, 1907.

———. *Experiments in Government and the Essentials of the Constitution.* Princeton, NJ: Princeton University Press, 1913.

Rosen, Jeffrey. *William Howard Taft.* New York: Times Books, 2018.

Scalia, Antonin. "Originalism: The Lesser Evil." *Cincinnati Law Review* 57 (1989): 849–865.

Schambra, William. "The Election of 1912 and the Origins of Constitutional Conservatism." In *Toward an American Conservatism: Constitutional Conservatism during the Progressive Era,* edited by Joseph Postell and Jonathan O'Neill, 95–120. New York: Palgrave Macmillan, 2013.

Schlesinger, Arthur, Jr., ed. *History of American Presidential Elections: 1789–1968.* Vol. 3. New York: Chelsea House Publishers, 1971.

———. *The Imperial Presidency.* Boston: Houghton Mifflin Co., 1973.

Scholes, Walter, and Marie Scholes. *The Foreign Policies of the Taft Administration.* Columbia: University of Missouri Press, 1970.

Schultz, L. Peter. "William Howard Taft: A Constitutionalist's View of the Presidency." *Presidential Studies Quarterly* 9, no. 4 (1979): 402–414.

Skowronek, Stephen. *Building a New American State: The Expansion of National*

Administrative Capacities 1877–1920. Cambridge: Cambridge University Press, 1982.

———. *The Politics Presidents Make: Leadership from John Adams to Bill Clinton.* Cambridge: The Belknap Press of Harvard University Press, 1997.

Starr, Kenneth. "William Howard Taft: The Chief Justice as Judicial Architect." *University of Cincinnati Law Review* 60, no. 4 (1992): 963–976.

Stewart, Charles. *Budget Reform Politics: The Design of the Appropriations Process in the House of Representatives, 1865–1921.* Cambridge: Cambridge University Press, 2006.

Stoner, James. "Rational Compromise: Charles Evans Hughes as a Progressive Originalist." In *Toward an American Conservatism: Constitutional Conservatism during the Progressive Era,* edited by Joseph Postell and Jonathan O'Neill, 209–234. New York: Palgrave Macmillan, 2013.

Storing, Herbert. "The Presidency and the Constitution." In *Toward a More Perfect Union,* edited by Joseph Bessette, 377–385. Washington, DC: AEI Press, 1995.

Story, Joseph. *Commentaries on the Constitution of the United States.* Vol. 2. Boston: Billiard, Gray, and Company, 1833.

Strauss, David. "Can Originalism Be Saved?" *Boston University Law Review* 92 (2012): 1161–1170.

———. "We the People, They the People, and the Puzzle of Democratic Constitutionalism." *Texas Law Review* 91 (2013): 1969–1982.

Taft, Helen Herron. *Recollections of Full Years.* New York: Dodd, Mead & Co., 1914.

Taft, William Howard. "Address of Hon. William H. Taft, President of the United States. Delivered in Boston, Mass. Thursday, April 25, 1912." S. Doc. 615, 62nd Congress, 2nd Session (1912).

———. "The Administration of Justice—Its Speeding and Cheapening." *Central Law Journal* 72, no. 11 (1911): 191–198.

———. "The Attacks on the Courts and Legal Procedure." *Kentucky Law Journal* 5, no. 2 (1916): 3–24.

———. *The Collected Works of William Howard Taft.* 8 vols. David Burton, general editor. Athens: Ohio University Press, 2001–2004.

———. "Delays and Defects in the Enforcement of Law in this Country." *North American Review* 187 (June–July 1908): 851–861.

———. "The Jurisdiction of the Supreme Court under the Act of February 13, 1925." *Yale Law Journal* 3, no. 1 (1925): 1–12.

———. "Message of the President of the United States: Transmitting The Report of the Employers' Liability and Workmen's Compensation Commission." S. Doc. 338, 62nd Congress, 2nd Session (1912).

———. "The Need for a National Budget: Message from the President of the

United States Transmitting Report of the Commission on Economy and Efficiency on the Subject of the Need for a National Budget." H. Doc. 851, 62nd Congress, 2nd Session (1912).

———. *Our Chief Magistrate and His Powers.* With a foreword, introduction, and notes by H. Jefferson Powell. Durham, NC: Carolina Academic Press, 2002.

———. "Possible and Needed Reforms in Administration of Justice in Federal Courts." *American Bar Association Journal* 8, no. 10 (1922): 601–607.

———. "Speech of William Howard Taft: Accepting the Republican Nomination for President of the United States." S. Doc. 902, 62nd Congress, 2nd Session (1912).

———. "Three Needed Steps of Progress." *American Bar Association Journal* 8, no. 1 (1922): 34–36.

———. William Howard Taft Papers, Manuscript Division, Library of Congress.

Thomas, George. "As Far as Republican Principles Will Admit: Presidential Prerogative and Constitutional Government." *Presidential Studies Quarterly* 30, no. 3 (2000): 534–552.

"To Make Mistakes Is Human." *American Economist* 49, no. 1 (1912): 8.

Troy, Gil. *See How They Ran.* New York: The Free Press, 1991.

Tulis, Jeffrey. *The Rhetorical Presidency.* Princeton, NJ: Princeton University Press, 1987.

Turner, George Kibbe. "How Taft Views His Own Administration: An Interview with the President." *McClure's Magazine* 35 (January 1910): 211–221.

Urofsky, Melvin. "The Brandeis–Frankfurter Conversations." *The Supreme Court Review* 1985 (1985): 299–339.

Wilson, T. Woodrow. *Cabinet Government in the United States.* Stamford, CT: Overbrook Press, 1947.

———. *Congressional Government: A Study in American Politics.* Cleveland: World Publishing Co., 1973.

———. *Constitutional Government in the United States.* New York: Columbia University Press, 1964.

———. "The Study of Administration." *Political Science Quarterly* 2, no. 2 (1887): 197–222.

Index

Hamiltonian theory of presidential
power, 101, 102, 107–108, 110,
114, 115
Hammer v. Dagenhart, 154–155
Harding, Warren, 163
Harlan, John Marshall, I, 142, 156
Harrison, Benjamin, 8, 22
Hepburn Act (1906), 48–49, 50, 93
Hilles, Charles D., 81–82, 83, 84
Holden v. Hardy, 150–151
Holmes, Oliver Wendell
agreement with Taft's majority
opinion in *Bailey,* 155
on commerce power in the *Swift* case,
139, 140
dissent in the *Adkins* case, 153, 156
dissent in *Truax v. Corrigan,* 148, 150
infirmity in the Taft Court and, 164
Taft's efforts to obtain strong
majorities for key Supreme Court
decisions and, 169, 170
*Home Building & Loan Association v.
Blaisdell,* 157
Hoover, Herbert, 134, 163–164
House Ways and Means Committee,
42
Hughes, Charles Evans, 156, 157,
163–164, 166, 175, 178
Humphrey, William, 134–135
Humphrey's Executor v. United States,
134–137

income taxes, 43–44, 56, 185
independent regulatory commissions
(IRCs), 134–137
industrial courts, 152–153
industrial relations cases, 152–153
inferior executive officers
congressional power of removal and,
121–122
Taft's defense of civil service reform
and, 123–128
In Re Debs, 104
International Harvester Corporation,
30
Interstate Commerce Commission
railroad regulation and the Hepburn
Act, 49, 51, 52

railroad regulation and the Mann–
Elkins Act, 48, 50, 52
Taft's enforcement of the Sherman
Act and, 31
Taft's oversight powers as president
and, 34
interstate commerce regulation,
139–144, 156
IRCs. *See* independent regulatory
commissions

Japanese American internments, 115
Jefferson, Thomas, 101, 115, 179
Jeffersonian theory of presidential
power, 101, 110, 114, 115
Judges' Bill (1925), 158, 159, 167–168,
173, 174
Judicial Conference, 158, 160, 161,
166
See also Conference of Senior Circuit
Judges
judicial reform
certiorari jurisdiction and the
Supreme Court, 158, 159, 160,
161, 167–168
overview of Taft's efforts in, 158–159,
171–172
Taft's efforts to expand protection of
individual rights, 174–175
Taft's efforts to reduce the cost of
litigation, 159, 172–174
Taft's expansion of the role of the
chief justice, 158, 159, 160–166
judiciary
Commerce Court, 48, 50–51
Taft's managerial role and oversight
of the federal judiciary, 165–166
Taft's prepresidential career in, 7–8,
78
See also Taft Court; US Supreme
Court

Kleinerman, Benjamin, 204n9
Knapp, Charles L., 49
Knott, Stephen, 88
Knox, Philander, 61
Korzi, Michael, 78
Kutler, Stanley, 151, 157